You are the Book

A Spiritual Memoir

RABBI TAMARA MILLER

Rabbi Tamara Miller (signature)

THREE GEMS PUBLISHING

Three Gems Publishing
www.ThreeGemsPublishing.com
8121 Georgia Ave, Suite 600
Silver Spring, MD 20910

ISBN-13: 978-0998973333
ISBN-10: 0998973335

Author Photo: Lloyd Wolf

Advance Praise for *You are the Book*

"Rabbi Tamara Miller is an authentic voice of pure spirituality. Her inspirational words need to be widely read. She blesses all of us with this offering!"

> —Rabbi Shmuel Herzfeld, American Open Orthodox rabbi and senior rabbi of Ohev Shalom Synagogue in Washington, DC.

"Tamara Miller is a woman of courage, resilience, and deep faith. Her memoir invites us to join her honest, and insightful and unique spiritual journey, a story of an American Jewish feminist."

> —Rabbi Sue Levi Elwell, PhD, Spiritual Director, Hebrew Union College-Jewish Institute of Religion

"Rabbi Tamara Miller reveals the transcendent light of meaning in the everyday details of her remarkable journey. In *You are the Book* we hear an authentic voice of Wisdom that has been honed and refined through deep reflection, soaring inspiration, and a sparkling humor that is born from well-earned humility and wide perspective."

> —Rabbi Shefa Gold, author of, *The Magic of Hebrew Chant: Healing the Spirit, Transforming the Mind, Deepening Love*

"Rabbi Tamara Miller presents an eloquent and revealing exploration of her life and her struggle to find religious authenticity and spiritual fulfillment as she served Jewish communities throughout the United States. She represents the strength of Academy for Jewish Religion alumni, many of whom are second-career students, who use the many aspects of their rich backgrounds to relate to and serve many different communities and segments of the American Jewish community. I think that readers will find in this spiritual memoir hope for fulfillment of their own long-held dreams."

> —Dr. Ora Horn Prouser, Executive Vice President and Academic Dean Academy for Jewish Religion

"Rabbi Tamara Miller illuminates her persistent and rocky road to the rabbinate with elegant, engrossing prose and steadfast spirituality."

—Faye Moskowitz, author of *A Leak in the Heart*,
Professor George Washington University, English Department

"You feel, in every line, an open and honest heart: quietly elegant, unblushing about love and unflinching in self-examination, addictively interesting, with a storyteller's gift for keeping you turning the pages. And the more you read the more you understand that the loss of innocence can be continuous as one confronts in one's own life the kinds of human cruelty so evident in history's darkest chapters—but also that such intensities of pain can inspire greater humanity, hard-won wisdom, and true grace.... *You Are The Book* is more than a memoir: it is the making of a great friend, sentence by sentence, and you want to introduce that friend to everyone you love—which is exactly what I intend to do."

—Tim Johnston, author of *New York Times* bestseller *Descent*

"Rabbi Tamara's spiritual journey into the rabbinate illuminates not only her personal emotional and spiritual journey, but the history of struggle between the Old World Orthodox life-style and contemporary struggles around paradigm shifts in the role of women and the role of religion. Written in a compelling style, this memoir will appeal to all searching for their authentic voice in the face of personal challenges and injustice."

—Rabbi Shohama Wiener, D.Min,
—President Emerita, Academy for Jewish Religion

YOU ARE THE BOOK

Written on my father's tombstone
at Cedar Park and Beth El Cemeteries
in Paramus, New Jersey

נ"פ

זקיננו אבינו בעלי

דב יצחק הרב

ה"ע אייזיק יצחק ברה'ב

ועייל שייף

ונפיל שייף

תדירא באורייתא גרים

לנפשיה טיבותא מחזיק ולא

RABBI BEN MILLER

ז"תשס שבט ז"כ נפטר

February 15, 2007 – Age 94

Here lies my husband, our father, our grandfather
Yitschok Dov, son of Rabbi Yitzchok Isaac
Of Blessed Memory
He entered this world quietly
He left this world quietly
He spent his time studying the holy Torah
And lived a life of humility,
Rabbi Benjamin Miller
1913-2007

Once or twice in a lifetime,
a man or woman may choose
a radical leaving, having heard
Lech l'cha -------Go forth.

God disturbs us toward our destiny
by hard events and by freedom's now urgent voice
which explode and confirm who we are.

We don't like leaving,
but God loves becoming.

Norman Hirsh
Mishkan T'filah, Reform Prayerbook

Table of Contents

Dear Reader,

While writing my own book, I came to understand how little I knew about how life works. I share with you, however, how much I have learned.

Writing this memoir has been an act of courage. I knew I had a story to tell, but how would it be received by family, friends, strangers? Would my composition matter? Could it teach as well as inform? Would my personal story influence others to take a leap of faith to experience their full potential? Would my own spiritual crises resonate with theirs?

With every story, I tried to find the transcendent in everyday living and to forge my own spiritual path within the traditions of my youth. Once destiny led me toward the rabbinate, I made a vow to myself: to be authentic and available to those who entered into the book of my life.

Blessings,
Rabbi Tamara Miller
Washington, D.C.
2017

PROLOGUE

THE ENDINGS THAT STARTED IT ALL

To enter the United States Holocaust Memorial Museum in Washington, D.C., you must first be screened by security.

The entryway is darker than that of many museums. To the right begins the journey through the hallowed spaces of history. But one important piece of history hangs on the wall in the entryway. It is a large photo of a young man in a uniform. The plaque beneath it reads:

While protecting visitors and colleagues, Special Police Officer Stephen Tyrone Johns was fatally shot on June 10, 2009, by an avowed anti-Semite, Holocaust denier, and racist. Officer Johns's outgoing personality and generous spirit endeared him to all who entered this museum, which was created to confront the very hate that took his life. His sacrifice shall never be forgotten.

I was the Director of Spiritual Care at George Washington University Hospital when Stephen Tyrone Johns was brought into the emergency room. His life would end that day, and mine would never be the same.

The hospital chaplain who had received the call told me what had happened: an 88-year-old man dressed in a Confederate coat had walked up to the museum entrance. Officer Johns, seeing only an elderly man approaching, moved to open the door for him. The man pulled out a rifle he had hidden under his coat and opened fire. He shot Johns at close range. The museum's other security guards immediately felled the perpetrator; I am not going to name him here, because I do not want to give him the attention he sought.

Officer Johns and the perpetrator were taken to George Washington University Hospital.

I was called to the emergency room to attend to Stephen's wife, Zakiah, who had recently arrived. The waiting room was chaotic; in addition to two other chaplains, there were many hospital administrators, concerned about the patients and the hospital during this this high-attention incident. Meanwhile, Stephen and the perpetrator were in surgery side by side, attended by two different medical teams.

More of Stephen's family and friends began to arrive, and the group was moved to a larger waiting room. We were joined by Pastor John McCoy, the leader of the Word of God Baptist Church in Southeast D.C. I introduced myself, and though he towered over my petite frame, it was clear we saw eye to eye. He took my hand and leaned toward me.

"I know you understand this kind of suffering, Rabbi. Your people and my people share a common history."

"Yes, sadly, it's true," I said.

The room was filling up around us, the group encircling Zakiah as if they could protect her physically from the pain. A temporary calm settled over us. We waited.

The operating nurse assigned to our case came in. "I will be monitoring what is going on in the operating room with your loved one," she said. "I will brief you from time to time. Should you have any questions, please have Rabbi Miller come and get me."

As a hospital chaplain, I became the bridge between the operating room staff and the family in crisis. The nurse returned each hour to give us an update, but she had no consequential news.

After several hours, the nurse approached me and asked if I would follow her out of the waiting area. As I left, I could feel the air in the room change. In the corridor, she whispered, "I have to give the wife the ring and tell her that her husband didn't make it. Can you come with me?" She squeezed my hand tensely. I could see that she wanted me to comfort her, too; this was new and disturbing territory for all of us.

The waiting room had become a makeshift sanctuary, containing hope and fear simultaneously within its partitioned walls. I glanced at Pastor McCoy and gave him a nod he instantly understood. I put a steadying hand on Zakiah's back. The nurse placed the wedding band in Zakiah's hands and gently said, "I'm sorry we couldn't save him." Someone caught the widow as she fell to the floor in shock. Stephen and Zakiah Johns had been married for only a year.

Wails reverberated around the room; what had been a sanctuary became a place of despair. I allowed myself to cry as I thought about "Big John," the gentle giant, the innocent victim. I heard Pastor McCoy call his congregation to worship.

"Let us pray. Hold hands. Gather us, Lord, in this time of unbearable grief. Help us to comfort each other as we say goodbye to our beloved brother Stephen."

The nurse returned to lead us to the room where Stephen lay. A white sheet covered his body, but his face remained in view. The noises of grief had given way to quiet tears and murmured goodbyes. There was nothing else to do.

Only a few hours ago, they had rushed to assemble here, friends and family answering a distress call on a bright summer day. Now they dispersed slowly, reluctantly, newly minted mourners straggling down the corridors and out into the night.

Wandering back to the post-op room to collect my things, I bumped into one of the emergency surgeons. Our professional paths had crossed many times, so I could tell he had something he wanted to say. He stood in front of me, not letting me by, and stared into my eyes.

"Explain this to me, Rabbi. How does this happen? We saved the wrong man."

The perpetrator, apparently, had survived his wounds. But what could I say to this physician, whose job it was to save human lives irrespective of their deeds?

"There is no answer," I said. "You did the work you were trained to do. The rest is out of our hands."

It had taken me years of study, prayer and experience, to know to speak these simple words—and to believe them.

THE BOOK OF MY FAMILY

I was 10 years old when I began dreaming of the Holy Land. Ever since I had learned that my Uncle Joe's brother, Avraham, had survived the Holocaust and was living in Israel, I wanted to go and meet him in person. The word *Zion* was often on my lips. Every Jewish prayer yearned for a return to the land of milk and honey; "Next year, in Jerusalem" was sung at the end of every Seder.

You could say that Jerusalem was my utopia, my paradise, my Shangri-La, my spiritual home. I believed that this far away State of Israel was the perfect place for the return of the Jewish people. How we longed for a safe and holy place where Jews could practice their Judaism without fear or trepidation, without pogroms and constant distress! My imagination soared with each passing Seder, and the longing flourished.

In prayers, in our books, and even in conversation, the act of returning to this Holy Land is expressed both metaphorically and metaphysically as an ascent, as "going up." That's the literal meaning of the word for going to Israel: *aliyah*.

It also means being called up for the Torah reading during certain prayer services.

It's a geographical ascent, as well. Anyone traveling to Israel from Egypt, Babylonia, or the Mediterranean basin, where many Jews lived in early rabbinic times, climbed to a higher altitude: Jerusalem is 2,700 feet above sea level.

I felt that to live in Israel, to "go up" in the footsteps of my patriarchs and matriarchs, would be the ultimate privilege.

Yet at 10, both dreams of aliyah seemed far away—that of going to Israel and that of being called up to read the Torah.

The fragments and reports I heard of news from family and acquaintances only fired my imagination. Some had relatives who had fled Europe at the time of World War II and had taken the route to Palestine instead of to America.

In 1950, Israel had passed the Law of Return, granting every Jew in the world the right to settle in Israel. I would have my chance.

Israel is made up of immigrants and refugees. The first wave of immigration, known as the First Aliyah, took place prior to political Zionism, in the late 1800s, as people in Russia and Yemen moved to Palestine. The Second Aliyah, prior to World War I, was made up exclusively of Russian Jews fleeing anti-Semitism and pogroms. After World War I and until 1923, the Third Aliyah was also out of Russia. The Fourth Aliyah, from 1924 to 1929, was largely made up of Jews escaping anti-Semitism in Poland and Hungary.

The Fifth Aliyah was the largest. One quarter of a million people entered Palestine between 1929 and World War II, as Nazism spread across Europe.

And in recent years, about 30,000 Jews have made *aliyah*—mostly from Argentina, France, and Britain. Whenever there is an uptick in anti-Semitism, there are more Jews being welcomed at Ben Gurion airport.

Eretz Yisroel, as my Yiddish teacher pronounced it, was the land of our beginnings as a Jewish people. My Eastern European family would often talk with excitement about the future of this biblical land, but no one I knew personally had ever visited it.

But this dream was far from the Bronx, where our extended family took up three apartments in the same apartment building, the Lindbergh Apartments on Prospect Avenue. I lived in one with my parents and my sister, Khana, four years my senior. In the second were my Aunt Paula and Uncle Hymie and their three daughters. In the third were my maternal grandparents and my Aunt Ruthie, my Uncle Joe, and their two children. We were often joined by my uncle Aaron, an itinerant rabbi who seemed always to be carrying a suitcase packed to bursting.

Every Passover, my grandparents' living room became a festive dining hall; chairs and tables occupied the entire space. Once everyone was seated, it was difficult if not impossible to move. Stuck at the Seder table, we performed rituals, sang songs, recited prayers, and waited endlessly for our dinner. Finally, plates were prepared in the overstocked kitchen and passed to the aunts, who passed them along to those at the end of the table, who passed them to the elders at the head of the table. The children were served last, dining from smaller plates. During all of this Passover passing of plates, I sat in my uncomfortable chair, smelling my mother's heavenly matzo balls, feeling lucky to be squeezed between my cousins. It was crowded and cozy.

Our family had survived pogroms, the Holocaust, poverty, and humiliation. Each song told a tale—making a book from which I could learn how to transform suffering.

Papa Abraham, the family patriarch from Volkovysk, was my mother's father, and he led the Seder, recalling Moses's flight with the children of Israel. Papa's own exodus story had begun in the impoverished *shtetls* in Poland, continued through the big Atlantic crossing, and ended in the borough of The Bronx. He was 40-something when he arrived at Ellis Island with his wife and four children. His profession: fishmonger.

On an ordinary day, Papa wore a crisp white button-down shirt with no tie, no beard, no yarmulke, and no other garb from his European boyhood. I frequently found him in the Chippendale-style chair in the far corner of the living room, holding the Yiddish newspaper, *Der Tog*, fully in front of his face. As a young child, I imagined him someday listening for my footsteps and quickly moving the paper into the chair while summoning me to sit on his lap, with a smile. But he never looked up. He never smiled at me, and our curt conversations were only in Yiddish. I longed to hear him speak a few English words, acknowledging that he understood mine.

Papa rarely went to work, but his wife, Fannie—or Feigele, the Yiddish name our family used—spent full days at the fish store on Tremont Avenue. She, too, spoke nothing but Yiddish. I often visited the store with my mother, but I never stayed long enough to get nauseated from the stinky smell of the fishery. Perhaps, I thought, after all his working years, Papa had developed a similar disdain for the stench of the sea creatures. When he no longer sat in the choicest chair in the living room, he would lie down in his bedroom, ghost-like, in a bed blanketed in white.

But on the Seder nights, Papa perked up. He was still strict and serious, but his white button-down was adorned with sterling-silver cufflinks that seemed to twinkle in my direction. With every dominating, glittering wave of his hand, Papa maintained control over the family's raucousness during the formal Seder proceedings, with an outstretched arm and a mighty hand, as God had for Moses and the people of Israel.

Papa Abraham died of cancer when I was 12, and my Bubbe Fannie followed him five years later. My cousins married and moved away—and after college, so would I. One by one over the years to come, we vacated the Bronx apartment building on Prospect Avenue and scattered to separate neighborhoods. My uncle moved to New Jersey, my aunt to Riverdale, the eldest aunt to Co-op City and my parents to the Grand Concourse. Many of their solemn stories remained untold, especially the ones about the Holocaust.

Vague stories of the horrors of Nazi Germany trickled down to the cousins. Uncle Joe never spoke about his parents or his life before he immigrated to America. Uncle Hymie and his brother Morris contained all of his family's memories. My friends Emily and Sy were only children in a sea of larger Jewish families. Their parents had them late in life. The war had interfered with generations of normal procreation.

My neighborhood friend Paul Bermanzohn had been born in a displaced person's camp before his parents and his sister immigrated to the United States. I never inquired about the how or the why, but the consequences of the war swarmed around me on the playground, in the classroom, and in every relationship. How much did I want to know? How much did they want to tell?

In my 20s, when the Seders of my youth had become the Seders of my past, I began a decades-long effort to piece together this genealogical jigsaw puzzle, a quest that was interwoven with my sense of who I was—as a Jew and a woman—and who I would become.

But even then, it would be hard to look squarely at suffering and death. I was drawn even as a child to the lessons the Holocaust might teach me. Over and over—along with love and happiness, suffering and injustice —death reached out to become a part of my life, writing the book of who I am, until I had learned enough to write the book for myself—and for others.

A FAMILY OF RABBIS

When she was 10 years old, my mother left her Polish *shtetl*, or village, in Pruznia to come to the United States of America. Her family—mother, father, two sisters and a brother—left the land of their birth to escape pogroms and anti-Semitism. Yes, it was a good move for this Jewish family. The longing to be in a country where religious freedom was an inalienable right became their lived reality. They would always be immigrants in a foreign land. Their children, however, were American-born. Now that, they felt, was an accomplishment!

My mother's twin brother, whose name we do not know, died at three months. The assumption was that he had been premature and had a weak heart. In order to try to save their son, my maternal grandmother, Fannie, nursed him solely, while my mother was given to a wet nurse to be nourished. This boy child buried in their *shtetl* remained in the Old Country, but the memory of his loss was painfully carried by the family. Another boy was born soon after. He was the youngest child of the Sietz family and the only boy. Uncle Jack survived and flourished in the *goldene medina*, the land of prosperity.

I have a black-and-white picture of my mother and father at their wedding, in an oval wooden frame, hanging in my hallway. My mother's dark, wavy hair stands in contrast to her white wedding dress and crowned veil. She holds a large bunch of white lilies that enliven the portrait. My father, in silk cravat and tuxedo, stands slightly behind her. Both are looking straight into the camera, which, today, means they are looking directly at me. They are in love.

My mother, short and petite like me, was a fighter until her death. She could be outspoken and opinionated about family issues and practical choices, but silent and withdrawn in social situations where she did not feel comfortable. Her world was limited to her extended family, where she played hostess and confidante. Because she had a rebellious streak from her youthful past—she had joined the Beitar revolutionary Zionist youth movement—she could be fiery, even hostile, about the injustices she saw around her. But when it came to her eldest daughter, Khana, she would simply say: "She is your sister above anything else. She has chosen a different path, and we must respect it."

My father had some rebellious and unconventional beliefs as well. He believed in the power of women—or rather, he believed in the power of all people to pursue their divine gifts, irrespective of their gender.

He once told me that in his community in Lodz, Poland, the rabbi's wife—known in Yiddish as the *rebbetzin*—was as well-informed as the rabbi. Women came to her for advice about the laws of *kashrut*, or keeping kosher; Shabbat; and *taharat mishpacha*, or family purity—the three mainstays of Jewish life. And when the rabbi died, it was the *rebbetzin* who counseled and provided continuity to the *shtetl* community.

And in the days before fathers ever thought to take over doing the laundry, my father was in charge of the laundry. My mother was not a physically strong woman, and he wanted to spare her those hundreds of arduous trips to the basement. He recognized that he could do the job more efficiently, and so he simply did it. He left the cooking to my mother, not because it was women's work, but because he didn't cook. I grew up with this unusual model, always aware that it was not the norm.

As a young girl, I delighted in going along with my father to accomplish this Sunday morning laundry ritual. Before we entered the elevator, we collected all our quarters, which we needed to operate the washer and dryer. I would press the mysterious "B" button so we could descend into the basement of our eight-story apartment building. We would always manage to complete the several loads of undershirts and underwear, the towels and turtlenecks of our daily life, with the coins we had been hoarding in sundry containers throughout the house.

In between loads, we would visit the nearby park, where my father puffed joyfully on his cigar, away from my mother's watchful eyes. His smoking was our secret, and I faithfully kept it. Unless, of course, my mother stared into my eyes and asked me directly: "Was your father smoking outside? Tell me the truth."

Smoking or not, my father mingled with neighbors and strangers alike. He was gregarious and garrulous. I enjoyed his chatter with the people who presumed to know me: "You must be Benny's little girl," they would say. But of course. Who else would I be? Did they not notice how firmly I held onto my father's hand?

Back and forth we went from the park to the basement and up again until the folded laundry was in our shopping cart and upstairs under my mother's scrutiny. She separated the laundry into two piles. One belonged to my sister and me; the other to her and my father. The laundry ritual continued this way until I was married.

This was not the only regular ritual I had with my father. From my earliest memory, my father and I spent Saturday mornings together in *shul* after *shul* in the Tremont avenue corridor of the Bronx, so my father could hear as many different sermons as his heart desired. My mother visited the synagogue only during the High Holy Days, Rosh Hashanah and Yom Kippur; my sister stayed home as well, until her teenage rebellion took her out of the scene altogether.

So I had my father to myself on Shabbat mornings, and I would wake up extra early lest I miss walking with him to services. We would hold hands as we strolled down the elegant tree-lined streets of the Grand Concourse to reach the Kingsbridge Heights Jewish Center, our Orthodox community synagogue. He prided himself on being there from the beginning, with time to spare, so he could schmooze with his buddies and help make the *minyan* —the quorum of 10 men necessary for the full Orthodox service to be recited.

Until I hit puberty, I was tacitly permitted to sit in the main sanctuary next to him with all the rest of the men. Because of my gender, I stayed hidden from open view, under my father's well-worn silk prayer shawl. I was warmly accepted by the other male worshippers, who ushered me into the wooden pew reserved for sons and grandsons. I was untroubled by the knowledge that I would one day be relegated to the women's section, the balcony of the synagogue that put the women out of sight, supposedly so they would not provide a distraction, and which effectively hid the pageantry of the services from women's view. It was a fact of life in the Orthodox world. But surprisingly, neither of my parents had internalized the gender biases of our community. And I was always good at compartmentalizing.

My father, my grandfather, my great-grandfather, one of my uncles, and my father-in-law were all rabbis. It certainly never occurred to me as a young girl that I could follow in their footsteps, and I'm sure the thought never crossed his mind back then; it was not customary, or even accepted, for a girl to learn the traditional texts. Still, my father taught them to me. I was his Yentl, the boy he never had.

Yentl was Isaac Bashevis Singer's fictional character—made famous by Barbra Streisand in the movie of the same name—who masqueraded as a boy in order to study Talmud, her love of Torah leading her to take desperate measures in order to circumvent the strictures of her era. I, too, had a longing to learn what my forebears had studied, to do so without fear or judgment.

I can still feel my father's silk prayer shawl, his *tallit,* slide through my fingers. I would pull on the fringes during prayers. He never chided me. He was sincere in his praying; he sang every word and mumbled through every paragraph, our bodies and souls energetically attuned. To this day, whenever I am in a synagogue, this memory connects me back to my father.

MY NEW WORLD SYMPHONY

Our household was Orthodox, but even so, my sister and I went to public school. As an Orthodox rabbi from a prominent Brooklyn *yeshiva*, my father would have preferred me to study Jewish texts and *halachah*, or Jewish law that is based on the Talmud, at an all-girls school. But my more liberal-minded mother was vehemently opposed.

"My American-born daughters are not going to wear long-sleeved dresses in the heat of summer. We have left the *shtetl* behind. New world. New customs."

So my sister, Khana, and I went to the local public school together with our numerous first cousins. There, we even had different names: my sister called herself Carol, and I called myself Iris.

Four afternoons a week after school, all the cousins walked a half-mile each way to study Yiddish language and literature as well as biblical Hebrew at the David Pinski *Folkshul*. This one-room storefront schoolhouse had only one teacher: the fervent Zionist and Yiddish linguist, Chaverah Miriam Herschberg.

Chaverah means "friend" or "comrade," and indeed, many of the students' families had Socialist or Communist backgrounds. But it also referred to the atmosphere of tolerance and openness she cultivated in her classroom. Though Yiddishists were often anti-Zionists interested in secular Jewish nationalism, Chaverah Herschberg was different: she made room for all ideologies, including my observant lifestyle.

I knew it was imperative for our Bubbe and Papa's sake that we cousins learn to read and write Yiddish, the *mamaloshen*, or mother tongue. But it was when Chaverah Herschberg taught us Hebrew that her Zionistic zeal was in full flower, and I was inspired by it, even long before I ever heard about my Uncle Avraham living in Israel. Decades later, I would visit Chaverah Herschberg in her Tel Aviv apartment, and we would speak only Hebrew.

Thus I became trilingual. With my elderly grandparents, it had to be Yiddish. They never uttered a word of English in my presence.

My family was the observant one in my public school as well as in my Yiddish school. Public school exposed me to the broadest range of humanity, but even my fellow Jewish classmates at the *Folkshul* came from many diverse cultural, political, and religious backgrounds—Bundists, Communists, Socialists, Zionists, and secular die-hard Yiddishists. Through studying the Bible in Yiddish translation and reading Sholom Aleichem stories in the original, we became Yiddish enthusiasts. *Folkshul* was my first entry into the colorful assortment of America's homegrown Jewish persuasions.

But because we maintained our observance, my social life centered around a third group, the kids I met at synagogue every week, who understood the restrictions I had to maintain. In this way, I lived with a part of me in each world: I was one part feminist, one part religious Jew, one part streetwise public school student, one part fluent Yiddish speaker. I tried to belong everywhere, so I never completely belonged anywhere.

Those restrictions were what my mother objected to, that the girls and boys were taught differently, that our genders dictated our Jewish perspectives in the world. But my mother's decision to send us to public school also had an unintended consequence: I had to forego the textual and ritual knowledge that my orthodox peers all acquired in *yeshiva*.

In fact, my mother was only intermittently progressive; in the domestic realm, she was as old-fashioned as any woman her age. In reality, it was my father who maintained an extraordinarily open-minded and egalitarian attitude in everything he did. He was an anomaly: a man born in 1913 who regarded each person, whether man or woman, wealthy or poor, black or brown or white, as having an equal voice in the world. And he had complete conviction in his daughters' ability to write the story of their own lives.

It did not occur to me, as I went through life and chose my partners, that most men did not share my father's attitudes. I had to learn this through experience.

My father's spiritual lessons would also take years to emerge in my life in a practical way. He taught me that the beauty of Judaism is that each of us is responsible for our own spiritual development. The authority comes from within: everybody creates their own rituals based on tradition, but contained in the private world we create, or co-create, in partnership with our beliefs.

We write not only the story of our lives, but the book of our beliefs.

Our family in those years was also marked by a shadow of suffering. Khana, four years older than me, had a major growth spurt as she entered her teens. As she became taller than all the other women in our family, her congenital scoliosis worsened, leading to a visible spinal curvature. My mother had one, too, but hers didn't really worsen until she was older.

Khana's teenage years were anything but carefree. She spent them in and out of a New York State rehabilitation center, either in a full body splint or recovering from major back surgery. The scoliosis did not respond to a lower-back brace, nor to intense physical therapy, so a medical team from the Hospital for Special Surgery inserted a rod to fuse her spine and make her crooked body straight. Every day, for more than two years, she wore a full-body plaster cast. She required assistance for all her physical needs. She ate in the cast, slept in it, dreamt with it. The rehabilitation center was an hour's train ride away, in the bucolic suburbs of Westchester County. During her long convalescences, our family made one or two visits every week.

Finally, when I was 12 and Khana was 16, the last cast came off. We celebrated by dancing at the wedding of cousin Shaindle.

I did not know that this reunion would be short-lived: soon after her sweet sixteen, Khana departed from the ways of our pious parents and grandparents. She flaunted her freedom by shopping on the Sabbath with her public high school girlfriends. She rarely came home for the festive Sabbath lunches that my mother cooked every week.

She was gone again.

It was a dynamic that would mark our sisterhood throughout our lives: her suffering, her independence, her pointed pursuit of what she believed was correct, and her conviction that the rest of us would mold ourselves around it. I was always a few steps behind, struggling to reach her, to make contact, to be a bridge. Whether I was 10 years old or 60, I admired her—

and I was afraid for her.

My mother and father never argued with Khana. They knew she had endured isolation and disability while bedridden, so they accepted her choices, even when these choices betrayed our traditions and caused heartache. We were a family suffocating in silence.

"The child has suffered enough," said my mother. "She deserves a little fun in her life. I will not stand in her way."

But my sister's choices left my father without choices, and I knew that even then. He would not betray his rabbinical lineage or his Orthodox praxis. My father never drove a car or used an elevator during the 25-hour Sabbath day. He never smoked his coveted cigars or carried his worn brown-leather wallet. He never ate even a cracker that was not kosher. He remained an observant and faithful Jew, attached to the form and content of his childhood—and his eldest daughter's defiance cut his open heart into shards.

I couldn't understand Khana's defection. Yet there were things about her that I envied: her statuesque height, her well-proportioned waist, her full breasts. When we walked together down the sidewalks of our Bronx neighborhood, my sister's lanky legs propelled her, and I was left behind, skipping and running to catch up. If only God had fashioned me a taller torso, I would think to myself, my sister and I could see eye to eye, and no one would question our bond. Our very different appearance revealed a deeper difference that would unfold over time.

In those days, I was always looking up to Khana. When she started dating, I hungered to know all the details of her social life. When she was accepted to City College of New York with my two female cousins, I knew that in a few years, I would follow.

And at age 24, she pursued a dream we both treasured: She would make *aliyah*, to teach English as a second language in a prestigious Tel Aviv university. I admired her bravery. I hoped someday I would do the same.

My parents were alarmed: they did not want to lose sight of their once-fragile daughter. I thought they should have been pleased at this development; after all, she would finally be fulfilling not only her own dream, but our mother's dream, the one she had cherished as a girl in the Volkovysk *shtetl*.

During the pogroms of the 1920s, my mother had joined Beitar, the Revisionist Zionist youth movement that preached political independence from the British Empire. She and her friends planned their journey to Palestine, determined to rebuild the Jewish state, to champion the cause of religious freedom and open the gates for Jews from every corner of the world.

"If we lived in a Jewish state, the Cossacks would not be banging on our doors in the middle of the night looking to punish some innocent Jew," my mother reasoned, trying to reconcile herself to Khana's decision to make *aliyah*. In a family album brought over from the "old country," a picture of my mother as a rebellious activist portrayed her teenage struggle. Dressed in a peasant uniform, she stood defiant with her Zionist friends.

"I'll miss you, Khana," I said. "Maybe I can visit one day soon."

"Let me get settled first, and then I'll have a place for you to stay," she said, hugging me too tightly.

My mother, too, sought her embrace, and Khana leaned over and held her caved-in body. They wept together. My normally loquacious father stood by, silent and stoical.

Khana spent five years in Israel. Her reverence for the Sabbath soared as she connected more deeply to her Judaism and her Jerusalem address. Soon she had returned to the rituals and regulations of our childhood—and more.

By the time she came home to New York City to marry, she had traded in her miniskirts and T-shirts for button-down blouses and full-length skirts. Her religious transformation had given rise to a rigidity that pained our tolerant father as much as her previous rejection of religious practices had. I had continued on the path he had chosen for me, and I, too, found Khana's doctrinaire approach distressing—even embarrassing.

"Every child has a path," he would announce, as if to reassure himself. Then he would offer me a prediction: "You will also find your way in the world." He'd reach into his prodigious Hebrew memory and quote a verse from the prayer book he kept in his head: "*Do not forsake the teachings of our Torah.*" (Proverbs 4:2).

SINGING TO THE WOUNDED

Every week for six weeks, our Hebrew choir, the Zamir—it means "nightingale"—turned an ordinary classroom at the Jewish Theological Seminary on Broadway in upper Manhattan into a concert hall. It was spring of 1967, and we had been selected to sing at the Zimriyah, the annual Israeli song festival that attracted choirs from all over the world.

Sing in Jerusalem? Meet Uncle Avraham? Perform with my group of friends on stages throughout Israel from the Golan to Eilat? I sang my heart out.

But on June 5th came the news: Israel had launched a series of preemptive airstrikes on Egyptian airfields in reaction to the mobilization of Egyptian forces along the Israeli border in the Sinai Peninsula. We continued to rehearse, and we waited for a miracle.

We could not have envisioned that it would only take six days for Israel to win this war against Jordan, Syria, and Egypt. Only a week after the war ended, our choir landed at Ben Gurion Airport. Within a few hours, we had mastered Naomi Shemer's popular song, "Jerusalem of Gold," *Yerushalayim Shel Zahav*. It would become our theme song for the seven-week tour.

As we were based in Tel Aviv, I was easily able to meet my Uncle Avraham, who had settled there, thousands of miles apart from the only other survivor in that family, his brother Joe, married to my mother's sister, Ruthie. He was tall, dark, handsome, and kind, and meeting him sparked a romantic feeling in me for the land and the refugees it embraced.

So when one of the baritones on our private bus began to tease me, perhaps I was more receptive than I would ordinarily have been. Michael had been at rehearsals throughout the year in New York, but it wasn't until we traveled together that summer that our friendship began. Michael was several years older than I and had just completed his first year of medical school. I was a rising senior at the City College of New York.

After dinner, when we had free time, we would walk along the Yarkon River outside our youth hostel, and talk unceasingly about the future of Israel.

"I never could have imagined a summer in Israel like this one," Michael said. "We're so lucky to have come on this trip now. So much hope everywhere! I wish we didn't have to leave next week. "

"It's true. Everyone here is so brave and alive! It'll be hard to go back to New York. I'm going to miss this place. It feels like another home."

Our group was asked to appear before the servicemen being treated at the Soroka Medical Center in Beersheva. We made our way clumsily down the aisle strewn with wheelchairs and hospital beds. When we reached the stage, we turned around and faced the soldiers, many bandaged from head to toe. I tried to look away from their bandaged faces, but they stared directly back at me. My throat closed.

"These men are my brothers," I told myself. "They have risked their lives so I could live securely as a Jew."

This was the price of freedom. Until then, war had always been something remote, but now reality intruded on my naivety. In this sea of broken bodies, I uttered a quiet prayer of thanksgiving.

We began our concert with the song that was being played on every radio station throughout Israel, describing the victorious reunification of the city of Jerusalem:

> *Jerusalem of gold, and of bronze, and of light*
> *Behold I am a violin for your songs …*

The audience sprang into song. Their faces were jubilant. We sang with them and for them.

After the concert, we walked slowly back up the aisle. This time, I looked straight at the soldiers and smiled. I used my elementary Hebrew to thank them. I no longer saw their wounds; instead I saw their hope.

Michael and I got back on the bus with our companions and talked about what had happened, how this concert in the sterile hospital setting had felt so much more significant than the ones in the overbooked concert halls. We agreed that brokenness was just a state of being, and we felt our power to heal with music.

After we returned home to the United States, Michael and I didn't see each other for six months. Then he called and asked me out for New Year's Eve. I already had a date, but quickly added, "Maybe we could meet another time while you're still in town. When else are you free?"

We dated for a year, shuttling from New York City to Syracuse on a monthly basis. For our summer break, we decided to apply for jobs at a Jewish summer camp in the Berkshires. Michael and I worked together as co-counselors for the high school program; we organized a potpourri of Jewish experiences in and out of camp, and spun our dreams of joining our siblings in Israel. Mixed in with all of this Zionistic ardor was some physical ardor as well: in the fevered romantic setting that only summer camp can create, I decided to set aside my Orthodox mindset and take the next step and I became truly intimate with Michael.

I was 21 when we got engaged, and Michael was 23.

Michael and I thought we were grownups, and we were prepared to make our own family within the traditional world we had always known. My future father-in-law, also a rabbi, had sent his two sons to the Hebrew Institute of Long Island, a modern Orthodox *yeshiva* where Michael and his older brother studied and translated modern and biblical Hebrew, studied the Talmud, put on *tallit* and *tefillin* every morning, and maintained their kosher practices at school, at home, at all times, in all circumstances. Michael had a much deeper knowledge of Jewish law and text than I did, because the Orthodox world afforded him access to those subjects from which I was barred as a girl.

I thought I wanted to honor the tradition of immersing in the *mikveh*, or Jewish ritual bath, before my wedding day. I signed up for *kallah*, or bride, classes at a local Orthodox synagogue, a six-week course that taught young women about the practice of *mikveh* in their married lives. In ancient times, Jewish men and women performed purification rituals in natural bodies of water—springs, wells, rivers—to reach a heightened spiritual state. *Mikveh* means "collection," which alludes to the more modern practice of collecting that living water in an indoor pool for ritual use. There is nothing holy about the water in the *mikveh* per se; the water is sanctified simply by the act of using it for the purposes of transformation. It is a status changer.

Throughout Jewish history, unmarried women have ritually immersed in the *mikveh* prior to their weddings. Submerging in a pool of water expressly to symbolize a change of soul seemed like a deeply spiritual way for me to mark this new station in my life, when I would be moving from single to married. I imagined that the waters of the *mikveh* could make me pure again.

All the girls in the *kallah* class were products of the neighborhood girls' *yeshiva*, a Jewish day school providing secular and religious instructions. I alone was the product of a public school.

I learned that girls immerse in the *mikveh* to be restored to a state of purity before their wedding night. Though they are sexually innocent, the teacher explained, menstrual blood renders them ritually impure. Married women who observe the Jewish laws of family purity continue with monthly immersions, seven days after the end of each menstrual cycle, in preparation for the resumption of intimate relations during their most fertile days.

I began to feel uncomfortable. I had been dating since I was thirteen, and now I realized that many of the girls in the class had just recently begun meeting boys, and some of them only vaguely knew their husbands-to-be. My girlfriends from *shul* never talked about sex. Now I could see why my mother had questioned my motivation in signing up for the class: "*Mikveh?*" she had asked. "Why would you want to take on that degrading custom from the Middle Ages?"

Yet our family lived an Orthodox lifestyle—observing the Sabbath, never eating non-kosher food, celebrating all the holidays and fast days, going to *shul* every week. And though everyone in *kallah* class thought of me as a rabbi's daughter, I felt I was fundamentally flawed. None of these girls had gone to public school. I looked around the room and realized that they were all still virgins. I was a virgin wannabe.

Week after week, with every lecture about the laws of family purity, my guilt heightened. Discipline and pure intention were required, but also a state of innocence I did not possess. I believed in the power of this ritual, though the lectures themselves were legal and practical. My fellow classmates giggled with every sexual suggestion. I knew things they didn't know, but I felt unworthy to be in the same room with them—or in the same *mikveh*. I was not giggling. I was squirming inside. What if they were right to have held on to their virginity? If they were right, then I had been wrong. I began to question everything they took for granted. I was ashamed.

One week I just stopped going. I never completed the *kallah* class or sanctified my marriage through immersion in the *mikveh*. At that age, I wasn't even conscious of the split in myself, but I was beginning to grapple with it: how to hold onto my traditions and still live in this contemporary world. The voice of my progressive mother mingled with the voices of the 1960s—the sexual revolution, Betty Friedan's *Feminine Mystique*. In their parlance, losing my virginity early was a badge of honor, not a sin to confess on Yom Kippur.

On June 29, 1969, Michael and I were married, at the Fort Tryon Jewish Center in Washington Heights. Our choir came back together to sing for our wedding. We walked down the aisle to the song we had learned together in Israel, "Jerusalem of Gold," and were reminded of another aisle on a different continent. Our hopes for the future merged under the *chuppah*, the wedding canopy. Everything in that moment felt right.

Throughout our marriage, Michael and I maintained our religious backgrounds by celebrating Shabbat, keeping a kosher home, and attending synagogue services. But I never could bring myself to observe the laws of family purity—customs such as the separation of husband and wife during the women's menstrual cycle and a monthly visit to the *mikveh* to restore one's ritual purity.

I didn't know how to elevate the spiritual act of going to the *mikveh* above the fact of my shame, and my internal voice was not yet loud enough to shout over the fence of expectations erected by the Orthodox community. At 21, I didn't have the vision or the courage to live a modern life and still maintain a connection to these rituals. I had no guide and no internal map to navigate the waters of the *mikveh*.

I thought it was all or nothing. So I chose nothing.

Soon I began to make other compromises, to look for a more egalitarian Jewish philosophy that would give me permission to use my voice. These changes in our religious life didn't really affect my husband, and he was comfortable with them as long as everything stayed the same in our domestic life.

Our marriage was built on our mutual desire to make *aliyah* and raise a family in Israel. With every choice we made, both personal and professional, we had the Holy Land in our sights.

"I wish we were in Israel already!" Michael would say.

"Me, too, but what about medical school?"

"I know. I know. Even Gaya and Lewis are making plans to leave."

"Well, they can make all the plans they want. But I bet she'll finish school here in America first. And I don't think we have a choice. Do you?"

"No," he sighed. "It's going to be a while before we can make the move."

Many of our Zamir friends had already returned to Israel as new immigrants. They studied Hebrew in the intensive *ulpan* schools; some entered the Israeli Defense Forces; others went to Hebrew University to pursue careers.

We, too, saw an opportunity to shape a young nation and be part of its destiny. But it took us another 15 years and three daughters before our dream became a reality. By the time we entered the Holy Land as *olim chadashim*, new immigrants, the dream had changed shape.

MAN PLANS AND GOD LAUGHS

There is a Yiddish folk proverb that resonates with my life: *Mann Tracht un Gott Lacht*. Man plans, and God laughs.

At age 29, my sister was the last of the cousins to get married. On one of her visits home from Israel, she had been introduced to Joshua, a *frum*, or ultra-Orthodox, man from Monsey, New York. He had pursued her back to Israel and enticed her to return to New York. He was too smug and self-righteous to get my vote, yet I wanted the marriage to work for my sister's sake.

To live a *frum* life you have to follow the rules of the group: you must marry as soon as possible and produce many children, to hold up the sacred task of perpetuating the Jewish people, a charge that took on even greater importance after the Holocaust. It was a worthy cause, but it did not take into account the importance a good partnership has in bringing up children well.

Khana and Joshua's engagement was short, as is the custom for that community; a large wedding took place just two months later. I was not there.

Our first daughter, Naama, had been born less than a week before. She had arrived three weeks after her due date, and with every passing day, I had grown more anxious.

"Michael, what if I can't go to Khana's wedding? Would you go without me?"

"We could bring the baby with us, so you could nurse," Michael said.

"It's only an hour and a half away."

I had a long and difficult labor, and the baby had to stay at Long Island Jewish Hospital for an extra five days. Michael's residency was at the same hospital, and our apartment complex was accessible through a large, verdant backyard. I went home without Naama, but continued to walk back and forth to nurse her several times a day.

Naama came home just two days before the wedding, but all the walking back and forth had taken a toll on my postpartum body. I started to hemorrhage, and even when I stayed quiet, it didn't stop. Michael agreed to go to the wedding only if we hired a nurse to stay with me the entire time he was gone.

I nursed Naama throughout the night to increase my chances of clotting. I still remember that lonely, dark night in our little apartment, with a stranger keeping watch over the baby and me, while everyone I loved was dancing at my sister's wedding. I was overjoyed when Michael returned home.

"How did it go?" I asked.

"Everyone asked about you and the baby, and I told them you'd be fine. The wedding was very *freilach*, lively with all the men dancing. Khana looked happy. Your mother even wore a *sheitel*—it was very becoming on her, actually. "

A *sheitel* is a wig worn by some Orthodox Jewish married women in order to conform to the requirement of Jewish law to cover their hair.

"Wow. A *sheitel?* Khana must have asked her to do that. I still can't believe I missed it. Now there will always be this story of how I missed my only sister's wedding."

A few days afterward, the newlyweds came to visit. Joshua peeked in on my infant daughter in her crib, and said, "It would have been better if she were a boy."

I was shocked and dismayed by his words. Did his prodigious learning of sacred texts not teach him manners or values?

But as I was to realize again and again, religious observance is neither a guarantee for nor a detractor from being a mensch.

Joshua was tall, dark, handsome, and rich—and, we would learn, a sociopath. It was not until Khana was pregnant that she learned of his pathological habit of lying: it turned out he had been married before, and had a son whom he did not support. Khana learned all this from his ex-wife, in a shocking phone call. It was too late. They were already expecting a child, and Khana felt she had no option but to stay.

After their child's birth—Yaakov, a son—Joshua began to stay out all night. Though Khana tried to tell herself that he was studying late at the *yeshiva*, she really had no idea where he was. I knew nothing of this until I took Naama and went to visit Khana and her baby boy in her Monsey, New York apartment.

She opened the door to me and said, "Josh is gone. I don't know where, but I don't think he's coming back."

"What? Khana, my God! How long ago?"

"I don't know. A few days," she said, her voice flat. "Don't tell Mommy and Daddy."

"Khana, they're going to find out anyway. That's the last thing you need to worry about. Do you have money? Have you been to the bank?"

"No … why the bank?"

"Khana. Josh has been lying to you from the start! You have to protect yourself. Get your money out before he empties out your bank account."

"Don't be silly. He would never do that," she said.

But it was already too late. Josh had withdrawn all funds from their joint bank account. Khana had no way to pay rent, no way to buy food. It took little convincing to get her to move in to our one-bedroom apartment in Queens. It was crowded with the two babies, each crying at different times of the night. Michael was very tolerant about the situation. He knew this was the right thing to do.

We bonded over our two babies, and I felt good that I, the younger sister, could provide Khana with a safe haven. But she was miserable; her whole future was now under review.

"He really fooled me, didn't he? But how could I have known? Tova called me today. She feels so guilty about making the match that she offered me money to help Yaakov and me while we make this transition. I tried to reassure her that it was nobody's fault. Bad things happen. Even to me."

Even to me? I repeated to myself. I wondered if she imagined her piety would be a bulwark against more of the kinds of misfortune that had plagued her childhood.

I felt sorry for my sister, just as I had when we were girls, and she was trapped in a plaster cage. Now she was living in a different sort of cage, one much more difficult to escape from. She had left behind her successful life in Israel as an assistant professor in the English department at Bar Ilan and a wonderful social life in a warm and loving modern Orthodox community in Jerusalem.

After Khana filed for divorce, some friends found her an apartment in

Far Rockaway, in another religious community. The next four years were difficult for Khana. Joshua claimed he was disabled and could not provide any child support. Khana began to use food stamps and had to go on welfare.

And once again, I could not be there for her. Michael and I continued to make plans while God laughed. Michael received acceptance to a two year residency in child psychiatry at the University of North Carolina at Chapel Hill. We moved south.

Chapel Hill was a welcome change from the rushed life of New York, and we fell in love with the natural charm of this Southern university town. Although we missed our family and friends, we had the local Hillel and soon made new friends with a diverse group. We stumbled over a college friend of mine from the Bronx, Paul Bermanzohn, who was receiving his own medical training in nearby Durham. In the following year, our second daughter, Elisheva, was born. I was grateful for the uncomplicated labor: I was out of the hospital within 24 hours.

Yet we were no closer to our dream.

Several years back, during the Vietnam War lottery, Michael had signed up for "The Berry Plan" to avoid a possible draft. This agreement allowed him to delay conscription to complete his medical residency. By the time his training ended, in June 1975, the Vietnam War was over, and we were grateful to serve in peacetime. Uncle Sam ordered now–Major Dr. Michael Ende to serve a two-year tour of duty at Fort Carson in Colorado Springs.

While we were there, we decided to round out our family with a third child—maybe a son, we thought. But after my protracted labor ended in an emergency cesarean section, we were just grateful to have a healthy baby, and we wept tears of joy when our daughter, Sariel, was born. It seemed we were not destined to have any sons, as our friends and family were fond of commenting, but we shrugged and laughed. We were content with our family.

With the single-mindedness of youth, we turned our attention back to the dream of Israel. But everyone we made contact with, including our Zamir friends, discouraged us. The shocking losses of the 1973 Yom Kippur War had caused an economic and emotional upheaval in the country.

"We are in a state of *dika'on,*" the Hebrew word for "depression," they would say. "Return when times are better. Now is not the time to come."

We felt like we had failed. Standing under our wedding *chuppah,* we had been filled with certainty. We never thought about what would happen if the plan did not work. We had even given our daughters Hebrew names, had envisioned them fitting right in with other Israeli kids: Naama. Elisheva. Sariel.

We returned to Fort Carson, Colorado in our own state of *dika'on*. The line from the poem "Harlem" by Langston Hughes rang in my ears. "What happens to a dream deferred? Does it dry up, like a raisin in the sun?"

Where would we go from here, we asked ourselves?

But unlike Khana, at least we had a broad range of choices.

I received word that Khana was getting married again. A matchmaker had found another husband for her, Shmuel. Again, she did not look too closely at her prospective groom, and again, she assumed that his religious observance guaranteed him a certain moral compass. It was as if her first marriage had brought her grief without wisdom. She was content to know she would have a father for her son, Yaakov, and a partner to complete her vision of a religious home.

I wanted to give Khana's new mate the benefit of the doubt, but I saw right away that Shmuel's personality was very similar to Joshua's— headstrong and belligerent, obstinate and rigid. And both masqueraded as righteous men in the religious community. Shmuel insisted loudly on living by the letter of the law and had a sarcastic, intimidating manner of speech.

Shmuel had also been married before, and had full custody of his two daughters; his ex-wife's health issues prevented her from being able to care for the children. Khana had sole custody of Yaakov; Joshua had moved to Israel, remarried again, and had no contact with either of his previous families. From these difficult beginnings, Khana's new blended family was created. I felt uneasy about her decision, but I could not have foreseen that her unswerving faith would lead her to a lifetime of tribulation.

Khana moved to Shmuel's childhood neighborhood in Philadelphia. Wanting to be accepted into the ultra-Orthodox community, Shmuel and Khana did away with family planning and began to have one child after another. Mordechai was born a year into their marriage. Twins Aaron and Avrummy were born less than two years later.

In toddlerhood, all three children began to exhibit behaviors not appropriate for their development: they were non-verbal, contrary, and frantic. Shmuel ignored them and continued to study Talmud. Khana was at a loss, and the boys' pediatrician did not seem to have any ideas.

It was my husband, Michael, a child psychiatrist, who finally pointed Khana in the direction of proper testing: all three children were diagnosed as profoundly deaf. The irony of Shmuel's wish for sons, it turned out, was that it was only in males that the chromosomal marker for the disorder that caused their deafness could appear.

When her twins were about 18 months old, Khana called to tell me that she was pregnant again. Though I had a sizable family of my own by now with baby number three, it was hard for me to delight entirely in Khana's fruitfulness—it seemed to come with so much new suffering.

"Have you had any genetic counseling?" I asked.

"No," she said. "Not yet. There's never any time." She sounded somewhat embarrassed.

I was frankly shocked, though given her religious practice I should not even have been surprised.

Her true thoughts were clear in what she said next: "And no matter what, God will provide."

Another boy, Shimon, was born, and he was not deaf. After that, Khana asked her rabbi if she could use contraceptives, and he gave her permission, but only for a Lippes loop—a device unpopular because of its failure rate. Two years later, Yossi was born, also deaf, and finally, a girl, Penina, with intact hearing.

My sister was 46 when she stopped giving birth: she had seven children and two stepchildren. Four in her family were deaf.

Soon after the twins were born, Khana began a search to secure schools that would provide the sign language and other support the boys required, the English studies they would need to live as Americans, and the Hebrew and Judaic studies she and Shmuel wanted for them. She faced compromises and difficulties: she sent them to Philadelphia's Pennsylvania School for the Deaf in the mornings, and in the afternoons she would accompany them to the *yeshiva* nursery school and interpret everything into sign language for them. Shmuel taught history until the afternoons, and then went off to *yeshiva* to learn until evening.

Khana saw that there was a void for parents like her. She took the initiative to establish a nonprofit organization, called P'tach, to provide for the combined Jewish and secular educations of Orthodox children with disabilities. P'tach still helps families today.

This was typical of her dedication and determination. But for herself, for her own life, she accepted perhaps more than was good for her. It was a pattern I would see many times in women I encountered in my life—and, to a lesser extent, in myself. We did not want to confront injustice—or we were willing to confront it anywhere else but in our own lives. And we often let pass another kind of injustice—the kind we do to ourselves.

Away from school, the lives of Khana and her children were filled with bullying and neglect at the hands of Shmuel. He yelled and screamed at them all—though many of them could not hear him—and often slammed out of the house without telling anyone where he was going.

My sister continued to show resilience and courage every day in the face of her challenges. Maybe it was her faith that kept her going, or simply her ability to see what needed to be done and to do it. She never wavered in her loyalty toward her family.

THE GREENSBORO MASSACRE

Violence—both its threats and its consequences—was threaded through my family's Eastern European history. Yet I had always seen it as mythic and distant. I had never expected it to visit my own time and place —and never in such a place as peaceful as Greensboro, North Carolina.

It was springtime in 1977 when Michael called, fresh from an interview at the Greensboro community health center that needed a director. I could hear the excitement in his voice. He described a small but active Jewish day school in a wooded neighborhood. "This could be our next home," he said.

By June, we were driving to North Carolina, transporting a six-month-old baby, two toddlers, three car seats, and a load of optimism.

Michael was right about Greensboro being a charming city, decorated with trees and verdant grass that stood in stark contrast to the desert landscape of Colorado Springs. On most days, a clear sky surrounded our Dutch Colonial house on Watauga Drive, with its screened porch and children's swing set in the backyard.

Greensboro was a family town, with two synagogues, a day school, a Jewish Federation, and plenty of people with commitment to Jewish values and causes. We were immediately accepted. Southern hospitality became our new reality.

The spread of feminism in the late 1970s coincided with my discovery of my feminist Jewish voice. I became president of the local chapter of Hadassah, the Women's Zionist Organization of America, a volunteer organization that inspires a passion for and commitment to the land of

Israel.

When I learned about Henrietta Szold, the founder of Hadassah, she became my guide. She founded Hadassah in 1912, at age 49, on a trip to Palestine, where she witnessed deplorable health conditions. Upon her return to America, she began her work in health care. Hadassah Hospital is a tribute to her healthcare activism on behalf of people of all faiths—Jews, Muslims, and Christians—living in the region. Mount Scopus opened in 1939 as the first modern medical facility in the region. Its second campus, in Ein Karem, opened in 1961.

I identified with Henrietta Szold: like her, I was a sister with no brothers, and born to a rabbi named Benjamin. I admired her passion for Jewish learning, the way she defied convention and studied at the Conservative movement's Jewish Theological Seminary in New York in 1902. Its rabbinic school was for men only, so Szold took classes there in advanced Jewish studies. She begged the school's president, Solomon Schechter, to allow her to matriculate. According to her biography, he agreed, but he restricted her from seeking ordination.

The story of her mother's death moved me as well: With no brothers to say *Kaddish,* the mourner's prayer, Henrietta took another bold stand for Jewish women: She recited it herself. It was 1916. It was not the norm in Orthodox or Conservative Judaism for women to say *Kaddish.* Hayim Peretz, a male friend, had offered to say it for her. She refused, and her response became famous:

> *I know well, and appreciate what you say about the Jewish custom; and Jewish custom is very dear and sacred to me. And yet I cannot ask you to say* Kaddish *after my mother. The* Kaddish *means to me that the survivor publicly and markedly manifests his wish and intention to assume the relation to the Jewish community, which his parent had, and that so the chain of tradition remains unbroken from generation to generation, each adding its own link. You can do that for the generations of your family, I must do that for the generations of my family.*

Eventually, her answer to Peretz was adopted unanimously by the Va'ad Halakhah, or Law Committee, of the Rabbinical Assembly of Israel, and used as the basis for the right of women to recite the Mourner's *Kaddish* in public when a quorum (or *minyan)* is present. Years later, when I lost my father and mother, her legacy would come back to me in a deeply personal way.

Everything I needed to know as a Jewish leader I learned through my work in Hadassah. I developed a fundraising strategy and raised tens of thousands of dollars; I created *Sefirot*, a Jewish women's literary circle that lasted 12 years, and I led the first all-women's Shabbat morning service at the conservative synagogue, Beth David, just a few blocks from our house. I had become friends with Dr. Sarah Malino, a feminist historian. She gave the sermon at this first women's service, thus bridging for me the feminism of the 1960s and the religious feminist movement that emerged in the 1980s.

We would find our voices. What we learned would be needed more and more, as the years went on and conflict and violence burst into our lives in ways we had never expected.

Paul Bermanzohn, my childhood friend from the Bronx, visited us in Greensboro from time to time. Now working as a doctor in Durham, he had become a committed civil rights activist, fighting for the cause of race relations in the South.

With another doctor, Michael Nathan, he helped to organize the Communist Workers' Party for the purpose of helping textile workers form unions for better workplace conditions. A whole group of medical staff became involved in this cause.

The textile mills were headquartered in Greensboro, and Paul and his colleagues were based in Durham, the epicenter of the tobacco industry. They were surrounded with evidence of racial inequality in the workplace. Paul shuttled back and forth between the two communities as he became more deeply entrenched in his radical political activities.

"Who would have thought two Bronx Jews would find their way to the South?" I said to him, on one visit. "Do you remember those City College student union meetings? How they went on and on. So many crises. Week after week."

"I took them all very seriously," he said. "The sit-ins. Vietnam protests. Strikes for union rights. It's amazing that I actually graduated with damn good grades."

One Shabbat, Michael and I decided to relax at home with our three daughters instead of attending services. Friday evening's dishes were still stacked in the sink. The girls wanted to go on a bike ride. I wanted time to read for the next gathering of my book club. I had reserved Simon Wiesenthal's *The Sunflower* at the Greensboro library, but I hadn't had the time to retrieve it.

"Michael," I said, "Will you watch the girls? I want to go get my library book. I'll be back in a half hour."

When I walked in the door of the library, there was an audible buzz. *That's strange*, I thought. *People here are usually so polite and respectful, especially in the library.* The voices around me were no longer whispering; people were standing and talking in groups of three and four. They held up the Greensboro *News and Record*, a local newspaper with headquarters right down the street. A large picture dominated the front page. I could only see part of the scene: a man pointing a gun at someone on the ground.

"What happened?" I asked, nervously.

One of the men talking offered me the paper. "Here, read it for yourself. A shooting. It was less than an hour ago. The photographer must have run straight to the news office with his camera to make the late morning edition." He pointed out the window to the streets.

I sat down to read the details, which looked something like this:

> *This morning, as activists were mustering for a "Death to the Klan" parade and rally in the Morningside Heights housing project, members of the Ku Klux Klan and the American Nazi Party opened fire on the demonstrators, killing five people and wounding ten others. Dr. Michael Nathan, the chief of Pediatrics at Lincoln Community Hospital in Durham is among the dead. He and another Durham physician, Dr. Paul Bermanzohn, were fellow organizers of the march and members of the Communist Workers Party. Bermanzohn was shot in the head and is now being transported to a local hospital for surgery.*

Paul's name grew larger and larger on the page as I read and reread the story. How had such terror suddenly appeared in the midst of my picturesque suburban life in this sweet Southern city?

I had been living in Greensboro for only two years, and I had no grasp of the sphere of influence the KKK and the American Nazi party had in North Carolina, but I was soon to learn much more.

It came as a shock to me to find out that the state I had found so peaceful was far and away the most active Klan state in the nation. In 1979, at the time of the shooting, more than 12,000 members resided in the state, and most of their activities were centered near Winston-Salem, a mere 30 miles from our home.

Confrontations between the Klan and the Workers Viewpoint Organization or WVO—which had recently changed its name to the Communist Workers' Party—had been heating up throughout the South. The Klan targeted the both white and black organizers of the WVO, whom they knew to be a threat to their white supremacist mission: when the shooters stopped their van on the curb next to the Greensboro demonstrators and emptied their weapons, they killed five of the central figures in the workers' rights organization.

Paul had been one of the organizing members of the WVO, and had been involved in the decision to rename it the Communist Workers' Party, as its mission had shifted farther to the left. I understood that his decision to use the term, *communist*, rose out of our common heritage, the Yiddish-centered community. There, that word was not fraught with paranoia and frightening implications, but rather, pointed to the original, Marxist definition: It meant advocating fair treatment and compensation for workers according to their abilities and needs. But most of America in the 1970s knew nothing of that context; it had long since been occluded by the era of Joseph McCarthy and the Cold War.

The Communist Workers' Party had acquired a legal marching permit for that day in Greensboro. The marchers had posted leaflets throughout the community along with *Death to the Klan* posters. They had two goals: to bring attention to the racism of the Klan and to further the cause of the textile workers. Months before, group members had infiltrated the textile mills in an effort to organize the black workers into unions where their rights would be defended. As a known leader, Paul had made many enemies in the KKK.

Sitting there staring in shock at the newspaper that day, I realized I was still clutching my book, *The Sunflower*, in its bright yellow jacket. The book is Simon Wiesenthal's recounting of his internment in the Lemberg concentration camp and his meeting with a terminally wounded Nazi. I remembered that Paul's parents were also Holocaust survivors. How would they be able to live if Paul died? The nightmare played itself out in my mind.

In the library, discussions were quieting down and people were leaving. I remained seated, knuckles white against the book, as tears streamed down my face.

I need to go home and see my girls. I need to find Paul.

Carrying my book and my bad news, I walked out the door and drove home on autopilot. When I reached the driveway and saw the girls playing, I tried to pretend that everything was okay. I hugged them a little tighter than usual, but I didn't start crying until I went inside and saw Michael in the kitchen.

"The KKK ... Paul ... shot in the head!" I said between sobs. "Where could they have taken him?"

"Slow down," Michael said, "Start at the beginning. What happened?"

After I told him the story, he said, "We'll find him. Let me call around to the hospitals. But I need you to stay calm. The girls are right outside, and if they see you so upset they'll want to know why. We have to keep this to ourselves."

Calling around as a physician, Michael found Paul at the Greensboro Women's Hospital—the closest trauma center—about 10 minutes from our home. I said goodbye to the girls and headed to the hospital. There in the waiting room was Paul's wife, Sally. We had never met, and I introduced myself as a childhood friend of his. I sat next to her until the news came that Paul had survived the surgery. What that meant for their futures would take months to unfold.

I wrote my name and number on a piece of paper and told Sally to call me if she needed anything. "I'll be back tomorrow," I said.

I slept fitfully that night, and prayed for the victims and their loved ones. I prayed for Paul to recover. I prayed for my own young family and for our safety, which had truly been called into question for the first time.

Praying for me in those days was a release of emotion, but it was accompanied by a deep conviction that my words would enter into God's field of receptivity. I often turned to the *Shema* prayer, that most iconic of Jewish utterances: *Hear, O Israel, the Lord our God, the Lord is One.* To pray was to have faith that my words were received by a Being who would listen, and because I believed that, it calmed and soothed me.

When I was growing up in the Bronx, we had heard about gangs and knifings, but I had encountered nothing as terrifying as this shooting. My fellow high school students sometimes got beat up in the back alleys, and once, when my sister, my cousins, and I were walking back from synagogue on a Friday night, a group of girls from the neighborhood encircled us in the dark street and prevented us from passing. They called us "Jew-girls." We were scared, but there were no bats, no knives, no guns. We held hands and sidestepped them, and walked away.

In my sheltered world, violence was something that happened elsewhere, in musicals like *West Side Story,* or in real-life but far-flung places like Vietnam. Of course I remember where I was when John F. Kennedy was shot. I had known the horror of the back-to-back murders of Martin Luther King, Jr. and Robert Kennedy, in 1968. Those were traumatic events for my generation, and they had left their mark. But now, it was my childhood friend who was fighting for his life.

47

When I got to the hospital waiting room the next day, I saw Paul's parents, two elderly, frightened people, huddled together, holding each other up so neither of them would fall.

"Mr. and Mrs. Bermanzohn, it's me. Tamara Miller? Paul's friend from Prospect Avenue. I live here in Greensboro now. How is he?"

They recognized me, and time fell away. They both began speaking Yiddish, their *mameloshen*, their mother tongue. It seemed to soothe them. In Yiddish, they could speak from the depths of their anguish in the voices of their childhood. I, too, switched into the language of my parents and grandparents.

"Dos is gefehrlich, vos hut passiert," I said. *It's terrible, what happened.*

"Far vos?" they asked, over and over, without waiting for an answer. *Why? For what?*

Paul was still in intensive care: he was alive but not yet breathing on his own. Surgeons had removed bullets from his head and his hand. He was heavily sedated.

We sat in silence with a tissue box between us, waiting for the doctors' update and for Paul's sister, Frances, to fly in from Boston. When she arrived, the weeping began again, until we all ran out of tears.

"Where are you staying?" I asked them.

"Where *can* we stay?" Mrs. Bermanzohn answered my question with a question. "We know no one here. Where can we get kosher food?"

"You will stay with me and my family," I said. "I keep kosher and we have a guest room where you can sleep."

I didn't ask Michael's permission. I knew this was the right thing to do, and the only thing I could do to ease their pain.

"A shaynem dank." We can't thank you enough. *"Mir seinen ferlohren."* We are lost.

That night, after dinner, and after the girls were put to bed, the five of us gathered in the den. The two Holocaust survivors spilled out their stories of deportation from Poland and degradation at the concentration camps. Mrs. Bermanzohn, Tema, took the stand, our family room becoming a silent courtroom laced with her vivid truths. She had lost her parents, grandparents, three brothers and a sister, aunts, uncles, and cousins. After surviving her stay at the Majdanek camp, Tema escaped the Nazis several times by jumping off trains that were taking her to the Treblinka concentration camps, but was caught. She proudly told us that the Nazis had nicknamed her "The Bird," for her efforts to escape.

Leibel Bermanzohn had lost his entire family as well: parents, grandparents, three brothers, three sisters, cousins, aunts, and uncles. He described how they were starved in ghettos, shot by Nazis and left in mass graves, or finished off in the camps. Paul's father had survived in a work camp.

They were liberated together, and lived for several years in a Displaced Persons camp in Munich, where Paul was born, in 1949.

"I knew this would happen!" Paul's mother said now. "I told Paul to stay out of the limelight. To stay neutral, a *groyer mensch*. But he was a sensitive child. He has always been an activist for justice. Even when he was a small boy, he wanted the kids to play fair. And, yes, he grew up with our stories. He knew about hate and how indifference leads to tragedy. He wanted to create a better world.

"But look what happened. And here in America, no less! How could there be Nazis here? They came back and tried to kill my boy. *Oy, Gottenu!*"

Frances went to her mother and held her. She had heard these sorry tales many times, but who would question why the story unfolding in the present had brought them all up again?

"Hitler started by killing small groups of people, intellectuals, and ended up killing six million Jews. This is how it begins," Tema wept.

For the next few days, I drove them back and forth to the hospital, carrying sandwiches and drinks for their long days of waiting. In between trips, I drove my children's carpools and did our household chores. One morning, I took a spontaneous detour and went to visit the office of the rabbi of our Beth David Synagogue. I told him how outraged I was by recent events and asked him to get involved.

"Tamara, I know you want to help," he told me. "But Paul was a member of the Communist Workers' Party. This is shameful. I would suggest you lower your profile."

"But, Rabbi!" I said. "Never mind about the Communists. Paul is *Jewish*. The KKK probably singled him out because of that, or shot him because he was organizing black people. He's still fighting for his life. His parents are Holocaust survivors.

"And Michael Nathan—he was a Jew, too, and murdered in cold blood on our streets here in Greensboro! He died trying to defend the rights of the black textile workers. What are you saying? Because they described themselves as Communists, we have no obligation to them as Jews? They were doing good work! We should be holding a memorial service for Dr. Nathan and a prayer vigil for Paul in *this* synagogue. They were not the ones who were doing the killing. They were *victims*, of the KKK and the American Nazis."

He shrugged and rolled his eyes. He had no comment. He stood up to usher me out. I could see he was not going to get involved.

"That's it?" I said. "You're not going to do anything?" No response.

I was furious with him. I walked out of the synagogue wondering if I would ever return. In the parking lot, my hands were cold and shaking. As I fumbled for my car keys, a friend approached me.

"I heard your old friend was shot at the rally, and that you've got his parents and his sister at your house. Is that right?"

"Yes," I said.

There were no secrets in this small town. Everyone knew my connection to the events of the past few days.

"I'm not sure that's such a good idea, Tamara," she said. "I know you want to help, but this is a federal case, and you never know what could happen. The FBI could come to your door and investigate you and your family. It's just not safe. They're Communists, after all."

After that, I was in such a state of disbelief about my fellow Jews that it caused me emotional pain. I continued housing Paul's parents; I continued my vigils in the hospital waiting room. I did not question my moral compass, but I felt small-mindedness was all around me.

It was hard to fathom. This town had come into the public eye in February, 1960, as the site of the country's earliest non-violent sit-in, at the Woolworth lunch counter, where four black students who had never been permitted to sit with white patrons took a stand for racial justice, sitting there in shifts around the clock. No one shot at them or even hit them—and six months after the sit-in started, the Woolworth's company reversed its policy of racial segregation in the southern United States.

But here it was nearly 10 years later, and nothing had changed in the town. And I realized that until Paul had been hurt, I, too, had been guilty of willful blindness.

Now I understood. What had happened at the corner of Carver and Everitt Streets was not an isolated incident, but the result of prejudice, widespread and deeply entrenched. I felt alone in this revelation.

As I am writing today, in 2017, similar events of anti-Semitism, racism, and police brutality are taking place in our American cities. And over the years, I have met many people who knew nothing about the Greensboro

Massacre. I had to explain that innocent men and women, mostly African-Americans, were murdered while doing nothing more than protesting for better wages for a better life.

The hate and violence caused by anti-Semitism and white supremacy would appear over and over again in my life. I would see what we as Jews had in common with African-Americans, and where we differ, in the realm of justice.

I would discover help coming from places I would never have expected—and learn ways to keep my positive view of the world despite this pain. Yet on some level, I think, as I did then, that nothing has really changed. It is hard to believe that we are still fighting for the basic human rights for everyone no matter their color, religion, or economic position in life; it makes me sad to think that our basic human character is so flawed and failing.

Of the 40 Klansmen that had come in their nine cars with the intent to kill, not one was even under arrest. Not one of them had been wounded. Meanwhile, five protesters were dead, and Paul still lay in the hospital, the only injured protester to survive.

He had a long road before him. He was transferred to a rehabilitation center where he spent months learning how to walk again. He was paralyzed on his left side and never regained use of his wounded arm.

The gruesome details of the shootings were rehashed again and again on the nightly news by the four major networks. The lack of police force at the rally was being investigated. There was a question of collaboration between the police and the KKK. Who was responsible for these deaths?

Yet, as would happen many times in my life, people wanted me to play only one role: the mother and housewife. Even simply extending help to a family in need was seen as going dangerously out of bounds.

Something had changed for me: It was no longer possible to live the quiet life. When you are called, you have a choice: you can deny the voice that whispers in your ear, or you can turn up the volume and act.

We had moved to Greensboro for practical reasons, but after November 3, 1979, I felt destiny calling me. The Greensboro Massacre became a seminal event in my life, and the next paving stone on my path to the rabbinate.

Late one afternoon, our friend Jonathan Malino dropped by the house.

"Tamara, I need a Jewish presence at the rally on the steps of the Guilford County courthouse next week," he said. "I've already asked both rabbis in town, and neither of them is willing to speak. I can't speak again. Everyone knows me and my position. We need a new voice … your voice."

Jonathan was both a rabbi and a professor, a distinguished presence with a booming voice. He towered over me both physically and professionally.

"Who am I to speak?" I said, unconsciously mimicking Moses. "I have no title. I have no clout. I'm the mother of three daughters. A housewife. I'm sorry, but I think you should find someone else."

I meant what I said at the time. I believed in speaking truth to power, but I thought that the truth-speaker should be someone other than me. But this was personal.

Jonathan called me again the next day and pleaded with me to reconsider. "We invited an interfaith group of speakers who will give a three-minute talk each. One of the widows will speak. There will be plenty of security and plenty of press. Please. Three minutes, that's all."

I gave in. For the next few days, I wrote and rewrote what I would say that could bring a Jewish perspective to the crowd. By the time I took the microphone in front of the county courthouse, I felt more than prepared. I had called upon the prophet Isaiah to help me:

Drop down, ye heavens, from above, And let the skies pour down righteousness; Let the earth open, that they may bring forth salvation, And let her cause righteousness to spring up together; I, Adonai have created it. (45.8)

I can still see the crowd standing in rows before me, black and white intermingled in a sea of faces. How many of us were Tema Bermanzohn's *groyer mensch,* as I had been, trying to stay safely in the grey area, giving lip service to these causes without really doing anything?

But I knew that black and white did not make grey. There was work to do. I did not want to sit on the sidelines of history. I was on the stage, speaking as much to myself as I did to them, my voice amplified so I could fight injustice where I found it.

ALIYAH AND *YERIDAH*: UPS AND DOWNS

Time and the shared experience of fear and loss forged a strong kinship with my community in Greensboro. By the time our daughters were 4, 7, and 9, I realized that somewhere along the line, I had let go my dream of *aliyah*, going to Israel.

The question had come up again and again in our marriage. And Michael was still racing toward the dream. After protracted negotiations, we settled on a compromise: we would go to Israel for two years. After that time, it would be up to me to decide whether we stayed on.

Apartments in Israel are very small, so we purged our non-essential furniture, books, and toys. We sold our home. Getting ready to leave was bittersweet. Our friends knew how much Israel meant to us, so they didn't discourage us from pursuing our pilgrimage to the Holy Land any longer. My own family—my parents, sister, cousins, aunts, uncles—wished us well. If we didn't go, we would regret it. Yet the leave-taking was rough.

We were temporarily housed at an absorption center, Beit Canada in Talpiot, a neighborhood in southeast Jerusalem. We shared the space with a group of Russians, who were overwhelmed by the desert heat of Israel's summer and complained loudly in Yiddish to each another. Because of my own Yiddish fluency I understood them, and in that way, found some unexpected new friends and a sense of linguistic competence I badly needed.

None of us had a working Hebrew vocabulary, except Michael. His Hebrew language skills were exceptionally good, and he was able to start his job at Hadassah Medical Center immediately. The rest of us joined an *ulpan*, a Hebrew immersion class, which met six days a week for six hours a day.

Naama and Elisheva went to school while four-year-old Sariel went to an Israeli-funded *gan*, or preschool. There, she had an intense Hebrew immersion experience; she spent the entire first week in tears. I would wait and listen outside the classroom door for her crying to stop. Some days were more difficult than others, but eventually she began to enjoy her playmates. Her English shifted easily to Hebrew and her distinctly Israeli accent made me smile.

Michael's parents—Bubbe Sylvia and Zeyde George to our children—came to visit several times during our time in Beit Canada, taking us out to dinner so I could take a break from cooking for the five of us on a two-burner hotplate.

After three months, we found an apartment in French Hill, a neighborhood in northeastern Jerusalem, within walking distance of the Hadassah Medical Center and the campus of Hebrew University. From our large *mirpeset*, or terrace, at the back of the tiered apartment, we had spectacular views of the Judean Desert, the Dead Sea, the Old City, and the Dome of the Rock. Nearly every day, awestruck at the sight, I would recite the prayer for entering a holy space: *Mah Tovu*! "How good are your tents, Jacob—your dwelling places, Israel." I can still close my eyes and recall the panorama.

French Hill offered us proximity to Ramat Zion, a conservative synagogue with an American structure of religious observance. Ramat Zion had to overcome opposition from the Orthodox bureaucracy who didn't understand or appreciate—who perhaps even feared—us newcomers and our approach to Judaism. We saw Ramat Zion as a safe haven. We participated in community programs and Shabbat morning services on a regular basis. For the most part, men and women in our congregation participated equally in rituals and learning, but this liberal approach kept Israelis from joining.

"I don't understand why you are so fixated on this idea of women having equal participation in the synagogue," my Israeli friend would say. "Who cares? Women have enough work to do at home. Let's leave the synagogue business to the men."

Again I was faced with an "all or nothing" mentality—but I was no longer willing to entertain it. I was surprised to feel a stronger sense of kinship with our American friends than with the Israelis who, despite compulsory military service for both women and men, had not seen the positive societal changes of the feminist movement.

Our apartment's small, overcrowded rooms gave us a sense of intimacy, but the oversize *mirpeset* lent an airy, outdoor feeling to the space. The three girls slept in one room, and at night I could hear them laughing and chattering in Hebrew.

I listened to them with pride—Elisheva might feel that she could not keep up in Hebrew, but here she was, speaking the language herself. And Naama was really stretching her wings. I remember thinking how resilient they were in the face of this upheaval.

Hebrew encircled me but I continued to struggle, linguistically and emotionally. I missed my aging parents and longed to see them. I hoped to bring them over for a visit. If we could all be together in the Holy Land, even for a little while, another dream of my mother's would come true.

But here, we had Michael's parents. Bubbe Sylvia was a joyful person, with a sunny disposition and two dimples to prove it. She loved people and played her role as the *rebbetzin*, or rabbi's wife, to her scholarly husband with great pleasure. They lived within an hour's drive, and she demonstrated her love for her six grandchildren by buying them gifts, taking them to restaurants, and spoiling them whenever possible. Her sons, Michael and Gabriel, indulged and adored her in turn.

In fact, we all did. At 69, she was a youthful and active grandmother. Because she was retired and did not have a rigid schedule to adhere to, she frequently offered her assistance with the children. We often went to Rehovot for Shabbat dinners at their home as well, and stayed overnight, sharing one bedroom. Bubbe Sylvia was a resourceful cook; nothing went to waste. She cooked with whatever was in her fridge, but I can still remember her chicken soup and the sweet taste of her noodle kugel. Like my mother, she always covered her head with a white lace doily as she lit the Shabbat candles. With her hands waving in concentric circles, she lilted the Hebrew blessing, embracing her three American-born granddaughters.

Yet even as we lived out our dream, there was pain to go with the joy. And once again, it was close enough to me that I could not evade it—death would demand to become part of my life.

Michael's first cousin, Ariel, and his wife, Rachel, had made *aliyah* long before us, and despite Ariel's prolonged battle with depression, they had happily settled into their orthodox Israeli life, with three daughters of their own. Michael had been looking forward to reanimating his relationship with his many cousins in Israel, and naturally saw our future in Ariel's situation. We were thrilled to hear they had had a fourth child, a boy, but soon afterward events spiraled out of control. Ariel decided he was so happy with his lot that he no longer needed his anti-depressant medication. All seemed well when the baby's *bris*, or circumcision ceremony, was held. Ten days later, a tragedy: Ariel went to the roof of his building and jumped off.

We grieved with Michael's large clan in Israel, and I held my three daughters close to me as I watched Ariel's daughters cry.

In Israel, going to the cemetery and visiting *shiva* houses of people in mourning was a frequent occurrence. Michael's Israeli family had already lost two of its own: Albert, his sister-in-law's brother, had died at 21, in the Yom Kippur War; and Yaakov, his second cousin, had been an 18-year-old *yeshiva* student when he was gunned down during Friday night prayers in Hebron. Loss always seemed to be lurking nearby.

But I loved the language and the land, and after months at *ulpan*, I made up my mind to put my linguistic competence to the test. I answered an ad in *The Jerusalem Post* and started working at the Office of Immigration and Absorption.

Fortunately, my job was geared toward the college audience of Anglo-Saxim, so I wrote in English: I was asked to create a news magazine about the study-volunteer programs available through the immigration center. Integration into Israeli society was the goal. I named the project "Manna," after the food that was miraculously supplied to the Israelites in the wilderness (Exodus 16:14-36). We would give our readers a taste of manna, nourishment for their experiences in the land of their ancestors.

In Israel our days were filled with feverish activity: Six days of work and school but only one day of Shabbat; no two-day weekends and no frivolous excursions. Shabbat in Jerusalem is like nowhere else in the world: No driving, no television, no telephone, and no movies. We loved the peaceful aura of the noiseless streets and the quiet, slow, deliberate way people moved on that day. We were spiritually satiated.

The weeks rolled into months. We finally started to adjust to our new surroundings. My parents made plans to visit.

Then Michael's mother collapsed. She was taken to the hospital with heart palpitations and diagnosed with late-stage diabetes. She went into a decline, and eventually into a coma, and our visits had a sense of dread.

Sometime during that period, Michael and I decided that we were done having children. I made an appointment to have a tubal ligation. Bubbe

Sylvia would often tease me with suggestions about having a *sabra*, an Israeli-born child, now that we were there to stay.

But now, the possibility of her help and support was receding, and when I pondered the idea of having a child in Israel, maybe even a son, I could not imagine it: all the children, boy or girl, went into the army at 18 and gave several years of their lives trying to keep the so-called peace.

The first Lebanon War had caused tension around the country; more lives lost and nothing gained. Soldiers with Uzis guarded the schoolrooms, and every field trip was accompanied by uniformed police. Bombs were going off in supermarkets. What would the future hold? I was scared.

I kept my gynecology appointment for the tubal ligation, though Michael did not come with me. Bubbe Sylvia had contracted hepatitis after months of hospital stays, and Michael began a vigil while I remained in Jerusalem with the children.

My pre-surgical consultation with the physician, a mild-mannered South African émigré, did not go as I expected.

After my exam, he blurted out, "My dear, you are pregnant."

Only denial kept me from hysteria. "Could you check again?" I managed to ask.

He gently reassured me of his diagnosis and reminded me to eat well and to rest as much as possible. I walked the streets of Jerusalem in a daze. God was laughing at me again.

That afternoon, I called Michael, who was at his mother's bedside, with the news. I was numb to everything. And Michael took it calmly, as if this had always been the plan.

"Is it okay if I tell my mother?" he asked. "Maybe she'll hear me and wake up."

Though it was too soon, he voiced a plan: "I'm sure it'll be another girl. We'll name her after my mother, Sylvia-Zahava."

Zahava, Sylvia's Hebrew name, means *the golden one*. "Her memory will live on in our baby," Michael said. I could tell this magical thinking gave him comfort: a soul dies; a child is born.

Michael and Gabriel shared the vigil for several nights in a row, Sylvia's very own guardian angels, but they could not save her. As if she knew her boys would never let her go, she died during the changing of the guard, leaving them both bereft.

Within a few hours, her body was brought to Har HaMenuchot, the Jerusalem cemetery where she was to be buried. We bundled up our three children and drove in silence to the cemetery.

My daughters and I stood in the designated women's area, while Michael went to stand in front with the other men. I was grieved by her death, and even more so by the archaic treatment that kept me apart from my husband as he grieved. There was nothing I could do except hold onto my daughters and think about my own mother, who was due to visit with my father in two days.

A busload of friends arrived from Rehovot; Gabriel and his family came from Tel Aviv; other family members gathered around the grave. Night was beginning to show her dark face. Rabbis with long beards mumbled prayers. Sylvia was draped from head to toe in a white shroud. No casket. No fanfare. Dust to dust. The sounds of moaning rose as the men stepped forward one by one to cover her shrouded body with shovelfuls of dirt.

I thought to myself that our *aliyah* had a purpose we never could have imagined: to bury our beloved Sylvia.

Michael spent the week of *shiva* in Rehovot with his brother and grieving father, but I could not go with him, as my parents were arriving on the second day of *shiva* for what turned out to be their only visit to Israel. The girls and I picked them up at Ben Gurion airport, and their first stop was the Ende family's house of mourning. Michael and I kept our secret as we mourned.

Upon seeing my parents, my father-in-law, always before so strong and statuesque, collapsed to the floor. The three remaining parents cried together.

While it was comforting to have my mother and father with me during this painful time, I couldn't help thinking that Bubbe Sylvia would have given them a big, warm welcome they would now never get to experience. Sylvia died at 70; my mother would outlive her by 25 years.

After 30 days, we returned to the cemetery, as is the tradition. We huddled together and repeated the Mourner's *Kaddish*. We read Sylvia's epitaph, which we had found among her papers during the week of *shiva*. Decades before, she had written it for herself as a journalism assignment. In it, she revealed her destiny: she would retire and move to Israel; she would die there and be buried on a mountaintop in Jerusalem. She would leave behind two sons, two daughters-in-law, and seven grandchildren.

Seven? Everyone whispered to each other. *There are only six. It was the only part she got wrong.*

Michael and I exchanged a look as we stood at Sylvia's grave and allowed the sun to warm us. We nodded at each other. Now was the time.

We told everyone: *No. Bubbe Sylvia counted right. There will be seven grandchildren.*

Something shifted once Bubbe Sylvia left this world. I became sadder and lonelier. My parents flew back to New York and I felt a profound emptiness. Michael's father became disoriented and despondent. He traveled back and forth from our house to Gabriel's house. He couldn't be left alone. We needed a plan. Always a plan.

One evening we had an altercation with the landlord who vehemently refused to fix our clogged sink unless we paid him for the work up front. I lost my temper with this bully and ranted at him in perfect Hebrew. I heard myself and realized I was becoming tough, maybe even harsh. My confidence had soared, but my emotions were always raw. It had been a long fourteen months.

"Michael, I want to go home," I said.

He was speechless. I had veto power, and now I was using it, something I could see he had never anticipated. He had made a promise, but sorrow and anger and blame followed us through every subsequent conversation.

"We've come all this way. We've overcome so much! How can we give up now?" Michael said. "Let's give it another six months, another year. "

"I don't want to give birth to a child here. I want to be back home, near my parents, where I feel safe."

"We're perfectly safe here."

"You know that's not true, and the longer we stay, the more entrenched the girls will be with their friends and the culture here. It will be harder to leave," I said. "I feel like an immigrant now, and I'll always feel like an immigrant. I know how my parents felt—they struggled for their entire lives with the American way of life. You know we'll never fully be accepted here. Please, I just want to go home."

In the end, he conceded. We had made a deal, and though he wasn't willing to admit it and I was not going to be the one to point it out, it had been a difficult time for Michael as well.

Despite this strife between us, I thought of the life growing in me as a chance for greater closeness with Michael; this was our "love child," not because it was conceived outside of our marriage, but because it was going to bring more love into it.

Yeridah means going down. It is the opposite of *aliyah*. Usually climbing up a mountain is more difficult than coming down, but not in this case. Leaving Jerusalem left us rudderless as a couple. That dream had cemented our relationship, and now we were letting it go.

Not wanting to pay for another transatlantic shipment, we sold everything we had shipped from the States—the couches we had purchased in a North Carolina showroom, the piano we bought in Colorado while doing our time for Uncle Sam, the mahogany dining table from Greensboro at which we had celebrated our children's birthdays. We let go of all the things we had accumulated in our 13 years of marriage. We would never again make a home for our family in this holy place.

LIFE, POST-DREAM

Leaving Israel meant leaving behind the dream.

Michael and I grew up believing that this land of milk and honey was our spiritual home, a place of continuous connection with our tribal lineage. Would this physical departure disrupt our spiritual footing? How would we reinvent ourselves and our marriage to adjust to this new reality?

If home was more than a place—if home was an existential feeling that lived within us—then maybe we could weave this experience into the next phase of our family life.

We returned to America with no plan for home or work. It seemed pointless, when our plans were always being overturned.

My parents were waiting for us at JFK Airport. They cuddled and kissed each granddaughter as if the girls had escaped a hurricane. I had never seen them happier. We were home.

I was six months pregnant, physically and emotionally drained. Michael was sad about leaving his Israeli family and anxious about providing for the soon-to-be six of us. When and how would we find our way again? Where to live? What to do? We would need to rebuild.

It was a different time than today, 1982. We had no internet to research housing or apply for jobs. Long-distance phone calls from Israel were prohibitive. We went to ground in the Bronx, in my parents' one-bedroom apartment. It was impossibly overcrowded, and could be only a way station, though they were thrilled to have us.

After many job interviews in the northeast, Michael ended up getting his former job back in Greensboro. We were relieved to be returning to familiar territory, but also embarrassed at the failure of our grand experiment.

Still, our friends were happy to have us back. Our old neighbor Joan, a devout Catholic, said she had prayed for us every day. Linda found us a rental apartment that was fully furnished. As my due date approached, our friends Ruth and Sarah babysat often for the girls. Thanks to my friend Susan, I began teaching Hebrew at the day school. A month before the birth, we bought a house not far from the first house we'd had, on Watauga Drive. The homecoming was complete.

When people asked us about our *aliyah*, Michael would say: "I never wanted to leave. Israel was my dream come true. My clinic work at Hadassah hospital gave me a new perspective on children from many different cultures and being close to my brother and his extended family was an added bonus. Frankly, I would never have left if it hadn't been for Tamara's reluctance to integrate into Israeli society. She was always pining for her family in America."

I felt compelled to tell my side of the story.

"Before I made *aliyah*, I could not have comprehended the difficulties of being an immigrant in a Jewish state like Israel. I was studying Hebrew every day, but my lack of verbal fluency kept me from integrating fully into Israeli society. And did I mention the lack of a feminist consciousness among men and women? Shocking, in a cosmopolitan city like Jerusalem. They're two decades behind us."

Our friends grasped the tension that surrounded this issue between Michael and me. Our disparate points of view remained throughout the next several years of our marriage as a reminder of all that kept us from being happy together.

I had spasms of nostalgia for the clear, crisp Jerusalem air and the energy of the Israeli people, but my life was on a fast track as we prepared for our fourth child. As a family, we voted on girl's names only, trying to find the right one to memorialize Bubbe Sylvia.

The nurses at Moses Cone Hospital made me comfortable as the anesthesia drip entered my body, I dozed off until I heard the chant from the surgical team, "It's a boy, it's a boy."

Cold and confused, I began to cry and shake. "Please don't play games with me," I remember saying. "It can't be a boy. I know it's a girl."

The doctor whispered in my ear. "Tamara, it *is* a boy. I will bring him to you. Your son is eight pounds and healthy."

He was wrapped in a white hospital cotton blanket, with its blue-and-pink stripes. I saw his spirit face for the first time, the phantom shadow of Sylvia that I imagined had passed through him at the moment of her death. I cried again, and then I faded back into sleep.

But for the first few days, it was not his gender that intrigued us, but rather the unimagined grace that had created another child. Michael and I came together as loving partners and parents. The fact that the baby was a boy added another dimension.

Three female siblings rotated holding him, patting him to sleep, and walking him around the house. I regained my physical strength more quickly than after the birth of Sariel, and I prepared myself for my son's circumcision, the ancient commandment for Jewish boys.

Eight days later, over a hundred people from the Greensboro Jewish community came to our house to witness our son's bris. The children from B'nai Shalom, the Jewish day school, walked for twenty minutes with their teachers and when they reached our home, they burst into song. My parents came from New York. My sister came from Philadelphia. Michael's father came all the way from Israel.

We had little furniture, but that just made it easier to set up rows of tables for the foods. The extended greenhouse where the actual bris took place was surrounded by glass doors and windows, so we could see the verdant outdoors. The panorama of our Jerusalem apartment was a memory; we had traded views as well as communities.

I did not feel queasy or unsettled about the circumcision. I felt blessed to bring a son into the covenant of the House of Israel. The children all sang cheerful Hebrew songs and the Rabbi and the *mohel*, the person who performs the rite of circumcision, recited the necessary prayers. Then, baby boy Ende was placed in my hands while Michael spoke.

"We are calling our new son *Zachary Shai* after my late mother *Zahava*. In Hebrew, *zechariah* means 'God has remembered.' *Shai* is the Hebrew word for gift and an abbreviation of the prophet Isaiah's name. Bubbe Sylvia, as we called her, would have been overjoyed with her seventh grandchild. We feel so blessed to have you all here today to celebrate with us. Thank you for coming."

People started clapping and singing *Mazal Tov*, while our friends danced circles around the three of us. Baby Zachary slept through all the commotion as he was carried through the adoring crowd. I remember thinking that this communal embrace was just what I needed to fill me with renewed hope for the future.

I couldn't articulate it then, but this kind of ceremony made me want to be able to provide this for others—the sense of community, of togetherness in values and history.

Michael and I would spend a total of 20 years raising our family in the Bible Belt, though our sense of rootedness in this community was not enough to sustain our bond, any more than our shared delight in this gift of a last child.

Still, I felt a sense of gratitude on that sun-drenched fall day. The decision to return to our American life in this small town of Greensboro, North Carolina had been right. Within a few months, we were even able to buy back our old house, on Watauga Drive. Starting over again would be easier here than anywhere else.

In my sister Khana, I saw some of the most destructive aspects of male-female relationships and the most unhappy ways religious rules can shape a life. When we visited her family, we found a houseful of unhappy, uncontrollable boys racing around the rooms, making loud noises and ballistic movements with their hands. A typical scene was like this:

"Shmuel, do you think you could find out why Avrummy is crying?" Khana asks.

"You know I can't understand anything he does with his hands. Eventually he'll stop on his own."

Mordechai walks up to his brother and tries to comfort him while motioning with his hands in front of his brother's face. He sits on the floor next to Avrummy. "What matter? Tired?"

Shmuel abruptly leaves the room while Khana continues diapering the youngest boy, Yossi.

"Bring him to me," she signs while speaking to Mordechai. "If he doesn't stop crying, he'll wear us all out." Then, as if on cue, comes the sound of blocks hitting the floor; 2-year-old Aaron claps his hands in delight.

Khana had all she could do just to keep up, and though she had learned how to sign with her children, Shmuel flatly refused to learn the language, so his communications with them were reduced to gestures and grunts, and often slaps.

Sometimes we would meet at my parents' place in Co-op City, but things were no better there. My parents were grief-stricken to see what was becoming of their brave first-born daughter and her children. Where was my intelligent, confident sister, I wondered, the one who had moved to Israel, the one who had made a life for herself after a childhood filled with suffering? Where did she go, and when would she come back?

It was difficult, if not impossible, for me to show anger toward Khana. She had always suffered, and my troubles had never stacked up to hers.

What right did I have to question her way of navigating through her difficulties? To not question was what my mother had always taught me, and I had internalized it, but now I found I could no longer be a witness to her self-sabotage. I had my own family, my own challenges, and I separated myself physically and emotionally.

My visits with my sister dwindled, though I began to think about domestic abuse in a new way.

Khana was like Job. She lived her faith, though hardship followed her throughout her life. Each blow seemed to strengthen her belief in God's will. Perhaps she saw suffering as normal; she certainly did not shy away from it, and in some ways, she courted it. And though it was true that she did some good with the bad hand that was dealt her, I could no longer bear to watch.

I had not envisioned that my new joy, with my new child, in an old home, would contain the seeds of my deepest sorrows. I had yet to learn the dynamic that was shaping my life: whenever I was a witness to suffering in one part of my life, I would become an activist in another.

THAT'S NOT ALL THERE IS

"Isn't it great that we both had boys?" Sarah said as we watched them play in the sandbox. Sarah and Jonathan's son was, like Zachary, a "caboose baby"—the one that comes at the end.

"It's true, but the difference is you've had experience with boys. This is totally foreign territory for me. Somehow I really thought he'd play with his sister's dolls—but he's not even interested."

"Oh, I know! Believe me, I've tried with my boys! With my women's studies background, I felt like it was my responsibility to teach them neutrality. I've been surprised over and over by the way these tendencies are entrenched."

Sarah and I were both enthusiasts of the *Free To Be ... You and Me* recording released in 1972. A project of the Ms. Foundation for Women, these songs revolved around the post-1960s concept of gender neutrality and individual identity, that anyone, boy or girl, can achieve anything.

"Yes! I can see how Zachary and David go off into their own boys' world," I said.

Zachary had reconfigured our female-dominated family. He loved playing outside and was always more active than the girls. In that way, he was the stereotypical boy who loved sports and climbing trees. He was the only child of ours who ended up in the emergency room—a broken arm, after he jumped off the swing set in David's backyard.

Rearing a son was a different experience for me, and an eye opener: even though Zachary was surrounded by baby dolls and playhouses, he ignored them all and gravitated instead to basketballs, miniature metal cars, and model train sets. This was pure nature, and no amount of nurture could override it.

Having a son also led me to think differently about the gender roles Michael and I had so carefully established before our marriage. But in the wake of the financial strains of our grand experiment, I needed to work to stabilize our household budget. Before I knew it, I had enrolled in a six-month real estate course, where I met ambitious women trying to break into the real estate market, which at that time and place was nearly all male.

My other friends did not view this as a good fit. They flat-out discouraged my new career direction. But I was excited to learn something new and outside my comfort zone. I was delighted to be with men and women tackling the business world. I ignored friends' advice and pursued this profession with an honest passion. My first real estate job was in an all-women's firm, the first of its kind in Greensboro.

My world expanded. I opened my own checking and savings accounts to keep my earnings separate from the household expenses. I told Michael that because I was the better budgeter, it would be my job to save money for the family, and his earnings would cover our household expenses. But in truth, I wanted more independence: I wanted to pay for my own professional clothing and other incidentals as I moved out of sweatpants and into pantsuits. I wanted to feel a sense of control.

What was more, I was having a surprising amount of fun while working. My work partner, Jeffrie Ann—or Jeff, as we called her—had come from New York as well, and also had four children. We savored our connections, both past and present, covering for each other when one of us was out of town or preoccupied with family obligations. I admired her savvy way of carrying herself in the male-dominated business world, and she loved sharing her expertise with me, her young apprentice. We worked well together. We became soul sisters.

Michael had a mixed reaction to my new career. He had always encouraged me to work, and said it was important for women to find their own place. He quoted Freud: "Love and work are the cornerstones of our humanness."

But he was at the height of his own career, and certainly never offered to alter his schedule: quite aside from the fact that his work involved human lives and mine didn't, I don't think it would ever have occurred to him to change his life because mine had changed. In fact, it seemed to me that the more I worked, the more he worked.

Practically speaking, though, our life needed to continue on—the children had to be cared for and the house had to be kept running. A string of reliable-enough graduate students filled in the child-care gaps from a logistical perspective, but the effect was that the household center vanished. I realized that Michael and I had never been acting together as the center. *I* was the center, and when I was gone, there *was* no center.

Of course, I had less energy for Michael, too: I didn't worry any more about asking how his day was—I was trying to manage my own day. I didn't worry, either, about the state of my marriage, a subject that had consumed many hours of therapy for me until then. I had no energy for sex, or for argument, or for negotiation: I was too busy. For over a year, Michael and I circled in our own orbits, and these two orbits synchronized less and less.

My real estate work gave me a sense of agency. I started my own company with another broker, and we called it "Accommodations." Together we managed dozens of properties. Large companies sought us out to arrange extended residences for their business consultants. We matched each individual with conveniently located furnished condos and townhomes. I was busier than ever. I would close a deal, and go home with a check for $5,000. What power!

But how to juggle it all? My relationship with Michael was in critical condition. Had our failed *aliyah* created a fatal load of resentment? And why did it feel as though there was an unspoken competition between us? Was there any chance we could create a new vision for our marriage that tied us to one another again? In the midst of professional success, I was alone.

One afternoon, before the children returned from school, I was standing at the kitchen window and washing the dishes, as if in a trance. The water from the faucet dripped down endlessly as I peered between the wooden panes. Suddenly, I felt I was suffocating.

Is this all there is?

I removed my plastic gloves, walked to the back door, opened it, and stepped outside into the tree-filled backyard. I scanned the Carolina blue sky. I had my dream house, my shiny career, and my caboose baby, but I could sense a whole world waiting for me beyond this small Southern suburb.

I wept. The tears seemed to come from a deeply wounded place I had not been aware of until then. There was no one to hold me. I crisscrossed my hands and embraced my own small frame.

After putting the children to bed, I waited for Michael to come home from another consultation following an attempted suicide of one of his young patients.

He talked about his own inadequacy to stave off this violent act, and I listened sincerely to the pain he was feeling.

"Michael, I'm worried. I'm not happy. You're not happy."

"Tamara, this is the way it works in marriage. A few good years. A few bad ones. It will all work itself out. Don't worry."

"You're the most important person in my life. If we're not working well together, then nothing works."

A week later, Michael and I were in couple's counseling. We had several long heart-wrenching sessions, traveling the 45 minutes arguing all the way, and returning in silence.

Michael and I had lived together for 20 years, but we rarely told each other the truth about how we felt. Behind it was my reluctance to confront. I have always seen myself as the mediator of conflicts, not their cause. When Michael started a fight with me, I withdrew. I didn't like criticism, and I felt bullied into a stalemate. I stifled myself in order to protect myself.

A heavy fog seemed to cover every part of our lives. I could not breathe. The tension clogged my airways; headaches followed me throughout the day. My partner at work covered for me as much as she could. All I wanted was to run away and be alone. But how could I leave the children? Night after night, I tucked each of them in with a hug and a kiss and hoped they couldn't see the tears rolling down my face into my silk pajamas.

Every night I waited for Michael to come home, but he stayed out later and later, tiptoeing into the kitchen through the back door after I was asleep. I thought then that there would be no leaving for me. I loved my children, and I loved my life, and I had made a commitment under the *chuppah,* a vow in front of family and friends. It was clear that Michael was avoiding me, but on this we agreed: it was best to stay together. We would wait for the heavy fog to lift.

A few months later, I came down with what I thought was a stomach flu. The pain was so severe that I could not eat or drink anything. I took medication to relieve the cramping, but the pain only worsened. I was free only when I slept. So I slept.

I had no desire to see anyone or be anywhere but in my bed. I grew weaker and weaker. I thought it must be cancer. Michael brought in friends to help with the children. They took turns sitting beside my bed and holding my hand. All my tests were negative, said the doctors. But I felt cursed: I felt like I was dying.

One afternoon, when Michael got home from work, I cried out in agony: "Michael, just take me to the hospital!" He called his colleague, a gastroenterologist, who agreed to see me right away. After examining me carefully, he sent me home with Valium. I slept for 15 hours.

When I woke up, the curse was gone. In its place was an insight: I could no longer stay in the same house with my husband. It was too lonely. My health was in jeopardy.

Ultimately, the marriage failed us for the same reasons orthodoxy failed us: the pressures of trying to negotiate our conventional male-female roles were too much for us. I had maintained our domestic life so Michael could nurture his career, but he was not able to do the same for me.

I can't explain my recovery any more than I can explain the illness itself. But looking back, it seems to me that my stomach was the container for my emotional pain. The suffering paralyzed my body until I acknowledged the fact that Michael and I were toxic to each other. One of us needed to leave, and I told him so.

The next day Michael called me from work and asked me to meet him at a nearby park.

"Tamara, please don't leave." He sounded sincere and scared. "We can work things out. Think about our family."

"How exactly would that happen?" I said. "We've tried and tried. We went to marriage counseling for months. The children must feel our tension. We can't live together anymore. I know it's not what we want for our family, but I think it will be the best thing for both of us."

"How do you want to tell the children?" Michael asked.

I had rehearsed what I would say.

We love you very much. We will always take care of you and provide for you. But right now, your father and mother can't live together.

I had pictured us sitting in the den on our comfortable couches, talking things through calmly and lovingly. We would cry until we had no more tears.

Instead, Michael just blurted it out as we sat down for dinner in the kitchen: "Kids, your mother and I are separating."

Chaos ensued. Elisheva got angry and started shooting questions at us. Naama tried to calm everyone down while Sariel went over to her baby brother, hugged him, and began to cry. Zachary had just lifted his fork to his mouth and stopped, not knowing whether or not to eat.

"Maybe it would be best to postpone this conversation until after dinner?" I said to him, trying to keep the fury from my voice.

"Why is this happening to us?" Naama asked. "We're a good, loving family."

"What am I going to tell my friends?" Elisheva said.

Once we decided to separate, Michael and I had to navigate our living situation.

"Michael, you have the financial resources to find an apartment. You can take some furniture. Let me stay in the Watauga house and keep the family routine going."

"I don't want to leave. I'm the one paying the mortgage. You're the real estate professional. *You* find a place to live."

After all these years, I still regret that I left. I had created that home with our children. At the time I could not see another option.

I confided to my partner, Jeff.

"I have an empty townhouse on the market," she offered. "If you furnish the place with your things so that it'll show better, you can stay there for free. I'll help you stage it, and you'll be all set until we have a sale. When do you want to move in?"

I was 40 years old. I had never lived alone.

I did not count on the children's reluctance to leave their home. I thought they would follow me anywhere, but they were afraid and wanted to stay in the familiar setting. Sometimes the kids spent a night or a weekend at my townhouse, but I was the one who did all of the adjusting.

I was always on call for carpooling and late night pick-ups. I went out of my way and changed my schedule to catch a few minutes with each of the kids. My guilt had no boundaries. I had tried to confront, to stand up for what I thought our children needed, and nothing had come of it. It was emblematic of injustices small and large that I would try to push back against.

Each of our four children reacted differently. Naama used her status as the eldest child to take on new responsibilities. Elisheva faltered in school and withdrew from us. Sariel leaned on her older sisters to avoid the conflict around her. Zachary, only four years old, couldn't possibly grasp the consequences of his parents' separation.

Although I knew that divorce was the right choice for me, I blamed myself for the break-up of our family. I zeroed in on the children's needs. If I couldn't be the good wife, I would be the best mother. As I withdrew my energies from Michael, I directed all my waking hours toward nurturing my kids.

My schedule was a carefully calibrated strategy, plotted out, in these years before computers, with color-coordinated diagrams on sheets of paper. While the kids were in school, I went to the office. At three o'clock I might pick up Zachary and take him to baseball or soccer practice. At four o'clock I might take Sariel shopping for a new dress for her best friend's bat mitzvah. At five-thirty, I might pick up Naama from tennis lessons and rescue Elisheva from her babysitting job. We would rush home to cook dinner and do homework. I had phone calls to make for work to schedule the next day's appointments.

I heard that Michael had started seeing someone: the friend of a colleague's girlfriend. But I was so busy, I didn't have time to think about the future. *One day at a time*, I told myself.

The days turned into weeks, and then into months. I was just beginning to get used to the new normal when Michael called to say he was getting married. Before six months had gone by, it was done. I was confirmed in my feeling that I was replaceable, and even worse, Michael now had a very large circle of obligations: with his new wife, Barbara, and her teenage son, there were five growing children and two adults to shelter. When I learned that he had decided to sell the Watauga house and buy a larger place in the same neighborhood, I asked him to meet with me.

"Before you sell the house to a stranger," I said to Michael as soon as we had exchanged the requisite niceties, "maybe we could work out some financial arrangement? I'd love to move back into the house so the kids don't have to move again. Doesn't that make more sense?"

"How exactly would that work? I've got equity in the house. I need the money to buy another house. You can't just come and tell me what to do."

"I'm not telling you what to do. I just want you to think about what would be best for our kids."

"The kids'll be fine. Even better. They'll each have their own room, and they'll still be in the same neighborhood where their friends are."

"But they love the Watauga house! It's the only consistent home they know. The divorce is hard enough on them. Why can't you give them this one thing?"

"No. You're the realtor. You find someplace else. The house goes on the market in less than a week."

I had no control over the situation. The house was in Michael's name, and he had no interest in my wishes. I would drive past "my" house with its "sale" sign sitting in the yard—an interloper I had not authorized. I would look at the black mailbox with the red flag, the brick house with its manicured lawn, like a house in a storybook, and see my children running to pick up the day's mail, tripping over each other to be the first one to snatch the letters. I could hear them laughing in their rooms; I could feel Michael's body lying next to mine as we drifted from pillow talk to dreams that would never be realized. It was as if a tornado had touched down and scattered the pieces of my life. It was all gone.

The Watauga house sold quickly. Michael and Barbara's larger house had a bedroom for each of their five children. A recreation room in the basement became the teenage hangout for their friends from school. After a few months of traipsing back and forth with their backpacks and suitcases to the two-bedroom condo I had bought, they came to me and said, "We want to go and live with Daddy."

Children are so concrete.

Before I knew what was happening, Michael had asked for full custody. Our attorneys had negotiated a typical joint custody agreement, but we considered the kids old enough to decide where they wanted to live. We asked a family counselor to help decide the future accommodations of our children. Michael had continued on with his professional life and his personal life with seeming ease. But he didn't like paying child support; he wanted to hold onto his money. My professional life was in flux, as were my finances. And my personal life was in chaos. I didn't see that it was all rigged—that I had been manipulated into accepting a punishment for wanting it all.

Just contemplating losing my children threw me into a bottomless pit of sadness. I could not focus at work. My therapist, Henrietta, suggested I get medication, but I refused: I didn't want to appear even more helpless than I felt.

It took several weeks for the family psychologist to speak individually to each child and to each parent. After these sessions, he brought us together to give his expert adjudication.

"All the children want to live with their father," he said.

Pause. Silence. Heartbreak.

"This doesn't mean they don't love you. You're their mother. They know you are a strong person and that you'll work with them on an individual basis to spend time with you. Weekends, sleepovers, dinners together. But you can't offer them space: at Michael's they can have their own rooms and feel more settled. They want one permanent place to call home."

Speechless and paralyzed with fright, I stared into the void. The children embraced me solemnly.

Why had they deserted me? I couldn't make any sense out of it. I stood up. I wobbled. Michael had won—and I didn't even know there was a contest.

Prozac became my drug of choice.

Wrapped in my cloak of guilt and self-blame, I could not see then what Henrietta pointed out to me soon afterward: "You'll see," she said. "They'll all come around. Their father has bribed them with candy, but soon the candy will lose its appeal. Your love will sustain them. In the meantime, learn to love yourself. Seek out your friends. Go on vacation. You're a good person. Remember that."

I tried. I went to Club Med in Haiti. *Seven Days in Singles Paradise.* Haiti! What was I thinking?

I cried all week. I ate with strangers every day. I sat around the pool with sunglasses to protect my swollen eyes. I played tennis fiercely with a mournful-looking but adorable widower.

On Day Two, a man whispered to me at the dinner table: "I'm not really single."

"What?" I said, unable to stop my eyes from going straight to his unadorned left hand.

"I lied so I could get away alone. I couldn't take it any more at home. Please don't tell anyone."

Who would I tell? I sighed. We were all of us alone.

On Day Six, I brought the widower back to my room, thinking at least we could offer each other some brief comfort. He sat down on my bed and started to cry, and he didn't stop until I told him it was time to say good night.

Somehow, despite the pervasive misery of the trip, the time away renewed my physical energy. But still, I missed my kids and their laughter. I missed seeing their lunch boxes lined up in a row on my kitchen table. I missed tucking them in at night and reading them a story. I told myself that I was responsible for their every present and future heartache.

After work, I came home and made myself dinner. I slept alone and woke up from my nightmares alone. My polka-dot blue-and-white duvet lightened up the room and, on occasion, lifted my spirits. I was functioning. Slowly, I began to have friends over. I dated a bit. My parents came to visit.

The kids slept over on Shabbat.

I was aware that people were talking about me. My friends admitted that many in the community took Michael's side: I had become too career-oriented, and that was what broke up the marriage. Michael had no choice but to find someone who would be more present for his family.

One evening, Naama called out of the blue. "Can I come and stay over tonight?" she said, sobbing.

"But, of course! The bed is already made for you."

She arrived with a suitcase, still sobbing, and I held her in my arms. I was dying to know what had happened—a fight with one of her siblings? A breakup with a boyfriend?—but I thought I should wait until she wanted to tell me.

"I don't want to stay in that house anymore. Barbara's still a stranger to us. And Dad is never home."

"Oh, Naama, I never meant for you to get caught in the middle like this. Why haven't you said anything before now?"

"I don't know ... I wanted to be there for Dad"

"And now?"

"I want to come live with you."

"And what about the other kids? Have you talked about this together?"

"Yes! Of course we talk about it. We hardly talk about anything else. I told them that we all had to stay together—that the divorce was bad enough; we couldn't be apart from each other, too. I told them I'd work it all out somehow. But I can't live there any more. Can I stay here with you?"

"You can stay here as long as you like. I've missed you so much."

Naama and I cried together on the old couch where we had sat and watched television all together just a year ago.

The next evening, Elisheva arrived with her suitcase and backpack.

"If Naama is staying here, then I'm coming too. What's the point of having my own room? I'd rather be with you."

That night I slept in the bedroom next to my two daughters. The crying had diminished and they whispered to each other.

"I told you that we'd end up with Mom. I just didn't know how long it would take," Naama said.

"You can't hide from reality, even in a big house," said Elisheva, my future social worker.

Sariel followed the next night, and without discussion or interference from Michael, a new arrangement began. Before long, my four babies were sleeping all together in my 1,000-square-foot condo.

Henrietta had been right all along. One by one they all returned.

After a few weeks, Zachary expressed his solution to our housing problem.

"Let's go back to Dad's big house, and Dad and Barbara can come live here. That way we get the space we need, and they get the space they need."

It was hard to explain to my 5-year-old why this wouldn't work.

My four children and I remained squished together in my condo for several years. I often shared my bed with Zachary or Sariel, and sometimes I slept on the pullout couch.

"Mom, I love being here in your little house," Zachary said. "I know where you are every minute. You're never far away."

After a few weeks, I stopped taking Prozac. The sun rose again in my heart.

Like her two older sisters, my daughter Sariel made her bat mitzvah. Now she would have the rights and privileges afforded to her in this new feminist Jewish era.

And my rights? I realized that while my daughters had this opportunity, I had never taken it for myself. The girls had studied the art of Hebrew cantillation and were able to decipher the unpunctuated words that appeared on the parchment pages of the Torah. Maybe it was time for me to take my place beside them.

THE STORY OF JACOB

Do you know the story of Jacob wrestling with the angel? It shows up in multiple cultures and religions, in art, story, and legend. Friends have mentioned it in passing, as have people whom I meet as a rabbi. It seems to have resonance for almost everyone. But it also seems to have different implications for each person. Even in Judaism, there are several ways to interpret this story.

Through my life, I've come back to the story again and again. Each time, I find a new insight.

Yet it's the story that best reflects how and why I set out to become a rabbi at that stage of my life, and what happened since.

The story is from the book of Genesis. Jacob is preparing to meet with his estranged twin, Esau, after 20 years of separation. The night before —understandably stressed—he has a dream.

In it, he wrestles all night with a being part human and part divine—an angel, for lack of a better term. Jacob is the stronger one, but the encounter leaves him physically injured and spiritually altered. The angel, seeing he cannot win against Jacob, wrenches Jacob's hip from its socket. As daylight approaches, the angel asks to be let go. But Jacob refuses to yield until the angel blesses him, thus leaving him in a weakened state while at the same time imbuing him with spiritual power. Why would the angel wound him?

The angel has given him his wound as a reminder that he is human.

When Jacob awakens, doubt crouches in the corner of his tent. Will Esau overwhelm him with rage and physical destruction, or will their relationship survive 20 years of silent enmity? This state of "not knowing" produces fear and anxiety for Jacob. How can he be the spiritual leader of his people if he can't reconcile with his own brother?

Jacob comes to understand the idea of "not knowing" as he goes forward into that uncertain conflict with his brother, Esau. He must embrace it, even while wounded, and irrespective of the outcome.

Esau turns out not to be hostile as Jacob feared; on the contrary, he embraces his brother, and they weep together. Jacob learns what he was not willing to accept at the beginning of this dream: that certainty is not the hallmark of a great leader of people. His greatness lies in recognizing and tolerating his own human vulnerabilities.

In thinking over this story over the course of my life, I've realized one of its most important lessons: Certainty is not ours to keep. Uncertainty is the default setting for human existence. But knowing this is not the same as accepting it. For that, I still wrestle—and so do so many of the people in my life.

REJECTIONS AND RENEWALS

After the divorce, I took back my father's name, but what did that mean? What was the difference between my husband's name and my father's? No matter what I called myself, I was unsure of what to do with my freedom.

I left my synagogue and secluded myself from the community. In my new household there was no husband, no father to do the blessing over the Sabbath wine when I gathered my children to the table.

But I couldn't let go of the rituals that had provided me with spiritual sustenance throughout my life. Without even meaning to, I started to take on the male roles of my heritage. I knew the *Kiddush*, the Sabbath evening blessings, and the prayers over the wine and the *challah*. I could chant them myself.

The beauty of Judaism is that each of us is responsible for our own spiritual development. The authority comes from within: everybody creates their own rituals based on the tradition but contained within the private world we create, or co-create, in partnership with our beliefs.

But it took me until my 40s to realize that in order to rewrite my relationship to Judaism, I had to let the voices of other people's Torah mingle with my father's Torah. At 21, I didn't have the vision or courage to see that I could choose to live a modern life and still maintain a connection to these rituals. I had no guide and no internal map to navigate the waters of the *mikveh*. I thought it was all or nothing.

I fell into my first rabbinical role almost by accident.

In hindsight, of course, I see that there *are* no accidents, but at the time, the truth had to sneak up on me and slap me on the shoulder.

It was my friend Jonathan Malino, the rabbi who had first pulled me into the politics surrounding the Greensboro Massacre, who referred me to Ohev Zion, a small, rural Jewish community in Martinsville, Virginia that needed a new rabbi. It was a 45-minute drive over the North Carolina border.

Before I knew what was happening, I was hired as their interim "spiritual leader." I reminded them again and again that I was no rabbi, and I thought of my job as temporary, a stopgap while they found themselves a real rabbi. But it turned out that this work came naturally to me, and within less than a year, I had been given a proper contract. I would be a *para-rabbi*: a term coined for individuals acting as rabbis in communities where an ordained rabbi was an anomaly or not available.

Shortly afterward, a reporter from the New York *Jewish Week* came to interview me about my para-rabbi role. I explained to the interviewer how I had come by my knowledge of Jewish law, biblical text, and prayer services: I was an educated observant Jew, and the daughter of an Orthodox rabbi. I had absorbed by osmosis all of the tools I needed to serve this community. They in turn had placed their trust in me, and supported me in my quest for more meaningful work. My being there served us all.

A week after the interview was published, a hand-addressed letter appeared in my mailbox. I remember sitting down at my desk to read it. It went something like this:

> Dear Rabbi Miller,
>
> I read the article about you in the New York *Jewish Week*. You are now the first female rabbi at Ohev Zion and I want to congratulate you and the congregation for its progressive stance. Although you are not officially a rabbi, it is still an honor to write to you as the spiritual leader of this community.
>
> Decades ago, when I was a young man and a recent escapee from Nazi Germany, I came to Martinsville looking for work. I will never forget the many kindnesses of the people there. They found me shelter and helped me get on my feet. And I have made a success out of my life—now I run an international investment firm in New York City.
>
> Please feel free to read this letter to the congregation, in case someone remembers me from back then. Be sure to thank them for me. I never properly expressed my gratitude, so I am enclosing

a check for the continued preservation of the synagogue in your honor.

Sincerely,

Mr. Leon Bernstein

Scarsdale, New York

The following evening at Shabbat services, I read the letter aloud to the congregants. There were a few elderly people who remembered Mr. Bernstein from "the good old days" when the synagogue was considered Orthodox, and the pews were packed with worshippers. But in 1992, only two-dozen people were scattered throughout the sanctuary as we prayed. During *Kiddush* afterward, several expressed their delight at receiving Mr. Bernstein's generous donation.

I wrote him a thank-you note, and we began a warm correspondence, the first in a lifelong series of my unconventional friendships with men.

My calling came to me slowly. It had been hidden from me for a long time. But eventually the signs piled up so high it was impossible to ignore them: the faith of my congregants in Martinsville, the support of Mr. Bernstein, the spiritual inheritance from my father. Forty years after my birth on Shavuot, the Jewish holiday that celebrates the giving of the Torah on Mount Sinai, I applied to rabbinical school.

My friends were ecstatic for me. I was petrified.

"How will I be able to keep up with the other students? I'm over forty years old and I haven't taken a real class in twenty years. What if I fail?"

"I have total faith in you," my friend Ruth said. "Didn't I just finish my nursing degree after staying home with the kids for all these years? You'll be fine. You're made to be a rabbi."

Rejection is just another word for detour.

I know that now. But then, it was hard to see it that way. My third rejection letter came on a Friday afternoon just before I drove to Shabbat services at Ohev Zion in Martinsville. I tore open the envelope, only to read: *I am sorry to inform you…*

What was I going to do? I had applied to the top three seminaries in the Northeast corridor, and unless I wanted to move to California, I had come to a dead end. How could this happen to a smart, dedicated student like me? First came denial: they must have made a mistake. Then I tried to rationalize. Was it my gender? My age? My quirky kind of Judaism that didn't fit the mold? I cried.

Parker Palmer, Quaker author and teacher extraordinaire, wrote: *"People keep telling me that* Way *will open. But a lot of* Way *has closed behind me, and that's had the same guiding effect."*

"Okay, God. Now what?" I wondered. "You said the Way would open."

But I had no time to wallow in my disappointment. I had to lead services in one hour's time. So I grabbed my briefcase, a box of tissues, some powder for my smudged eye make-up, and collapsed into the front seat. I drove past the North Carolina state line into Virginia. For 45 minutes, I sang together with my tape: a mix of Shabbat chants and modern Israeli songs. It was my warm-up and my distraction.

No one was at the synagogue when I arrived, so I unlocked the doors and went straight into my office. I soon forgot about the letter and focused on the prayers for the evening's service. Although there were fewer than 30 people sitting inside this snug sanctuary, I began chanting as if there were several hundred, with a ringing voice that contained all my hopes for myself and for my congregation.

When I came to the *Kaddish,* which signaled the end of the prayers, I lingered.

I thought about all those who had no one to say *Kaddish* for them, and those millions who were murdered at Auschwitz, Birkenau, and Terezin. I felt like a sturdy partisan in the midst of the forest. I would persevere for them.

"Shabbat shalom," I said, and invited everyone into the social hall, where we blessed the wine and shared the challah. Like a loving family gathered around the dinner table, we schmoozed about everything and everyone.

"Rabbi, you really moved us tonight. I can't wait until you become our real rabbi."

"Rabbi, thanks. I needed that. My sister is ill and my teenage daughter is in drug rehab. Your singing carried me through my sadness."

I drove home thinking that prayer works, that it had transformed me in these three hours to someone confident and useful. Rejection had renewed my desire to serve. *I have what it takes,* I told myself.

What did it mean to act as a lay rabbi? It wasn't just about leading services and teaching Hebrew School. More than anything else, people needed help with their lifecycle events: births, weddings, funerals. But I was never sure in those days what I was qualified to do; I only knew that it was far easier to officiate at a joyous occasion than a sorrowful one.

When my friend Phyllis asked me to visit her friend, Fanette, who was struggling through the last stages of stomach cancer, I balked.

"The doctor thinks she only has two weeks left to live," Phyllis said. "She's looking for a rabbi to do her funeral. She called the two other rabbis in town, but they said that since she wasn't a member, they couldn't officiate at her funeral. So I thought of you."

"Phyllis, I'm not even ordained, and I have no experience with the dying. I've done only one funeral so far."

"Fanette doesn't care about that. She and her husband have worked out the plan for the funeral, you just have to implement it. And," she went on, "her house is right on your way home."

So I called Fanette. I told myself I had enough empathy in me to do what I needed to do.

Still, when I stopped in front of her house at the appointed time, I hoped that she wouldn't answer the door. How do I introduce myself to someone who is dying? "Hello? It's me—your neighborhood rabbi"?

I said a prayer: "Please God, put the right words into my mouth."

I knocked gently. Fanette opened the door.

"You must be Tamara. Welcome. Come in. We've been expecting you."

She was 65, and I was surprised to see that her illness hadn't aged her beyond her years. I realized I had been expecting a ghost—but her eyes glittered with warmth. She took my hand in hers and led me to the living room couch.

"Sit. Make yourself comfortable. I made some rugelach for you. Do you like rugelach?"

Before I could say yes, her husband came in from the kitchen with a tray of the homemade pastries. Okay, I said to myself, this is a good beginning. I relaxed. Tall and sturdy, Donald was built like an athlete. He stood in contrast to Fanette, whose slight body and thin arms were struggling to hold the teacup she offered me. She and Donald had been married 35 years and they had two children. Fanette loved baking rugelach. It was her Jewish soul food.

She talked about everything but her cancer. She wanted me to know who she had been, before she would tell me where she was going. She was alive with stories.

"Maybe you can come over again next week, and I'll teach you how to make rugelach."

Visiting with her became my Friday ritual. I would come and bring a fresh challah from the nearby bagel store. We would talk about her week and sometimes we would bake together. Week after week, my understanding of her deepened; where I had previously been frightened, I was now eager to see my friend.

"I've had a pretty good life," Fanette said. "Marriage, children. Lots of friends. I've traveled a fair amount. I worked some. Made my own money. But now as I face the end of my life, I do regret a few things." She began to cry.

I had never seen her break down before.

"We spent too much money. We didn't save enough. And when Donald lost his job, we went into debt. We can hardly pay our mortgage." She cried some more. "It's worse being poor than being sick."

I was stunned by this statement.

I leaned over and put my arms around her skinny body. She reminded me of my own mother, whose small body always made her look and feel more fragile than she actually was. Fanette was showing her vulnerability, and I wanted to ask her why this issue, of all things, was the one that made her so. I wanted to know whether she was really implying, as she seemed to be, that she was more distressed over her money woes than the fact of her imminent death. But I knew those questions would not comfort her. They were only for me. Instead, we stayed still and let her words hang in the air around us.

I was beginning to learn that, although holding silence was more difficult for the listener, it was more satisfying for the patient.

I remained unsure of what to say and when to say it from one week to the next. It was clear to me that Fanette was looking to me for spiritual support, but I was looking to her as well, to help me define my pastoral identity. I was hungry for information about the process she was going through: What was she thinking? When she went to sleep at night, what images floated through her mind? Did she cry when no one was looking? Did she pray to God or did she curse him? What was it like for her to know she was dying, to cede control to an unknown force?

"I'm ambivalent," she said as the weeks went by and she remained stable. "I thought for sure that I'd be gone by now. But, somehow, I'm still here. Before you came, I was planning my funeral, but now I think I have some life left in me, and I don't know what to do with it."

"What do you want to do with it?"

"I don't know ... I want this time to mean something."

"Well, it means something to me, I can tell you that."

"What does it mean?"

"When Phyllis first called me. I thought, why is she calling *me?* I don't even know what I'm doing. But look at us! Laughing and crying and baking together for all these months. Your honesty and courage have deepened my compassion; you've challenged me to live my life more truthfully. I'm so grateful for the time we've had."

THE WOUNDED HEALER

It was 1990, and women entering the clergy were still pioneers. Like many pioneers, I wasn't sure where my next steps would take me. But also like many pioneers, I wasn't alone.

I carpooled to my Hebrew classes at Duke University with another woman working her way toward a role in the clergy, Dale Walker, who was studying Greek to fulfill her seminary credits in the Presbyterian church. Though I had known Dale from my neighborhood, I learned more about her, as our carpool became a mobile classroom for interfaith dialogue. And she proposed an idea that would prove life changing.

"Dale," I said as we drove to the Duke campus in Durham, "I've been rejected from seminary three times. I don't know where to go from here. You're going to finish seminary in a year and a half, and I won't even have started."

She didn't respond immediately. I could tell she was thinking about what to say.

"You know, Tamara," she finally said. "You could always become a chaplain."

"Chaplain!" I laughed. "Have you ever heard of a Jewish chaplain? There is no such thing. Chaplaincy grew out of the Christian ethos. Jewish girls can't become chaplains. It's an oxymoron."

"No, seriously," Dale said. "The chaplaincy world is very diverse. They pride themselves on bringing different faiths together to foster mutual understanding. Let me introduce you to the head of the Duke University chaplaincy department. Let's see what he has to say."

A week later I was in Reverend John's office on the Duke campus. He was the first Lutheran minister I had ever met.

"I have no experience in chaplaincy, and also, I'm Jewish. Is there any place for someone like me?"

He laughed. "Of course there is. I don't personally know any Jewish chaplains, but that doesn't mean that you wouldn't be welcome here. Unfortunately, I just completed the next cohort of chaplains, and I won't have any openings until the fall." He paused.

"Where do you live?"

"Greensboro."

"Well, in that case, let me send you to George Karl at Wesley Long Hospital. I'll write a letter right now and you can give it to him yourself."

I had never considered becoming a chaplain, but why not? In the Jewish tradition, *Bikkur Cholim*, visiting the sick, is a mitzvah, a religious duty. After spending all those years with Khana in and out of hospitals and rehabilitation centers, I was comfortable in that setting. Would the chaplaincy provide me another doorway into becoming a spiritual leader? Would it help to illuminate my murky relationship with my sister?

I went to Wesley Long Community Hospital, just 10 minutes from my home. I told Reverend Karl the basic details of my life: Jewish New Yorker transplanted to North Carolina, married, divorced, four children; my work at Ohev Zion; and my desire to become an ordained rabbi.

"Do you have any hospital experience?" he asked.

"My older sister was in and out of hospitals and rehab centers during her teenage years. Witnessing her suffering made me want to become a nurse."

"Well, chaplaincy is really about being an empathetic listener," he said. "Becoming a chaplain is a process of caring, not curing."

"I can appreciate that. For the past few months I've been visiting a woman who is dying of cancer. Because of Fanette, I learned that I need to put aside my own discomfort for the sake of the one who is suffering. She has told me how alone she feels, how this isolation can be even harder than the prospect of dying. I'd like to think that my weekly visits have reassured her. She has taught me that the most important thing is not what I say or even what I do, but just to be there."

"I can see you've already done a lot of groundwork. And we would love to have a Jewish person on our team," Reverend Karl said. "You would be our first. But don't worry! I can help you navigate. Our starting date is only two weeks away. Can you be available three days a week for our clinical pastoral care education program? You would have to commit to two years working and studying with us here at Wesley Long. After that, you would get your certification."

"Of course," I said, unable to believe my luck. Pastor Karl would become my supervisor, my counselor, my teacher, and the person I confided to about my inner life. The Way had opened.

People are afraid of the dying. The path to Fanette's death was prolonged; Fanette became invisible. Perhaps it was painful for Fanette's extended family and friends to see her skeleton body. Phyllis rarely visited, nor did I often see other friends of Fanette's. But I was there—the benign stranger—and Fanette shared her innermost thoughts with me.

When she stopped making rugelach, I knew that Fanette had begun her descent. A hospital bed was brought into the bedroom and round-the-clock nurses kept her comfortable and as free of pain as possible. She slowly disappeared into the white sheets.

The day after I was accepted into the hospital chaplaincy program, I went for one of my visits to Fanette. She beckoned me close to her. "Tamara, it's time. We need to talk about things. I don't want Donald to be stuck with all the details of my funeral. I trust you to help him through this," she said, without bitterness or discontent.

"Fanette," I said. "I want you to know that you've been a wonderful teacher. Yesterday, I was accepted into the hospital chaplaincy program at Wesley Long—and it's because of you, because you were willing to share so much with me. I'm a different person because of the time we've spent together."

"This makes me very happy!" she said, reaching out to clasp my hand. Her face blazed with delight, and I was amazed that she could still express such joy. "To know that I've helped you with your work means that all this dying hasn't been for nothing."

Fanette died at home the next day with her husband and daughters around her. Peace had come at her own pace. Eight months after we had met, I presided over her funeral. It was the beginning of my life's work as a chaplain.

People think that rabbis become immune to the deaths we witness. But every loss stays with me. Every interaction teaches me one more thing about the work. I am there to alleviate the suffering of the dying, even as I struggle to integrate my own emotions.

The sight of rugelach still reminds me of Fanette. "Another cup of tea?" I can hear her asking.

"Sure, why not? Let's have another cup of tea."

The Wounded Healer

Rabbi Joshua ben Levi came upon Elijah the prophet while he was standing at the entrance of Rabbi Shimon ben Yohai's cave.

He asked Elijah, "When will the Messiah come?"

Elijah replied, "Go and ask him yourself."

"Where is he?"

"Sitting at the gates of the city."

"How shall I know him?"

"He is sitting among the poor, covered with wounds. The others unbind all their wounds at the same time and then bind them up again. But he unbinds one at a time and binds it up again, saying to himself, 'Perhaps I shall be needed: if so I must always be ready so as not to delay for a moment.'" —*Tractate Sanhedrin 98B, Babylonian Talmud*

The hospital bed was raised so high that I could not even touch my sister's hand. I was 10 years old and she was almost 14 when she stayed at the Hospital for Special Surgery for several months. She wore a full body cast, only her toes and arms sticking out of the plaster. Her head and neck were also wrapped in plaster. The cast prevented her from turning in any direction, so the nurses had placed the bed in a position where Khana could see everybody coming and going. The sign next to her door said "Carol Miller."

This was the name she used outside of our little insular community, where everyone had trouble pronouncing the Hebrew "Kh" sound.

More than once, a nurse would lift me up onto her berth, so that we could be next to each other. I admired the nurses whose kindness eased my sister's struggle.

Because of such experiences with my sister, I had decided I wanted to become a nurse. Now, as a resident chaplain, I was as near as I would ever be to my childhood longing.

When I said "yes" to Pastor Karl, I had no idea what "clinical pastoral education" involved. The Christian clergy simply called it CPE. As a chaplain intern, I was paid four hundred dollars a month to work three days a week; I had two on-call rotations a month, and several supervisory and interpersonal sessions with Pastor Karl and my CPE unit fellows.

"On-call" was a 24-hour overnight stay at the hospital, and just like a medical intern, I had a beeper with me at all times. In an unoccupied hospital room on the top floor, I would undress and change into my nightgown, always hoping to sleep through, but anticipating that I would be awakened three to five times during the night. When the beeper would sound or the phone would ring, like a robot I would rise out of bed, get dressed and proceed directly to a patient's room, the emergency room, or, sometimes, the morgue.

One night when I was called to the intensive care unit, a young man was being revived after an attempted suicide. His bewildered 25-year-old girlfriend had called for a chaplain.

"Chaplain, I am so scared. This is the second time Dan has tried to kill himself after I told him that I wanted to break up. I feel responsible, but I know I need to leave."

She turned a bruised arm toward me. "He hits me. He pushes me against the wall and punches me. I told myself many times to leave him, but I always came back. And now, what if he dies? I'm the only one here for him. What should I do?"

I held her close as if she were my own daughter. The more she cried, the tighter I hugged her.

I pulled back and searched her bleary eyes. "Wait here a minute, Rose." I said. I went into Dan's room, where I found the doctor monitoring his blood pressure.

"He's in an induced coma," he said. "He's going to make it. What makes these kids want to give up on living? I just don't get it."

I went back to the young woman. "Rose, the doctor said that Dan will recover. He'll wake up in a few hours. Where is your car?"

"In the parking lot—and my suitcases are inside."

"Then go! Do you have someone you can go to?"

"Yes, I have a plan. I'm going to stay with a friend in Winston-Salem, and she's expecting me. But now that he has hurt himself again, I'm not sure what to do."

"Here's my card with my phone number. Drive away. If you hesitate, or want to turn back, just call me. You are not safe with Dan. You just said that he has physically attacked you. And you can't save him. You can only save yourself. You are a beautiful young woman, sincere and loving. You have a future ahead of you. Go find it. I'm rooting for you."

"Thank you, Chaplain. Thank you. I needed someone to tell me that I was doing the right thing."

"God bless you," I said and embraced her once more. I understood the power of those three simple words in a new way.

I walked back to my hospital room. I undressed and fell into bed. I slept for an hour and the phone rang again.

"Hello, this is Chaplain Miller."

"It's me. Rose. I can't stop crying. I'm thinking of turning around and coming back to the hospital."

Words slid into my mouth.

"Rose, don't do that. Keep going. Don't look back. Your friend is waiting for you. I will try to help Dan if I can. You have a life to live. Go live it."

"I don't know..." Her meek voice did not convince me that she had the strength to leave this traumatic situation behind.

"You can do this, Rose. You can do it. Call me when you get there."

I hung up the phone, emotionally exhausted. I prayed for her safety, and was gratified when she called again to say she had gone the rest of the way and was with her friend.

The Talmud says: if you save one soul, you have saved the entire world.

In being a domestic violence survivor, Rose was not unusual, except for the fact that she had not been the patient. My work as a chaplain often put me in contact with battered women. They arrived at the emergency room covered with bruises and cuts and injuries from the fists, knives, and sometimes guns of their boyfriends and husbands, whom they usually refused to implicate. They would grab my hand and in hushed tones beg me to keep their secret from the doctors. Weeks later, these same women would return again with new disfigurements. Only a few escaped, like Rose had.

Most of my patients were healing from surgery, or had just been diagnosed with a terminal disease. Some had come to the hospital to die without pain. After several months I realized how matters of the soul and spirit transcend all boundaries. People continue to ask the same existential questions: Why me? Why this illness? Did I do something to deserve this? Where is God?

I learned many lessons during my daily rounds, and I learned even more from Pastor Karl and my peer group. CPE was an opportunity for inter-religious dialogue: my peer group consisted of a Seventh-day Adventist pastor, a Moravian deacon, a Catholic priest, and a Pentecostal sister. None of them had ever met or been in contact with a Jew before—a reminder to me that outside of my little community, the world is a very large place, and Jews are a very small fraction of it. In our twice-weekly meetings, we dispelled our myths and stereotypes of each other and became colleagues, working together to reduce the pain and confusion we found all around us.

Not all of these collegial interactions were easy. I struggled most with Patricia, the Pentecostal sister. We were cordial to each other, but we didn't really accept or respect each other's belief systems.

One day, we had an altercation in the chaplain's office. I had just returned from attending a death in the intensive care unit. I had been working with the patient and his wife for several months before he succumbed to his disease, and afterward, the man's Pastor had recognized my efforts as we stood in a circle holding hands; he had offered a beautiful prayer that mentioned my service to his congregant, and had ended with, "In the name of Jesus Christ, Amen."

When I returned to the chaplain's office, I found Patricia there, and I said, "Patricia, why does every prayer have to end with 'in the name of Jesus'?"

"What do you mean? He's our Savior. Everything exists because of Him."

"I just don't think it's respectful for people to pray with me and for me, and to end their prayers with *Jesus,* knowing full well that I don't believe in Jesus. It seems disrespectful to my faith."

"I think you may not be looking at this from the Christian point of view. This is our prayer … this is how we pray, and we conclude with the name of our Lord."

"But don't you understand how uncomfortable this is for me? Jews have been dispersed and despised all over the world because we refused to believe in Jesus."

"Well, I had nothing to do with that!" Patricia said.

"You're from the deep South! You were probably told that the Jews killed Jesus! Do you still think that?"

Patricia walked right past me and out the door. I was shaking all over. Without a satisfying response, the fire between us would not die down. I was infuriated to be confronted with this wall of beliefs. How would I learn to navigate the Christian world when I was so unaccustomed to it?

In New York, my life had revolved around being Jewish. All of my friends were Jewish; in fact, Jews were visible in every corner of my life, at school, at work, at home. When I had first moved to the Bible Belt, I had been amazed to see a church on every corner, but I had still found my own little community where I was comfortable. Now I was really the Other.

Sam, the young collared priest, overheard my altercation with Patricia and decided to bring it up during our group time. When all was revealed, our peer group put us on the hot seat.

"Tamara, what is it about Patricia that pushes your buttons?" someone asked.

"To be honest, I don't appreciate her strict interpretation of the Bible. I wonder how she represents herself with this diverse patient population."

"Well, at least I know where I stand," Patricia jumped in. "You're so busy trying to please everyone that you don't even have a clear message. Where's your Bible?"

"You mean the *New Testament?* That's not my Bible! And what's wrong with trying to relate to everyone?"

The supervisor listened to this conversation, and then asked a question he often asked.

"Tamara, who does Patricia represent to you? Is there someone in your family or among your friends who she makes you think of?"

In an instant, I realized my blind spot, and my anger evaporated. "She reminds me of my ultra-Orthodox sister, Khana. She's so rigid! Her way of thinking is so different from mine. I can't seem to reconcile her lifestyle with mine."

Patricia looked startled. She moved closer to where I was sitting, took my hands into hers, and said, "I'm so sorry. That sounds painful ... We need to get to know each other better. We both have a lot to learn."

I wiped away the tears that had fallen on my blue button-down blouse. This was hard work. But we were pushing each other forward in establishing our respective theologies, separate from our childhoods.

Then, too, I had entered the chaplaincy just as my civil divorce became final. My emotional wounds were still healing, and I had not yet acquired the full vocabulary for this spiritual exploration. At the time, I was still wearing my badge with my married name, Tamara Ende.

One day, a resident said to me, "Oh, you must be Dr. Ende's wife."

"No," I said, blushing, and not wanting to embarrass him, I walked away.

In some way, I was always in my ex-husband's domain and my sister's house of rehabilitation. But I needed to reclaim this space for myself. I needed to create a role I could live with, even if others couldn't seem to grasp it. Behind the oxygen masks and the heart monitors lay a place I never knew existed: a place where I met God again and again in unexpected and magical ways. I had been put here to heal and be healed.

During my two-year residency, I rotated through every unit in the six-floor hospital building, from gynecology to orthopedics, from oncology to intensive care. The Jewish patient population was minuscule; the bulk of my patients were Christian, from a myriad of denominations.

I became genuinely interested in how their religious beliefs affected their daily living. I listened and learned. In turn, they would ask me about my "Jewish faith." I struggled to articulate the Jewish fabric of my life, and in time, I developed a sincere and articulate message. I was forming a new Jewish identity in the South, where I would live for a total of 20 years.

When my colleagues did come across a Jewish family, they would pass them on to me. It was a welcome change for me to be with my *mishpochah*, my Sinai family. I would see a fellow Jew and think: Our tribe began in the desert, and we share the imprint of the exodus. Our prayers and our paths have carried us through centuries of hardship. On a meta-level, we are all relatives.

I would chant in Hebrew and then in English, the *misheberech* prayer for the sick, adding in the Hebrew name: "May the One who blessed our ancestors … bless you, *Moshe ben Sarah*." When I chant this healing prayer, the mournful modulations of my vibrato seem to increase the listeners' compassion. I am humbled when family members cry at hearing it.

Visiting the sick is a mitzvah. It obligates the community to provide for the patient's physical and emotional needs. The concepts of healing of the soul and healing of the body are regarded as interrelated, and I have observed this to be true. I knew little about the science of medicine, but I could enter into the soul of the matter by asking the patient: "How's your spirit today?" The answer was always different, and that would tell me what question to ask next.

Through the vigorous pace of long nights and pre-dawn conversations with the sick and the dying, I was drawn deeper into my authenticity. The patients would not accept a masquerade; I had to be real. Time was precious, but I never rushed these exchanges. I gave weight to every one of my words, as I once again became a visitor in a world of pain and isolation.

As chaplains, we learn to use our own woundedness to connect with others. We are called the "wounded healers," a term coined by Catholic theologian Henri Nouwen:

> Our very humanity depends on crossing over to the other and reaching deep into their hearts as if it were our own. Nothing can be written about ministry without a deeper understanding of the ways in which the minister can make his own wounds available as a source of healing.

Suffering is not specific to any religion, and the gift of empathy comes when we listen and give credence to each other's suffering. As people who are created in the image of God; we all share the experience of being human. We all feel pain and the fear of our mortality. Through compassion, life's greatest challenges become opportunities for hope and renewal.

The rabbis in every age talk about God's empathy. After World War II, when someone would ask: Where was God in the midst of the Holocaust? They would answer: God was among us, crying for each and every victim. The real question should have been: *where was man?*

YENTL GOES TO SEMINARY

I knew as soon as I walked into the roundtable interview for the Academy for Jewish Religion that it would be the right place for me. I had no doubt, even though the admissions committee's last question to me had been a request to explain my three failed attempts to find a rabbinical cohort.

I had answered, "The reason I was rejected from those programs is that I didn't belong in them. I belong here."

I didn't have long to wait: decisions were made on the spot. After the last question, they sent me to an adjoining room.

Rabbi Shohama Wiener, the Executive Dean—whose upper West Side living room we were sitting in, and whom I knew to be a second-career rabbi like me—was the one who summoned me back and spoke the words that validated my optimism: "We on the admissions committee want to warmly welcome you as a rabbinical candidate to the Academy for Jewish Religion."

A few days before the start of classes, I flew into LaGuardia Airport on what had to have been the sunniest day of my so-called midlife crisis. Now I was beginning to see that it was not a crisis at all, but a reclaiming of my purpose and destiny. Now I was making my first flight toward becoming a rabbi. I carried a huge backpack with all my clothing for the next few days, a spiral notebook, a new package of highlighters, and a tape recorder.

I walked outside the terminal and found the taxi stand.

"Where are you going, Miss?"

"The Upper West Side," I said confidently, laughing at the *Miss*. "Central Park West and 86th Street."

As we exited the airport, I looked out the window to catch a glimpse of my beloved Manhattan. Could I go home again? Eighteen years before, I had left New York with a husband and a toddler to pursue my husband's dream of becoming a doctor. Now it was my turn. I was divorced, with two children in college at Chapel Hill, and two still in public school in Greensboro. I was returning to the city of my youth to study the books my father had read in his youth.

As the cab driver drove past familiar bridges and skyscrapers, my own sky opened up. I saw beyond the kitchen windows of my Watauga house into a new frontier. Although I was terrified of being a student again after 20 years, I was also excited to be back in the classroom where knowledge flowed like the river out of Eden.

The Academy for Jewish Religion was housed inside the Society for the Advancement of Judaism, a historic Reconstructionist synagogue founded by Mordechai Kaplan. This building was the first real home of the congregation, where the first American Bat Mitzvah was held on Saturday morning, March 18, 1922, for Rabbi Kaplan's daughter, Judith. I reached up to kiss the large wooden mezuzah affixed to this massive front door and took the first step into my progressive Jewish education, rooted in ancient tradition and set in contemporary civilization.

I walked up the two flights to the classrooms where we would be studying the classics: Torah, Talmud, Mishnah, and Midrash. I wondered, who would be my fellow students? I followed the noise and saw a room full of men and women standing and talking to each other animatedly. Was I the only one in the crowd who knew no one?

"Shalom," said Shohama Wiener, who I remembered warmly from my roundtable interview. "Welcome, Tamara. *Brucha Habaah!*"

We were told to gather our chairs in a circle, and someone began to chant a melody, a *niggun*. All my life, I had loved these wordless tunes. They are a mesmerizing form of prayer and had always seemed to me the easiest way to go back to the Old World. I had hummed them around the Shabbat table with my family, had sung them with my youth group as a teenager.

When the singing was done and we had all scattered, a friendly voice hailed me. "Let me introduce myself! My name is Judith Edelstein. I'm also a first-year student, and I'm your spirit buddy. We all get them—someone to talk to, so we don't feel alone here."

We were passionate about becoming rabbis in midlife.

During bad weather and before big exams, I spent the night at her three-bedroom apartment where her husband, Jim, daughter, Jocelyn, and son, Jacob, welcomed me. Jacob was the same age as my son, whom I missed every day; he reminded me of Zachary, with his soft-spoken, sweet disposition.

Most nights, after a full day of classes, I took the express bus to Co-op City, located in the Baychester section of the borough of the Bronx. My parents and my two aunts had lived in that co-op for over 20 years; my parents had their first air-conditioned apartment in this socialist-style neighborhood, where immigrants from all over the world gathered to form mini-communities.

Around the kitchen table, my mother, father, and I would eat a simple home-cooked meal with a quiet joy that warmed up the entire apartment. When it was homework time, we cleared the dishes from the table, and I took out the Talmudic dictionary and the texts for the following school day, translating for Rabbi Barth's class in Jewish Law, or *halachah*.

My father did not need the dictionary, because he knew it by heart; he was my walking encyclopedia, my living internet connection to all things Jewish.

Night after night, we studied the holy texts that, in another time or place, would have been forbidden to me. I became a daughter again, and a student, even as I was trying out the role of spiritual leader. Growing up in the Bronx during the 1950s and 1960s, I never felt my identity as the daughter of an Orthodox rabbi to be unique. But now it seemed to me that I was fulfilling a long-ago wish I never knew I had made.

Like my rabbinical journey itself, my father's acceptance of my new path was, perhaps, unusual. But you had to know my father to understand that his love for me was unwavering as his love for Judaism.

I am certain my father had an unspoken desire to have a son, and for that son to carry on his rabbinic lineage, but with two daughters and no sons, this longing was not going to be fulfilled. Or so my father thought. It was beyond the scope of his imagination to entertain the idea that his daughter would follow in his footsteps.

Thus, my declaration that I would be going to rabbinical school was an Abrahamic moment for my father. When God told Abraham that he would be the father of a great nation, Abraham still did not have a child, and he viewed the promise as preposterous. Then God announced that Abraham's wife, Sarah, would soon conceive a child. Sarah laughed at that, but somehow, the unbelievable occurred, and Sarah gave birth to Isaac. So what appeared impossible to my father at 30 became a reality when he was 79.

Unlike Yentl, I did not have to change genders to study Jewish texts. But there were many sacrifices: financial, parental, logistical. For four years, on a weekly basis, I left my younger children in the care of my ex-husband for three days a week, while I traveled 500 miles.

Acclimating to seminary life in the labyrinthine building that housed us was also a challenge. The cold marble steps of the hidden stairways and the rickety old-fashioned elevator that hummed from floor to floor sometimes made me feel like I was in Oxford, England, rather than New York.

Every room had the same decor: books on various Jewish subjects placed indiscriminately on tilted bookshelves; a scrawled-on chalkboard with small pieces of colored chalk left on the ledge; a long wooden table surrounded by mismatched chairs. A *mezuzah* was attached to each doorpost as you entered into the courtyard of learning. The SAJ building had a worn, warm, scholarly character; but the so-called Academy library was a closet shut with a padlock. It was clear what the priority was in this building: books came first. I quickly learned the combination so I could leave some of my heavier schoolbooks there instead of hauling them back and forth from Greensboro.

Once I was inside, I longed to stay in captivity. For me, this *yeshiva-style* learning was the Garden of Eden.

There is a Midrash that describes the Garden of Eden in luscious terms; it is filled with spices, trees, angels, perfumes, precious metals, and jewels: *"Who dwells there? All righteous beings. The great sages, the matriarchs, the patriarchs, the well-known biblical figures, scholars from all ages, and the messiah. In the midst of this, God sits and explains the Torah."*

Now my professors, rabbis, and scholars sat godlike in every classroom, explaining and redefining the tenets of my Orthodox childhood. I was not someone who carried a bag of belligerent Hebrew school memories; my bag contained the power of the *Sh'ma* chanted before bedtime, the sweet aroma of my mother's chicken soup on Friday afternoon, and the weekly ritual of Sabbath candle lighting.

Sure, I had questions about the meaning behind the Bible stories and their inconsistencies, but I came to the table engaged in the process of discovering truth in all of its manifestations. I wanted to fill in my blind spots about my Judaic heritage, but only after I delved into the books my father had lived and breathed.

The art and discipline of Talmud study still tantalized me. My freedom to learn brought back a very different time, when I was a junior at the City College of New York and leading a conventional observant life.

But my Orthodox friend Deborah and I had plans beyond the conventional.

"I'm so jealous of my three brothers who study Talmud every day at Yeshiva University," she said. "I want to study Talmud, too. Don't you?"

"Tahlmood," I said. "It sounds like the forbidden fruit in the Garden of Eden. Are girls allowed to study Talmud?"

"Why shouldn't they?" she said. "It's almost as important as the Torah. Some say even more important."

The Talmud is essentially the oral law in written form. It encodes age-old debates about the intent of the Torah. And the act of Talmud study is intrinsically holy. The rabbinic sages experienced the study of the Talmud as a walkway toward God. It was even more than that: it was a way to be *like* God.

But until very recently, women were not permitted access to the complexities of the Talmud. Certainly, during my teenage years, girls did not study Talmud alongside the boys in the *yeshivas* and Orthodox day schools in New York. The male authority figures said that women were "not well-suited for the intellectual rigor of Talmud study." Others said it was "inappropriate" and not at all congruent with women's role in Judaism.

"I did get a small peek at a page of Talmud," I cautiously admitted to my friend Deborah.

"The other night I sat next to my father while he was studying."

"Tatteh," I had said, using the Yiddish word for "daddy." "This page looks so different from anything I've ever seen! It's overcrowded, with different-size shapes and scripts and that big text in the middle. How do you make sense of it?"

"Aha!" he answered. "From where you're sitting it must look like a crossword puzzle, right? So you see, in the middle is the main text or phrase. And around that text are multiple commentaries by different rabbis who had other opinions or ideas about a certain law or the meaning of a certain phrase. It has a structure. Once you can see it, everything becomes clear."

"So, let's do it!" Deborah said, on hearing this. "Let's study Talmud together. It'll be our secret. We don't need to tell anyone." She was serious and determined. I was more skeptical.

"And exactly how would that work? Neither of us knows anything about it. How can we even begin to study it, let alone understand it?"

A week later, Deborah had a plan. She had contacted a rabbi at Yeshiva University who was willing to teach us. There was only one caveat.

We couldn't tell anyone that he was teaching two Orthodox college women the Talmud. (I continue to keep his identity secret—mostly because I don't remember his name!)

"It is prohibited. *Asur!*" he said. "And if you tell anyone about our meetings, I will deny it. I'm not going to risk my reputation over a couple of eager renegades. Understood? *Asur!*"

He regularly emphasized the word *asur* in rabbinical law. The irreversible certitude of the term's potency disturbed me. *Asur b'halachah.* Forbidden according to the law. End of discussion.

So why was he doing it? I will never know, but I would like to think he just loved Talmud so much that he wanted to share it. If so, how could he refuse us, when we came to him with all our youthful optimism?

Our clandestine meetings began. Could two college girls study the oversize scribbled pages of the Talmud and survive?

Every Thursday afternoon, Deborah and I traveled by train from City College in Harlem to Yeshiva University in Washington Heights. Once on campus, we surreptitiously walked down many circuitous corridors to find the rabbi's office. There weren't any other college women in sight. We looked out of place with our wool berets and black tights, amidst the 18-year-old boys who covered their heads with black crocheted *kippot*. I noticed how comfortably they carried several heavy volumes of Talmud underneath their arms.

Deborah and I feigned confidence as we sneaked past them, but we also felt defiant as we closed the door to the rabbi's office.

"So, young ladies, how is your Aramaic?" The bearded, cherubic man asked. "You know the Jews read the *Tanach* in Hebrew, but they spoke and wrote in Aramaic, and most of what the rabbis said was written down in that language."

Deborah and I looked at each other and giggled.

"Oh, no. We have to learn yet another language in order to get into the Talmud for real?"

"If you are expecting Talmud study to be easy, think again. The world of the Talmud is formidable. The rabbis did not organize or arrange their views like we do in the Western world of canonic thought. There is a great deal of legalistic minutiae in the discourse of these abstract broad principles. That is what I mean when I say *formidable*. New students must learn how to apply this methodology in order to tease out meaning amidst the chatter of six centuries."

During the winter months, in the rabbi's dark and damp office, Deborah and I studied the first page of the Tractate *Brachot* (or "blessings"). This volume deals with all kinds of Jewish prayer: daily prayer, special holiday prayers, fixed prayer, spontaneous prayer.

We lingered on the first sentence for weeks. "*May-ai-matay*? From what time may one recite the evening *Shema*?"

Deborah and I studied one chapter for six months with our unorthodox rabbi. We learned some Aramaic vocabulary. We delved into the mechanics of Jewish prayer and its legal ramifications. We familiarized ourselves with Rabbi Eliezer and Rabbi Joshua. We became detectives of the text. We immersed ourselves in the "sea of the Talmud" and we began to swim from one thought to another, from rabbinic commentary to rabbinic commentary in the hope of finding the answers to this riveting crossword puzzle.

Like Rabbi Shimon Bar Yochai, we were ensconced in a cave of splendor.

Fast-forward 22 years: I am sitting with my fellow students, listening to Rabbi Leonard Levy, a 30-something Professor of Talmud at the Jewish Theological Seminary.

"Studying the Talmud is not a practical activity. It is a religious experience. Are you ready to take the plunge?"

Was I ready? I had waited my whole life to study Talmud this way. "Yes!" I thought. "This is what I want. It doesn't matter if it's formidable. I want to know its secrets."

The first lecture was so intense that a pounding headache followed me for hours. Rabbi Levy's information cycled through my mind. Studying Talmud reminded me of freshman calculus, which I barely passed with a D grade. (It was the only D in my entire school career.) Would Talmud be like calculus class, where if I missed a concept, I would miss the entire equation? Would I drown in the continuous waves flowing tumultuously in Rabbi Levy's sea of Talmud?

Unlike my first teacher, Rabbi Levy was modern and animated, passionate and precise about every nuanced argument. He had us diagram every passage throughout the semester.

It was fascinating and frustrating. When Aramaic became a problem, we studied its grammar. When we needed to know what was behind Rabbi Akiva's reaction to a specific legal issue and why it differed from Rabbi Hillel's exegesis, we learned about their politics. What was their platform? What stories did their students tell about them? Every rabbi who stated an opinion in the Talmud had a backstory.

In a few weeks' time we all became researchers and archaeologists, lawyers and historians. To further develop our diagnostic skills, we were configured in *chevruta* style—a form of intense daily study in partnerships of two or three, originating in European *yeshivas*. Through this process, I came to understand Rabbi Levy's devotion to the science of Talmudic thinking.

One night after dinner, I asked my father to help me with a difficult passage from the Talmud that I had been given for homework. I couldn't translate the Aramaic or the Hebrew. There were just so many words I didn't understand. How would I be able to answer the homework questions if I couldn't even decipher the text? After two months of learning Talmud, I had to admit that I was still a novice.

"Come show me." My father moved next to me at the kitchen table. He put on his glasses in order to see the small print on my photocopied homework page. "Write down everything I say," he said.

I took up my Talmud notebook, and my father began, patiently to transmit his knowledge to me. He would read and then translate every word, so I could learn the vocabulary.

"You need a special dictionary for the Talmud," he told me. "So many words come from different languages that are now obsolete. Sometimes there is a Greek word that was used by Jews in conversation. Sometimes the word is slang, and though it was used centuries ago, today it has no viable meaning. Sometimes there are three translations for the same word and you will have to figure out which one makes the best sense inside the context of the sentence. But the more you study, the more repetition, the better you will be. Practice is all you need.

"Now, don't look so glum. Talmud is fun once you know the rules. Let me know how it goes tomorrow in class. I am going to bed now. I will wake you up and walk you to the bus in the morning. Get some sleep. "

I was exhausted. I quickly undressed and put on my nightgown, lying down on the dilapidated pullout couch in the living room of my part-time home. The kitchen was in the middle of the Bronx apartment, and it was the only space that separated us from each other. I told myself that once I got my first paid pulpit, I would buy my parents a new sofa bed. Several years later, I had a brown-mini-striped couch sent to Co-op City from the furniture warehouse in High Point, North Carolina. Although I never slept on it myself, it became my mother's throne as she aged. After my father died, my mother refused to sleep in their master bedroom ever again. Instead, she stayed in the living room on the couch I had bought them.

The next day, I was fully prepared for Talmud class. I knew everyone in the class: the six male students and the one other female student. Even though we were adults, the gender differences persisted in the classroom. The men shouted out answers, while the women raised their hands. The men cheated more than the women. There was competition between and among us. I just wanted to learn. I was not that second-grade girl in braids, sitting in the fourth row—the one the boys made fun of. I spoke my mind, most of the time.

But then as now, every now and then when the boys played around, it was the girls who got in trouble. The men went home to wives or girlfriends who cooked and did their laundry. I went home to several loads of laundry and two kids who needed my attention. From the beginning of rabbinical school, we were not on equal terms.

"I would like each of you to translate one sentence as we go around the table. Brad, why don't you begin?"

"I didn't get to do the homework. I will have to pass."

"Okay. Sam, what about you, were you able to decipher the homework?"

"I really tried, but I can't say that I made heads or tails of it."

"Really?" He stared down each student until he came to me.

"Tamara? I see you have something written down. Can you explain our verse?"

"Yes," I said. "The verse says: When one of your cows strays into another neighbor's pasture and does damage, you are responsible."

"How did you get that?" Bill said in a mean-spirited tone. "You must have cheated and looked it up in the English version. You're not allowed to do that."

But I had no hesitation about turning to my father for guidance. It was my spirit that led me to seek out those answers and take the time to comprehend them.

"I guess I'm just lucky, Bill. I have my own built-in encyclopedia at home. He's my father," I said beaming.

Today at Yeshiva University, there is a graduate program in Advanced Talmudic Studies at Stern College for Women. Since 1982, women have been receiving doctorates in Talmud from the liberal seminaries in America and in Israel. Rabbi Dr. Judith Hauptman was the first woman to achieve this distinction. She is currently the chair of the Department of Talmud and Rabbinics at the Jewish Theological Seminary, and she was ordained as a rabbi from the Academy for Jewish Religion in 2003.

But any beginner in Talmud study needs a teacher or a mentor to learn its intricacies. I was lucky to apprentice myself to my erudite father. In his old-fashioned but light-hearted way, he taught me the complex format of the Talmud. His steady guidance saved me from despair and turned my Talmud class into a dialogue between father and daughter that lasted a lifetime.

"Move over, Yentl," I would tell myself as I turned to my father yet again. "Sweet *Tatteh*, let's learn together again tonight."

"AT LAST WE MEET"

Leon Bernstein remained my patron for the duration of my rabbinical education. Every few months, he would send a check to my scholarship fund, set up by the Ohev Zion Board of Directors to defray my rabbinical school tuition so I could continue working for them while pursuing my studies. As it turned out, I stayed at Ohev Zion Congregation for seven years.

Women are less likely than men to go into ministry for many reasons —but a major one is that they can't afford the time or money for the intensive four-to-six years of study. My desire for this heritage of learning was so strong that I ignored the economic ledger and trusted in my destiny. Through unexpected donors, unusual grants, a good work situation and the generosity of friends and family, I was able to complete my schooling with only $10,000 in debt.

But in addition to his financial help, Mr. Bernstein's presence in my life, through the many phone calls we shared, brought me many lessons for my future rabbinate.

"You're probably wondering why I reached out to you in the first place," Mr. Bernstein said. "You see, two years ago, I lost my daughter. She was just about your age. I didn't want to write about this in a letter, but … she was murdered in a Los Angeles hotel. A burglary."

"How terrible for you. I'm so sorry."

"It was. Thank you."

His tone was stoical, but I could hear the emotion as he went on.

"Sarah was on a real spiritual path when she died. She loved Judaism, and was studying with a rabbi in California. She was so excited about her new life! I can't believe how it ended." He was silent for a moment. "When I read about you, there in Martinsville, it reminded me so much of her."

In one of our phone calls, he told me the story of how his own congregation had bitterly disappointed him after Sarah died. In his time of suffering, the rabbi and congregants were indifferent: once the *shiva* week ended, they vanished from sight. He had prayed for more than 40 years with this congregation, he said, and he had given much time and money to enhance the synagogue, but he had to walk away.

He never considered giving up on Jewish life altogether, however. He found the comfort he needed in another community. But the pain of that betrayal compounded his grief, and remained with him as he struggled to recover. He was resilient, he said. His business continued to thrive; and his ability to speak German, French, and Italian contributed to his financial and global success.

But his wife was bereft: she collapsed after Sarah's terrible death, and was never the same again. With their daughter gone, and their estranged son, Elliott, in the Midwest, Mr. Bernstein had only his bedridden wife to return home to. With the help of a caretaker, he had learned to manage, he said, but it was another sorrow to add to the scale that balanced out the rich life he had built.

In this way, Leon Bernstein had been much poorer than my own father, a man of around his same age. My father was not financially adept; though he provided for our family, there was never any extra. But now I was grateful to think that he had escaped the abundance of sorrow that had followed Mr. Bernstein through his life.

After years of phone calls and letters, I suggested that we finally meet. I was in New York City frequently, but it wasn't easy setting a date with this international entrepreneur. He was always planning for a trip or returning from abroad. After months of trying, we arranged to meet at Grand Central Station on a weekday in June.

When I walked into the station, I easily identified my benefactor. Wearing a superbly fitted linen beige suit combined with soft brown leather shoes, he looked like a sweeter version of the "Master of Suspense," Sir Alfred Hitchcock.

When Leon turned toward me, our eyes met and we smiled at one another. He was not a demonstrative man, but I already loved him, and being in his presence added a new dimension to our uncommon friendship. Like my own father, Leon believed in my worth, and was willing to invest in it. He trusted that I would pay him back in service to the Jewish people. On that June day, I realized, that just as I was a surrogate daughter to him, he had become my surrogate father, offering me the one thing my own father could not: financial security. With two fathers supporting my emotional and material needs, I felt doubly blessed. The fact that they were men was not significant. That was simply a sign of the times.

The heavy humidity prompted us to find a nearby kosher deli. I had my favorite, Dr. Brown's Cherry soda and a corned beef sandwich on rye. Leon ordered a pastrami sandwich with French fries.

We spoke effortlessly about school and work and family. Our correspondence and frequent phone calls had created a rare friendship. But as our chatter slowed, this reserved man let down his guard. He lowered his eyes, and said haltingly:

"Sarah was loving and kind. Her death destroyed my family. I miss her every day. All the money in the world couldn't protect her. And it can't heal my broken heart."

He recovered quickly from this outburst and took from his jacket pocket a compact prayer book.

"I bought this for Sarah, but I never got to give it to her. I even dated it." He opened the cover and showed me the date, scribbled in red ink: *9/11/90.*

He gently placed the *Artscroll Rosh Hashanah Machzor* into my open palm. The dark navy leather cover was laminated with raised gold Hebrew letters. I read his inscription for the first time: "At last, we meet. 6/2/94."

"What a gift you've been in my life!" I said. "I can never thank you enough."

"No need to thank me."

"Well, I have something to ask of you."

"What is it?"

"When I get ordained, I want you to be there, so you can see what your generosity has meant to me and my family."

"I travel almost every week," he said, "but I promise you, if I'm in town, I will come." He paused. "Yes, I would like to come. Send me an invitation."

We walked a few blocks back to Grand Central Station with him holding my arm and guiding me through the throngs of people who were passing us by. We stopped, and he gave me a gentle hug and a kiss on the forehead.

"Thank you for everything, Mr. Bernstein. Sarah's prayer book is safe with me."

I would graduate less than a year later. I sent him an invitation with its RSVP card nestled inside. I imagined introducing him to my entire family, especially my father. They would talk all night and become instant friends. I would thank him publicly, alongside my father. And most important, I would give him something he lacked: joy!

In the middle of a class on rabbinic Judaism someone tapped me on the shoulder. I jumped. "There's a phone call for you. They said it was an emergency."

I rushed home to Co-op City and found my mother sitting at the kitchen table clutching a bottle of Bayer aspirin and a tall glass of water. Her breathing was heavy and erratic. My father held a folded wet dishtowel on her forehead. Her blouse was partially unbuttoned and her bra was showing. She was sweating.

"Yaakov," she said, breathing the name of my sister's son. "He's in Jerusalem—Hadassah hospital. A bus. Hit him. A coma. I'm going with Khana. You need to stay with your father."

My mother, who hates flying, and was usually less than spontaneous, was decisive.

I hugged her frail and trembling body and said what everyone says when tragedy strikes. "It'll be okay, Mom. You'll see. It'll be okay."

She cried in waves. Had we lost Yaakov? Would he survive? It seemed impossible that God had devised another test for Khana. How much suffering could my pious sister endure?

Soon I was to hear the story behind Yaakov's accident. While Khana waited and prayed for her son to come out of the coma, a family friend who had been asked to check in on Yaakov in Israel told us what had happened:

"Yaakov asked me to find his biological father, Joshua. He knew the man was in Tel Aviv, somewhere in the B'nei Brak neighborhood. So I asked around. People knew him, and without thinking, I gave Yaakov his father's address. I didn't want him to go alone, and I told him I'd go with him as soon as I had a day off.

"But he didn't wait. And when he came back, he was a mess. He told me he had found Josh's apartment and knocked on the door. *It's me, Yaakov,* he said. Josh said he wasn't going to give him any money, and told him to go away. Yaakov just kept repeating those terrible words: *He told me to go away and never come back.*

"I tried to give him hope. I said maybe Josh would change his mind, and that Yaakov should give him some time. "

"But he was still so upset when he left. He must have gone off wandering the streets, and didn't see the bus coming. I'm so sorry. If only I had gone with him. I should have gone with him."

The doctors encouraged Khana to ask Josh to come to the hospital. Maybe his voice would wake Yaakov from his coma. But Josh didn't come and Yaakov did not stir.

After six weeks with no visible changes, the doctors advised Khana to bring Yaakov back to America, where he might be able to get additional treatment. An American doctor volunteered to accompany both of them on the airplane back to Philadelphia. And in a few months, Khana got her miracle. Yaakov woke up, but it was another year before he could walk or talk. His ability to use sign language enabled Khana and the hospital staff to understand him—but his brain injury left him with severe speech impediments, cognitive disabilities, headaches, memory lapses, and grand mal seizures. He never went back to school. He has never been able to hold a job.

ON THE WINGS OF EAGLES

After completing two years in clinical pastoral education, four years at the Academy for Jewish Religion which included seminary and a detailed course of biblical study on the laws of family purity, I went with two of my fellow female rabbinic students to an orthodox *mikveh* on the West Side of Manhattan. It was just a few days before our ordination.

The *mikveh* lady asked nothing from us except the minimum $18 charge. She showed us the accommodations and quickly left to administer to the other regular visitors. This was uncommon: *mikveh* ladies are the gatekeepers of the ritual bath, and are there to scrutinize every minute detail of the visit. This is not an act of aggression, but a way of ensuring ritual readiness: entry into the waters of the *mikveh* can only happen in a pared-down state: visitors must remove all makeup, dirt, nail polish, and other impurities that could act as a barrier between them and the water. Only the *mikveh* lady can decide when you are ready for immersion.

But in this case, we were female rabbinical students, an oxymoron within the orthodox world. Our *mikveh* lady didn't feel the need to supervise us because our immersion did not fall within any legal construct that she understood. So we became each other's *mikveh* ladies. After six years together, we offered each other the first glimmer of ritual authority. We recited the blessings and witnessed each other's immersions.

The *mikveh* is a status changer. I didn't go into it as a bride—I went in as myself, and I came out a rabbi.

People asked me all the time: Will your father be at your ordination? As an Orthodox rabbi, will he even be permitted to come? My answer was always the same. "My father is my best supporter and, not only will he be there, he will be presenting me to the *Beit Din.*" This was the rabbinical court that would validate the ordination proceedings.

I envisioned standing next to my father as he said the words, and I felt grateful that my fears for his health had been unfounded: he was 82 and doing well. Yes, he would be there.

My sister was a different story. When I told her about my ordination, she hesitated.

"I'm not sure if it's permitted," she said. Behind this declaration, I could hear the word *asur*, uttered to my Talmud-hungry ears with that same final tone of that teacher. "But I will ask my rabbi."

Didn't family count more than all the laws that separated us? I was heartbroken at the thought that my only sister would not be at this singular occasion of my life. What would persuade her to come?

I turned for advice to one of my favorite Orthodox teachers. Rabbi Meir Fund, a Kabbalist with Hassidic roots, said, "Although I respect all of you and your desire to learn Torah with such devotion, I, myself, cannot come because of my position in the Orthodox world.

"But your sister should come for your sake. After all, it is a graduation, not a prayer service. You have earned this degree with dedication and hard work. Perhaps if you put it that way, she will reconsider."

All four of my children—now 13, 18, 22, and 23 years old—came to New York to see me graduate. They piled into my parents' Bronx apartment, and we all slept side-by-side on two convertible couches and a couple of foam mattresses on the living room floor. No one complained.

It was May 25, 1995, my 48th birthday.

The Town and Village Synagogue on East 14th Street was the site of our ordination. We walked into the sanctuary as dozens of people began tumbling into the wooden pews. I sat in my black commencement gown, with my fellow graduates on one side and my father on the other. Just like all those long-ago mornings in *shul*, he was wearing his *tallit* and a small black velvet *kippah*. I would always be that young girl looking up to him while he prayed. But now there was an addition to the ensemble that would transmute our relationship into that of colleagues: as my presenter to the *Beit Din*, my father, too, wore a black gown.

The music began. The congregation grew quiet. Everyone stood in place as we walked down the aisle. Our black robes were punctuated by our black-and-white prayer shawls. I didn't look back until I reached the end of the runway. There in the second row sat my sister and Yaakov. It had been three years since the bus accident, and Yaakov appeared fine, but of course, it was the new normal. He smiled at me, signifying his delight in being there.

Despite the fact that Khana could not condone my desire to become a rabbi, she had found no law against her attending the ceremony. In a twist of irony, she could attend only because the rabbis who had made those laws could not even have envisioned such an eventuality.

So there she sat, with Yaakov on one side and my mother on the other, next to my Aunt Ruthie and my cousin Loretta. Aunt Edna and Uncle Jack were there, and so were my cousin Shaindle and my cousin Phyllis with her husband Al. My friends ViVi and Jan from Greensboro surprised me. For many, this would be their first rabbinical ordination. I gazed out at the audience, my past and present mingled together.

I didn't see Mr. Bernstein, though I scanned the crowd again and again.

When it was our turn, my father and I walked up the several steps to the bimah, the raised platform where the reading table and the Holy Ark was housed.

My father stood at the podium and consulted an index card imprinted with the precise, pre-written language of the presenter:

"Tamara Miller has completed her studies. She has written her thesis and has shown integrity and professionalism in her work. I therefore bring her before this *Beit Din* for her *smicha.*"

Instead of stopping there, he continued on without missing a beat. "But my daughter is not just any student. How many of you know the perseverance and dedication she showed in pursuit of this honor? Every week she traveled from North Carolina to New York to study, for four long years. And who carried her? God carried her on the wings of eagles, back and forth so she could complete her studies."

He went on to quote the Hebrew passage: *You saw that which I did to Egypt; and I carried you on the wings of eagles and I brought you to Me (Exodus: 19:4).* He trailed on as I stood next to the podium, paralyzed with embarrassment and love.

He preached the sermon of his heart, and when he finished, the audience erupted in applause. I looked at him standing at the pulpit: he was happy and proud; he was pleased with himself. I wondered how long he had planned this mini-speech, and thought: *once a rabbi, always a rabbi.*

We walked on together until we came to the other rabbis who were waiting for us under the Eternal Light, the *Ner Tamid.* They placed their hands on my head, they blessed me, and they called out my Hebrew name as a mark of my genealogy: *Tamara Khava Bat Harav Yitzchak Dov U'nieta, the daughter of Rabbi Yitzchak Dov and Nieta.*

Then they turned me toward the congregation and said: *From this place, go forward.*

It seemed that despite my confusion, I already knew what kind of rabbi I was going to be—and my speech reflected that vision:

> *I was genetically prepared for my rabbinic work at an early age, God knew. My family and friends knew. I was the last one to know, to really know.*
>
> *But don't be deceived. My rabbinate will be anything but mainstream. My very presence, my very femaleness, invites a re-interpretation of the past and a radical shift into the future...*
>
> *We live in a time when the order is continually being challenged; the teachings are changing, even as we teach them...*

I thanked my parents and my children, and surprised myself with this special mention: *I want to thank my older sister, Khana, who has taught me the meaning of courage.* It was true that Khana's life had been filled with adversity; I did not know yet the new ways this reality was going to have a direct impact on me in the months and years to come.

After the ceremony, all of the newly ordained rabbis and their families gathered for dinner. It was like the bat mitzvah I never had as a girl, only better. There were so many people to kiss and hug and thank. It wasn't until I sat down to eat my dinner that I realized again there was someone missing.

Mr. Bernstein. He had not come. I told myself he probably had something he couldn't reschedule, but I was very disappointed. I had so wanted to see him with my father, and to show him what I had done, what he had helped me do. But he was a busy man, and he didn't owe me anything.

Slowly, everyone left the social hall and wandered out into the city to find their way home. I flew back to Greensboro from New York City, having completed my mission. My older daughters went back to college. My younger children came with me to begin another chapter in North Carolina.

I wanted to call Mr. Bernstein, but I kept putting it off. My euphoria subsided: I had many thank-you letters to write. There was work to do at Ohev Zion, and a celebration planned in honor of my ordination. There would be a second celebration at my home synagogue, Beth David. I put it out of my mind.

When the phone rang, I almost didn't pick it up. I had invitations to get out, a choir to put together, another speech to write.

"Rabbi Miller? This is Elliott Bernstein. I'm Leon Bernstein's son. My father has spoken about you with great fondness."

"Oh, I am very fond of him, too. And I am so indebted to him." I paused. "Is he ok?"

"I am sitting at his desk and holding the invitation you sent him to your ordination. Congratulations. He was planning to be there. In fact, he was on a plane from Europe, heading to your ceremony, when he had a heart attack. I am sorry to tell you that he didn't survive."

This is not the way it was supposed to be, I thought, stunned. Yet another person who had become so vital to me, so quickly and unexpectedly, had just as unexpectedly died.

Or was this the right order of things? My dark premonitions about my father's health came back to me. I hadn't been wrong, but it was Mr. Bernstein who would die. Our connection had been deep.

"Rabbi Miller? Are you there?"

"Yes, Elliott. I'm so very sorry for your loss. Thank you for calling me and for letting me know what happened to your father. He was my guardian angel."

I thought back to my ordination, only 10 days before.

I had begun my teaching with a story from the disciples of Reb Zusya:

Reb Zusya sat in his usual place in the Yeshiva studying a page of Gemara. His students watched him sit in front of the same page for hours and hours, but Reb Zusya did not move. He continued to gaze at the words as he went deeper and deeper into the same sugya, or the same passage, again and again without turning the page.

"Why haven't you gotten beyond the beginning?" the students asked their master impatiently.

Reb Zusya looked up at his Talmidim, his students, and smiled.

"Because," he answered, "it feels so good where I am. Why should I go on?"

I continued: *Why should I go on when it feels so good just to stay here at the Academy ... to enjoy the sheltering atmosphere of this house of study? So who am I and where should I go from here? These are questions of the soul that many of us never figure out.*

We may struggle with God, language, and the nature of the divine; we may explain the difficulties of evil and justice in this world, and we may even come to terms with the boundaries of our observance, but when we attempt to understand our changing identities and our life's desires, many of us come to a major halt."

Therefore it is incumbent upon me to turn the page on this chapter of my life. What if God will ask: "Why didn't you get beyond the beginning, Tamara?" I want to be able to say, I fulfilled the work of my heart. I was who I was supposed to be. I did what I was supposed to do.

At least Mr. Bernstein and I had our brief encounter on the streets of New York City. I have the memory of that day, and a little blue prayer book, to bring him back to me during the intensity of the Days of Awe, the 10-day period between Rosh Hashanah, the Jewish New Year, and Yom Kippur, the Day of Repentance—the holiest times of our Jewish calendar. In this time for introspection, I remember him.

LOW POINT IN HIGH POINT

My first full-time job as a rabbi was at B'nai Shalom in High Point, North Carolina. It was to be a short and stormy stay.

My mother had offered me her wisdom. "With your gifts, you could cross an ocean, so it should be no problem for you to bring the community together. You have to give them the time to understand what it means to have a woman rabbi."

Six months was not enough.

I was the first woman in the history of the synagogue, established in 1920; the congregation and I had high hopes at the signing of my two-year contract in 1997. Set far back from the street, on two acres of rolling hills and tree-lined landscape, this imposing brick building told the story of an era of prosperity, when the Jewish community was flourishing and the Jewish population soaring. The structure stayed in shape while the community and its once-strong source of economic support, the furniture business, shrank. My job was to raise the visibility of the Jewish community and to "bring in more business."

With great enthusiasm, I set about to infuse this community with my spirit: I established inclusive healing services; I initiated Torah study groups; I ran from pillar to post in the enormous building, teaching Hebrew school, meeting with the board, hiring staff. I did home visits to shut-in residents and met with bar mitzvah students.

But within six months, my rabbinic presence had been hijacked. One male congregant stalked me whenever I was in the building. Several people consistently interrupted my Friday night sermons to ask unrelated questions. One of the board members barged into my office without knocking, while I was meeting with a congregant, and proceeded to scream at me for something he thought I had done. The all-male board mistook my femininity for submission. The married women saw me as a threat.

There was one big positive: The children and their parents were happy to have a good teacher. But that was not enough to contain the furor surrounding my leadership. Our honeymoon was brief and the divorce painful and public. I was fired *de facto* after five months, despite my two-year employment contract. The newspapers delighted in my failure and placed my story on the front page.

How did this happen? I asked myself. Had I not received the blessing of ordination and the promise of a lifetime of fulfillment? This effective vote of No Confidence was not just hurtful. I questioned my career choice, even the veracity of my perceptions.

When I confided to my friend, an Episcopal priest, and asked him for guidance, he smiled and asked back in Talmudic fashion: "So you thought that you would be immune to evil in this world? Look around you. You can decide to face it or fear it, but it will always be there. You have my blessing on your journey. Go in peace, my friend, and know that you are not alone in your suffering."

Like Jacob, I wrestled with my own expectations of divine immunity. Like him, I had engaged in hubris: I could not control the spiritual growth of my congregants, and they were not ready to accept who I was. My rabbinical training did not imbue me with God-like powers. My *tallit* could not protect me from an uncertain future.

At the time I told myself that certainty would be mine when I found the right job. I would inherit my spiritual birthright just as soon as I was given the space to really shine. But it turned out that wrestling with uncertainty would be my life's work.

While it was true that I went on to find many opportunities to grow spiritually and to enhance Jewish life for other people, it would take many more such reversals—in my work, in my friendships, in my family life— before I understood that the very act of questioning *is* my birthright. My decision to carry on the rabbinical line as a woman means that I am always walking the fence between tradition and progress. I am not certain of anything, but I continue to strive for meaning in my daily conversations.

Still, I needed to work, and to put the whole High Point fiasco behind me. I contacted my seminary, the Academy for Jewish Religion, and told them my tale of woe. I was hoping to find another position close to home; I still had a 14-year-old son to consider, and I had lived outside of the Eastern Seaboard only for a short stint early in my marriage, on the army base in Colorado.

Just before Passover, I received a call from the seminary dean, Rabbi Samuel Barth. A fellow classmate had accepted an interview near Seattle, a remote location called Bainbridge Island in Washington State, and then had changed his mind. Now the dean was offering me the plane ticket and the chance to interview for the job: rabbi of two adjacent communities, the island of Bainbridge and the city of Bremerton on the Kitsap Peninsula.

I accepted his offering—although I felt certain I would never want to move to the Pacific Northwest, nor that they would want me there. I was prepared for the work of a congregational rabbi, but I was not prepared for the dislocation of my life. At that time, my life priorities were shifting rapidly. The day-to-day work of motherhood was shrinking, and my life as a rabbi was growing. I was now financially responsible for myself, so having a job was imperative.

My daughters were all in Boston. Naama and Elisheva were rooming together while Naama was getting her Master's in Public Health at Harvard and Elisheva was completing her Master's in social work at Boston University. Sariel was an undergraduate in anthropology at Boston University and living in the dorm.

They had each other for support and friendship.

Zachary, however, was in seventh grade. At 14, his peers were more important to him than his parents, and his father more important to him than his mother.

"I've had my bar mitzvah. I'm an adult now, and I don't want to drag my stuff back and forth the between two houses," he said, his voice cracking. "I want to leave it at Dad's from now on."

It was like a recurring nightmare from ten years before. "Zachary, you probably don't remember this," I said, trying to control the trembling of my mouth and keep my voice neutral, "but it's not so easy at Dad's."

"No, you'll see, Mom, It'll be good. I'll see you all the time. I'll bike over after school. We'll have dinner. It'll be just like now, but without the pillows."

He started to leave his things at Michael's house. True to his word, he would ride his bike to me after school some days, and some days he would stay for dinner.

Sometimes I would go to see him play basketball. But often, I did not see him at all. He was already a shrinking presence in my household.

"Zachary, I got a job!" I said at dinner one night.

"Wow, mom," he said, in his adolescent monotone. "That's great."

I cleared my throat. "The thing is … it's in Seattle. Well … on an island off the coast of Seattle, called Bainbridge Island. You've probably never heard of it."

He shrugged.

"Anyway, it's the only offer I've had in over three months of searching. The season for rabbinical hiring is about to end. I'm running out of chances."

He looked up at me, startled. I tended to shield him from adult realities, and he was not accustomed to hearing about my worries.

"The thing is," I said, "if I took the job, would you come with me?"

He shrugged again. "My friends are here. And my stuff is already at Dad's. You go. I'll be fine."

It was clear to me he did not realize the implications of what he was saying. I wasn't even sure *I* did. But he was at that age when he needed Michael, I reasoned. And what could I do?

When I hesitantly told my mother that I had been offered the job on Bainbridge Island, she surprised me with her unequivocal answer: *move forward with your work and begin again.*

Begin again? Leave my family, my recently grown children, my teenage son, my friends and my comfortable environment, to begin again, at the age of 50? The memory of my itinerant Uncle Aaron and his fully packed suitcase came into focus and humbled me. I felt as if I could hear him saying, "Time to go, my favorite niece. Another opportunity awaits you on another shore. Do not despair, find a song to sing, and I will sing it with you as you travel."

My mother, who had never strayed far from her home in the Bronx, was encouraging me to leave my past in search of a better future? I had no feminine model for such risk-taking: my mother was the poster girl for staying at home. Did she have any idea where this adventure would lead me? Did she not wonder if I would ever come back East?

And within me were darker feelings. I could not shake off the idea that I was being punished—perhaps by God, for putting my desires to become a rabbi over the family's needs. Maybe I was too ambitious. I felt shame about breaking up the family that I had nurtured for decades. I would be leaving everything and everyone I had known, to be alone. Was I being exiled? What had I done to deserve exile? Was this a breakdown—or a breakthrough, to some higher purpose and place?

When bad things happen, we think it must be our fault. How else can we explain it? *I must have done something wrong. Life was unfair and my luck had literally run out.* All the good that I had done in my life didn't seem to count at all. I felt my separation acutely—I would literally be on an island, separated from the mainland.

Yet there was another way to see this: Everyone around me was advocating for a fresh start.

"Go. I hear it's beautiful out there," said one friend.

"You need to get away from here," said another.

"You'll see, it will be fun. We'll come visit."

I still could not decide. As I stopped to fill my car's gas tank one afternoon, I saw my friend Judith filling her car in the lane behind me.

"How's it going?" she said.

"Fine. Still trying to find a job after my fiasco in High Point. What about you?"

"I'm off to see my brother this weekend."

"I didn't know you had a brother."

"Well I don't get to see him much. He lives out west near Seattle, on an island. You probably never heard of it. It's called Bainbridge."

"Bainbridge Island? I can't believe it. I was there a month ago for an interview. I just got a job offer to be the rabbi of the Jewish community! Beautiful place. But I don't think I could leave everything behind."

"But … why not? I would think this would be the perfect time to start over. And it sounds like a great adventure."

I said nothing more, and she added, "Well anyway, if you change your mind, I'll put you in touch with my brother."

I couldn't help viewing the conversation with Judith as a sign: the coincidence felt like an arrow pointing me to parts unknown.

Less than two months later, I left the place I had called home for 20 years, and journeyed, like my forefather, Abraham, before me, to a place I did not know. I flew solo for the first time in my adult life. No parent. No husband. No child. No turning back.

NO WOMAN IS AN ISLAND

No man is an island, entire of itself,
Every man is a piece of the continent, a part of the main.
                                        —John Donne, 1624

I arrived in Seattle on an ordinary sunny day. The air is crisp during the summer months. Cloudless skies. No humidity. It was easy to feel that I was only on a long vacation. But in truth, I felt more like an explorer. What would it be like to be the only rabbi on an island? How would I, a divorced middle-aged woman, be received?

A few weeks before, I had made a trip to Bainbridge to find a place to live. A young married couple had rented me their bright two-bedroom garden apartment. The two communities had paid my moving expenses, and now the truck was on its way with my furniture and other necessities. I hadn't wanted to leave my belongings in storage: I thought it would be best if I were surrounded by my favorite things, and I needed furniture and bedding for my children and friends, who would visit.

From the Seattle airport, I took a bus into the city and waited for a ferry to cross into Bainbridge Island. I stared out on the scenic bays of Puget Sound, skipping my gaze over the small boats that dotted the waters. When I walked onto the ferry for the first time, the breezes whispered: "Take a deep breath. Inhale this beauty." Ah, yes. This was a new kind of living.

On the ferry, I imagined my grandparents crossing the Atlantic Ocean and arriving on Ellis Island on the way to Manhattan. What would it be like on the other side of America? Bainbridge Island, nearly three times the size of Manhattan Island, had a population of only 23,000.

I stood with others on the upper deck while the boat's engines churned. I wanted to float on this ferry forever—never to reach the other side. After years of rushing around with the four kids' everyday activities and my own back-and-forth to rabbinical school, I felt I was drifting toward a beautiful sanctuary.

I would ride the ferry dozens of times in the coming year, and it would always be like that first time: a wide-eyed wonder, with the still-snow-capped Olympic Mountains to the west and the majestic Mount Rainier dominating the horizon to the east. The locals call it "The Mountain" or "The Mystery."

There was an abundance of natural beauty, and I never lost the thrill of watching The Mountain rise out of Puget Sound. It was the first question people would ask when they met each other on the street: "Is The Mountain out today?" Seeing the Mountain when it was "out"—not fog-covered or obscured by clouds—was the sign of a consistent world.

But even when The Mountain wasn't visible, one had an existential awareness of it. It was like knowing God's immanence; and if God is found in Mother Nature, I was sensing God all the time. My childhood rhyme followed me. "God is here, God is there. God is truly everywhere."

As I drove around the island in my blue Honda Accord, I passed parks and forests and trails and verdant spaces in every direction. The stately cedars protected me. Because there were no street names and hardly any stoplights, my eyes became my guide. I would recognize a certain tree formation on the corner or a patch of green, and I would know where to turn.

At night, however, my guideposts were swallowed by the dense dark. The first time I got lost on the island at night, I stopped the car and put my head on the steering wheel and cried like a child who could not find her mother. I was a city girl in the wilderness. When my tears subsided, I took a deep breath, started the engine, and sensed my way home, feeling the island's terrain embracing me. In a few short weeks, we became friends.

My new home was at 350 Grow Avenue. This is not a made-up name. I was going to *grow*, whether I liked it or not. I did not know that while I was on this island, I would finally grieve the loss of my marriage and begin the process of clarifying my rabbinate.

The condo I had rented was under repair when I arrived, so I went to stay at a hotel a few blocks away, where I could see Puget Sound from my bedroom window. The scene quieted my anxiety.

Every day I would walk from my little inn to the Bainbridge town center, known as the village of Winslow, and meander in and out of the shops, make small talk with the owners, sit outside Starbucks and sip my latte while watching the people walk back and forth with their tethered children or puppies or both. The pace on the island was like a country ballad; people moved in slow motion. I would need time to adjust.

I walked daily to my apartment to check the status of the repairs, as if I were responsible for their completion.

"Do come in, Rabbi," Tom the carpenter would say, always friendly.

"You can call me Tamara," I said. "How's it going?"

"Well, the boards were very wet, so I had to wait until they dried. It may take a few more days."

It took 10 days until I was able to move in. During those days, I met with the leaders of each community and we set up a calendar for the High Holidays, which were approaching fast. There were many things to arrange. The community was still looking for an office for me to work in.

I had no choice but to slow down.

Tom became my first friend outside of the Bainbridge Jewish community. Once the carpet was down and the moving truck arrived, he offered to put together my bookcases. Together, we organized my books on the shelves. While he was at it, he painted the worn walls. When he was finished, the apartment looked brand new.

"We should celebrate," he said. "Why don't we go to dinner?"

I turned him down, saying I was simply too busy. This was true, but what I didn't say was that I hesitated to be seen on a date with a non-Jew. It wasn't fitting, I thought with regret. I would struggle with the right way to live out my role—and discovering it for myself—for years to come.

Meanwhile, I continued to meet new people every day, to go to new places, to find my way.

"Rabbi, I would like to show you our little cemetery," said Sarah, a member of my congregation. "Can I pick you up on Thursday morning?"

The young woman drove me to the Jewish cemetery nestled in a forest 20 minutes from the center of town. I gazed around at the land, made impossibly green by the abundant rain. This cemetery was strangely empty of headstones.

"Right now, there's only one grave," she said, walking in front of me. "My two-year-old son died four months ago. He had a genetic birth defect. His name was Bradley. The community bought this land in order to have a place to bury him."

Suddenly I understood two things: one was that this was truly a newborn Jewish community, and I had a unique opportunity to help it grow. But even more important, I saw that Sarah had been waiting for me to arrive just so she could bring me to this place and tell me her story. She was not only looking for my compassion; I was a witness and a repository. I could hold the memory of her son, extend its radius beyond her. It was another crucial part of my rabbinic role, I saw then: to come into people's lives at their most vulnerable moments, often as a complete stranger, and to justify their trust by providing some assurance that their human experiences were profound. It was a privilege I had glimpsed with Fanette, but now I saw that it extended outward infinitely.

"I'm so sorry for your loss, Sarah. What a tragedy." We stood in front of the little grave, holding each other around the waist. Her body shook with spasms of grief. Her face dripped tears. I thought of my son, so far away, and tried to imagine the enormity of her suffering. I wept with her, and gradually her sobs slowed. Her breathing became even and quiet. We stood there for a long time before she simply said, "It's time to leave."

The next time I returned to this cemetery, it was to bury the second Jewish person who would rest on Bainbridge Island.

Tom kept leaving messages asking me to go to dinner. I knew he was new to the island as well, and must be looking for some companionship. But I declined every time. I felt certain that as the new rabbi, my every move was being tabulated and discussed. He was very sweet, but I couldn't imagine how it would ever work.

I had been on the island two months and it was tough shepherding my flock. The initial excitement of the adventure had turned into shock as I realized just how much work there was to do here. I still had no office. Everything had to be found, or built from the ground up. I was all by myself.

I was in constant contact with my children, but I ached with loneliness. Even the natural beauty everywhere was not enough to ease my heartache. I cried enough tears to float a new island. The births of my children and the noisemaking of our young family came back to me in nostalgic waves. My friends were thousands of miles away and every phone call ignited a painful sense of disconnection from all the things I had known and loved. Here, nothing was familiar. This island had become my *midbar*, my desert. I tried to see the desert experience as the metaphor for my spiritual growth. Like Moses and Jesus and the Buddha, I was sent out into the barrenness. I must find my own Torah, I realized. I felt empty. God was emptying me.

One day Tom knocked on my door. "Hungry?"

I could not refuse him. We walked to the nearby seafood restaurant and sat overlooking the sound. We had a table for two, wine glasses, a friendly waiter.

"Tamara, I have to tell you that I was so impressed with you that first day we met. Anyone else would have been mad as hell. After all, you just got there! And all you found was a mess. But instead of making a fuss, you accepted it without blaming anyone. I thought to myself, that lady has style!"

I looked at him as if for the first time. He had curly black hair, a short beard that made him look chubbier than he was, and an arresting gentleness. Despite my trepidations, I began to relax. He was a Catholic from California and had come to Bainbridge Island to find new prospects as a carpenter. He had been married before and divorced. No kids. He was wandering the world, looking for roots.

We talked easily for several hours, laughed about the island and all its idiosyncrasies, smiled warmly at one another. He walked me home, and at my door he said, "May I call you again?"

"I just don't know, Tom," I said. "Maybe you don't see me this way, but I'm the *rabbi* here. I'm not sure what people would think."

He accepted my decision and walked away. It would be a long time before I realized he was the only one on that island who saw me simply as a woman.

I entered the apartment that had become my home. Everything was in its rightful place. The mantle held all the pictures of my life before Bainbridge. I looked at the smiling faces of the kids and smiled back at them, pushing down my tears.

The phone rang. At first all I heard was sobbing.

"Zachary. Is that you? What's the matter?"

"Mom, I really miss you," he said, sniffling loudly. "Can you come home?"

"I miss you too, every day, Zachary," I said, trying to keep the tears out of my voice. "But what's going on? Are you having trouble at Dad's?"

"Not trouble exactly. It's just that I'm all alone here. Dad's never home. And Barbara's … well … Barbara. She's not you. I hang out at David's house whenever I can, but that's not home either."

Barbara had been Zachary's stepmother since he was 5 years old, but they had never made an emotional connection. And since I had arrived here, Michael had never once called to tell me how his son was faring. It was clear that he hadn't stepped up to fill the void I had left. I had always been the nurturing one. This thought gave me no joy, especially now.

"I know this is a lot for both of us to handle," I said, fighting more than ever for control of my voice. "I want to see you, too."

"I didn't know it would be so hard. Maybe I should have come with you…"

"I would have loved that. But I know you need to finish junior high. And this isn't forever. I can come back for Thanksgiving and you can come with your sisters for Christmas break. That way we have something to look forward to."

After a few minutes, Zachary stopped crying and started talking about school and his activities. He was in public school and was playing baseball and basketball and soccer. By the time we finished the call, he was calm again.

But when I hung up, my guilt boiled over. Why me, God? Why did you have to send me away? Why couldn't I find a job in Greensboro? Have You no mercy? I feel like an outcast. What am I *doing* here?

There were no answers to these questions, but there would be many more such phone calls. I began to fly back across the country with dizzying frequency. Much of my income vanished into plane tickets, and I felt increasingly torn.

WHEN A BRIDGE IS NOT A BRIDGE

My congregations were two Jewish communities divided by water. My goal was to build a bridge between them. The Bremerton congregation, Beit Hatikvah, was decidedly more conservative, both religiously and politically. The Bainbridge folks, Kol Shalom, were Berkeley graduates, liberals, Birkenstock wearers. Each community paid half my salary.

No one had created such a bridge before.

With the support of a joint committee, I worked out a viable temporary plan to lead prayer services on an alternating schedule, one Shabbat in Bremerton followed by one on Bainbridge. Bremerton required a more traditional service—the *siddur* (Hebrew prayer book) was their guide and they rarely strayed from its pages. Bainbridge was always creating new forms of prayer with music, poetry, and discussions. I felt comfortable in both settings.

But melding the two communities and their philosophies was a much bigger challenge. I felt like Solomon, though I would have much less success in striking a compromise than had my biblical forbear.

We spent the High Holidays together, geographically midway between the two communities, in the social hall of a Lutheran church. Over 100 people sat in folding chairs facing the makeshift bimah, and I was delighted to hear the community sing out the traditional hymns, *Avinu Malkeinu* and *Adon Olam*, despite their relative isolation.

One of the congregants and board member, Don Shakow, had been instrumental in hiring me. Don was the appointed patriarch for the

Bremerton-Bainbridge community, not only because he had a storehouse of Jewish knowledge, but also because he understood the rebellion of the New Age, anti-religious Bainbridge residents. He represented their longing as well as their loathing of all things institutional; they were the anti-everything crowd.

But both congregations were individualistic, full of strong personalities, and quick to question authority. Sometimes, this created an exhilarating shared challenge for us all; other times, it manifested as a hurtful attack.

In preparation for the High Holidays, I met with Don and a few other congregants several times to put together an inclusive prayer service for the many interfaith families who had found a home here—not an easy goal to meet. It was early in my stay, and I was still far from getting to know everyone and understanding their greatly varying needs and levels of commitment. That, and perhaps overwork, led to a simple action that would have lasting consequences.

Our prayer book was from the Conservative movement, which meant that there was a great deal of Hebrew, and we had to be conscious of the flow of the long, complicated service. I had chosen the flow of the ritual details and choreography, and I thought we had built a lot of participation into our plans. But, I found that I was working very hard to fill in the missing pieces, and by the time we arrived at the main part of the Torah service, I was exhausted.

I searched the seated congregation for the person who would lift the Torah scrolls into the air, but no one came forward. I spotted a young man with a dark beard and curly hair in the front row—I had met him and remembered his name was Ken. I motioned for him to come up to the bimah. He looked over his shoulder behind him, then back at me. He shook his head "no." Still no one else stood up; I continued to motion to him, and finally he gave in and walked up to the bimah.

"Just take these two handles, bend your knees, and lift high so that everyone can see the letters."

I heard a gasp from the congregation. I did not stop. It puzzled me for a moment, but I told myself they were afraid that this young man would somehow falter. But he did a beautiful job. I remember being pleased at how wide he was able to open the scroll with his outstretched arms so the hand-scribed lettering was visible to everyone.

Imagine *tashlich* on this island! *Tashlich* is a powerful ritual of release on the afternoon of the first day of the Jewish New Year, when people symbolically throw out pocketsful of misdeeds in the form of breadcrumbs or handwritten notes. I was alarmed to learn that on Bainbridge there was a "no crumbs" policy, lest they disturb the digestive system of the fish; and a "no paper" policy lest we litter the Puget Sound. I was in a new world conceptually as well as physically, it seemed: the Pacific Northwest was blooming with environmental concerns—recycling was already commonplace in Seattle—but these practices were then still uncommon in the Northeast.

It was pouring rain by the time I led my ragtag group to the water's edge. We sloshed along in our Gore-Tex finery, my umbrella obscuring my panicked face as I wracked my brains for some way to practice *tashlich* without incurring the wrath of my flock. In a merciful surge of ingenuity, I asked the congregants to partner up with the person next to them, to talk about one bad habit they wanted to let go of, and make a declaration of intention to do so. This appealed to the group of thirty, who threw themselves into the task. I was drenched by the time we finished, but I chanted a few Hebrew prayers to ground the ritual, always cognizant of the traditions I had grown up with.

"*Shana tova,*" I called as I watched the crowd disperse hastily.

I lingered, exhausted with relief and sudden awareness. There was no better place to perform this ritual than on a dock in the Puget Sound. Water was all around, in every form: it lapped at my feet, it dripped from the sky and collected in puddles, it drifted in misty shreds across my vision. The view might be obscured, I thought, but I had begun to see things more clearly.

The maturing hippie generation trotted out their new forms of worship at every opportunity: they saw me as the "establishment" and did not confer with me about these new approaches, and I found myself polarized in spite of my own open-mindedness. It is remarkable how easily we can be pushed to take a stance we may not even believe in wholeheartedly when we are faced with a reactionary crowd.

It would take me several more years of rabbinical practice to understand that almost all congregants are wounded in some way by their past experiences as Jews, and they have a tendency to play out their ambivalences in the next generation of their adult spiritual practice.

Immediately following the holiday, I received a call from a congregant.

"Rabbi. Maybe no one told you this, but we don't call non-Jews to the

Torah, and we *certainly* don't let them lift the Torah on Rosh Hashanah. What were you thinking?"

I thought back to the young man with the dark beard I had motioned to the bimah. "Do you mean to say that Ken isn't Jewish?"

"Exactly," he said.

My face flushed with anger at his harsh, disrespectful tone.

"Well, I didn't know that. Nobody told me. I needed someone at that moment, and I pointed to him. He tried to refuse, but I insisted," I explained. "There was no malicious intent here. It was an accident. An unintentional mix-up. Please let everyone know what happened."

"Well, it's a scandal," the caller replied. "It's all over the community, and you haven't been here but two months." He hung up.

I was angry—but worse, dismayed at the intolerance of the supposedly liberal side of the congregation. But I set it all aside and called Ken. I asked him to come to my office.

"I'm so sorry my request has put you in an uncomfortable situation with the other members of the congregation."

"It's true. I was shocked when you motioned to me to lift the Torah. But now, after thinking about it for a few days, I believe it was meant to be."

"How so?"

"My wife Leah is Jewish and we have a two-year-old daughter. I've always wanted to convert, but I just kept putting my desire aside. Now, after lifting the Torah scroll, I know I'm ready. Will you teach me? I want to convert."

"Of course," I said quickly. I thought he must be right: God had a hand in bringing about these strange events.

I called Don to share this latest wrinkle in the story, and he invited me to Shabbat lunch at his home with his wife, Carol.

Warmth flowed from him unceasingly. Sitting at the table, I learned about his work in energy conservation, public transit planning, and sustainable farming for immigrants. I began to see that he was a visionary, a man before his time, with a deep moral commitment he applied across all aspects of his life.

I saw, too, his love for the Bainbridge Island Jewish community, as he explained to me the reasons for his unwavering support of my work:

"I understand these children of mine. That's why I brought you here. The strictness of a male rabbi might have been too reminiscent of their past negative encounters. I thought you would be able to soothe them, or teach them, or cajole them. Your background isn't so different from mine.

You have a lot to offer, but you have to do it without them realizing you're doing it. Not what they taught you in rabbinical school, right?"

I nodded and smiled, not sure what to make of these revelations. Was he saying my being a woman rendered me weaker as a leader, and thus less threatening? Or only that he hoped I would have a more conciliatory approach and that was why he had brought me here? But I could not ask those questions. I only said, "I don't mind. I'm not just here to teach. I'm here to learn. But already there's been this conflict over Ken."

"I know, but that wasn't your fault. How could you have known? Any rabbi could have made the same mistake. That has nothing to do with your gender."

"I'm glad you feel that way, but I'm not sure everyone shares your feelings. I'm still smarting from my last position, where being a woman was a major handicap."

"Well, you'll have to tell me more about that sometime. I have faith in you—and I'll do my best to make sure you have the information you need to do your job. But right now, there's something else you need to know," he said.

Carol, who had not yet said a word, leaned over suddenly and put her hand on his. There was a pause during which I could feel the connection between them.

"I've got cancer," he said. "I have less than a year. I want you to take care of my funeral and burial in the traditional way."

"Oh, no, Don. But you're so young. You can't be more than fifty! Are they sure?"

He nodded. "I'm fifty-one. And yes, I'm afraid so. It seems to have happened when I was teaching at Clark University in Worcester, Massachusetts. No one knew about the dangers of asbestos back then, but it was all over the place in those old buildings. Anyway, that's what the doctors think. There are other cases like mine."

"I'm so sorry. And of course, I'll do whatever you need me to."

His wife looked relieved, and I thought, *she will need me, too*. It was touching to see how attached they were to each other.

"Oh, don't look so sad," Don teased. "We all have to go sometime. As a rabbi, you know that. And this is my time. You're here just at the right hour to fulfill my last wish. I have an Orthodox brother in Philadelphia, and I want him to be able to be at my funeral, and for that he has to know that I was buried *k'dat v'chi din*, according to the most stringent Jewish religious laws. That's the only way he'll come, and I want to give him that *zchut*, that privilege. After all, he's my only brother." He winked at me with an impish look.

"I understand completely. My older sister, Khana, is also *frum*, and also in Philly, for that matter. And since we don't practice the same way, I'm constantly trying to appease her."

"This is good, Tamara. Then we understand each other. And we have work to do. Have you seen our little cemetery on the island?"

"Yes. That very first week, Sarah took me there to see her baby's grave."

"Well, I'll probably be the next one buried there. Carol and I have talked about this a lot, so everything's already written down. She'll call my brother when the time comes and we'll wait for the burial until he arrives. No eulogies. Just *tefillot*—a few prayers. *El maleh* and *Kaddish*. The usual. You'll facilitate. David, my brother, will not disrespect you. I've already told him about you, and of course he knows my situation. I mean, the cancer. I want to die at home surrounded by my family. There'll be a hospice nurse. Morphine will be my friend."

The world of Fanette returned to me, though I had traveled miles since then. I was not a novice any more, but neither was I numb to the prospect of such loss. On the contrary, each death piled upon the last, and I carried them as a remembrance, a tabernacle of tragedies.

"From the moment we met, I felt that we understood each other," I said to Don. "But how could I have known that inside you were suffering your own nightmare? I'm very sad. I'll do everything you want me to. Just don't leave me yet. We have work to do, right?"

"Right," he said. We stretched our hands across the table and squeezed fingers.

Carol stirred and said, "Let's say *birkat hamazon*." We sang the grace after meals together and brought back the Sabbath with our harmonizing.

The winter months with their incessant rains and overcast skies drew me into a fierce depression. I was still receiving distressing phone calls from Zachary. Most nights I cried, and often woke up drenched in sweat. The days were shorter than I had ever experienced; as early as 3:30pm, the sun would go down. But there were night meetings and study groups that I was obligated to attend and sometimes lead, so I would force myself to go out into the blackness.

I knew my "children" on the island were fighting me for control. As in High Point, my authority had vanished after the six-month honeymoon. And living on an island with one grocery store, one hardware store, and one main street meant that in the space of a few minutes I could meet several people I knew. There was a lot of gossiping, and I felt that they were always watching me.

During this dark time, there were some compensations: several of the congregants became my friends and often invited me for dinner. The Rosens, Nancy and Stephen, originally from Long Island, became my surrogate family, and took me in during a snowstorm when the power in my apartment went out.

Don's family, including his mother-in-law, Alice, who lived near me on Bainbridge, became an anchor for me. Their sense of family made me want to be around them. Sometimes Alice reminded me of my former mother-in-law, Bubbe Sylvia, who also had a zest for life, an abiding intellectual curiosity, and a maternal spirit.

Into all the coming and going of my island life, the art of meditating came as a gift that year, and it stayed with me forever. A white index card on the bulletin board outside the grocery store led me to Madeleine, who had assembled a group of four women who got together on a weekly basis for meditation. It was a life-changing experience for me: a new, deeply personal form of spirituality that pushed back the wall of my despair and further broadened my rabbinic practice. Madeleine taught me how to quiet my mind, and explained how we hold layers of grief and healing together in our bodies. When we let go of our over-active thoughts, our "monkey minds," then our bodies release those built-up tensions in the form of tears, shaking, and sometimes nausea. Often, the tears would stream down my face, unprovoked and continuous during our sittings, and eventually her visualizations allowed me to transcend space and time. Madeleine's lessons stayed with me for the entire week, and in befriending silence, I learned to embrace the texture of the night.

On Thursday mornings, I also began attending a weekly women's Talmud class with Rivke Kletenik, the *rebbetzin* at the Ashkenazic Orthodox synagogue in Seattle. Rivke was brilliant: insightful and forward-thinking, despite her prominent role in the traditional community. She created an atmosphere of scholarship and sisterhood that left an indelible impression on me.

The fact that she and Madeleine were women was not lost on me. I had so few female spiritual role models from my youth that the discovery of two in such close proximity got me thinking more deeply about this inequity.

Though it was not by design, men had provided the lion's share of guidance for me in this realm. I had, after all, grown up most deeply connected to my father; women in our community had not been in leadership roles like Rivke, who in the 1990s was still a maverick. The women I had known when I was young were great *balabustahs:* "masters of the home" who were fierce about cleaning and cooking for their families but rarely pursued deeper intellectual or religious aspirations. I had yet to understand the important truth I was now discovering: that deep learning and spirituality could come from anywhere.

THE COMMON GROUND OF OUR APARTNESS

It was a great relief when the president of the congregation, a real estate developer, finally found me an office space, within walking distance of my house on Grow Avenue. My office sat on the second floor, directly adjacent to a space occupied by a young Episcopal priest named Bill Harper. His friendship was a life-changer.

"Welcome to Bainbridge Island," said Bill, sticking his head in my door just after I arrived. "When I heard that you were moving into the office next door, I told everyone, *the rabbi is coming, the rabbi is coming!* And now you're here!"

I laughed. "Thanks for making me feel so welcome," I said, looking around at the stacks of cartons and files. "I'm more at home already."

"Well, I'll let you settle in a bit, and then maybe we can walk into town? We can have a bite of lunch and get to know each other."

"Sure, that would be great. I'm so looking forward to working in this sunny space … and having you as my personal priest!"

It was his turn to laugh. "Okay! I'll knock on your door at noon."

Bill was a walking model of the relaxed island culture. He wore khaki shorts and leather Birkenstock sandals. His button-down cotton shirt was his only nod to formality—and with his flowing blonde hair, his blue-diamond eyes, his pierced ears, and his mischievous grin, he was irresistible. Bill was known as the "hip" priest in town, and it was my good luck that we were office mates.

"So tell me," he said, as we ordered salads for lunch at an outdoor café, "What's it like to be a pioneer?"

"Me? A pioneer? I thought *you* were the pioneer! Taking kids into the wilderness and teaching them about God. I heard about your retreats."

"Well, they're a lot of fun, but you're the one who's really breaking new ground," he said. He never failed to make me feel good about myself.

Bill was a progressive Christian pastor who pushed the edges of tradition. When I learned we would be neighbors, I asked around and had been told that he was considered very unorthodox: he always preached his sermon standing among the congregants instead of up on a dais. Like me, he was liberal in his views, less concerned with the establishment than with his service to individual people, which he held as his highest priority. He believed that teenagers in particular, so full of doubt and existential anxiety, could most easily find God in the wilderness, where the evidence of Creation could not be ignored.

"We can only glimpse the truth of the Gospel, but we will never own that truth," he said. He was the real thing. He had been called to ministry at a young age, and at 35 he was pursuing his purpose with an authenticity I admired. I was close to 50 and still stumbling around in the dark.

But just having an office made me feel more legitimate. Every morning I would get up and rush off to the cottage, where I felt I could work more easily. I liked that people came into my space: I counseled congregants and held meetings; I felt new power there. And in between meetings there was always Bill. We shared stories and frustrations; talked about grief and illness, birth and marriage, politics and personalities; our mini-support sessions buoyed us with hope, and allowed us to share concrete ideas for how to cope with everyday problems in our respective communities. Aside from our obvious clerical roles, we were both involved in the work of building young congregations that were essentially homeless. We spent a lot of time brainstorming solutions to the problem of space.

Our offices were separated by a set of French doors, and we fell into the habit of knocking on the glass between us whenever we needed to talk. We even had a code for signaling each other as to the degree of urgency: one small knock meant: "Come over as soon as you're free." Two sharp knocks meant: "Help! It can't wait!"

"Knock, knock," I said one day, standing in his doorway with a smile. "Time to talk?"

"Sure," he said. "What's on your mind?"

"I heard there's a place in the Midwest where a church and a synagogue built a congregation together. They share everything except services: their budget, their administrative staff. Wouldn't it be something if we could do that?" I asked.

"Anything's possible," Bill said. "You just have to hold the vision and pray toward it."

I was often surprised at these shows of faith, so different from the rabbis I was used to learning with, who focused more on rituals and commentaries than on frank expressions of belief in the direct power of prayer. But it didn't matter that Bill was a Christian and I was a Jew. Our connection transcended it all. We were doing the same work, and I knew that no one else on this island could understand me as well. For us, this was where true friendship could reside: outside the clergy-congregant relationship, in the common ground of our apartness.

Meanwhile, I found a safe social space among the leaders of the Seattle Jewish community as well, as I was wrestling among the two camps I was intended to bridge. I escaped to the mainland, where I was wholeheartedly welcomed by the young rabbinate. We had regular meetings and social events. We all had stories to tell about our rabbinic practice, and it was good to know I was not alone with my challenges. We talked about our isolation: how our congregants, seeing us at dinner parties or on the street, often ignored us. Or worse, they accosted us with some pastoral concern when we were on personal time. We laughed together rather than cry about our situations. Many of them had already been in the rabbinate for over a decade, though they were younger than I, and I had more life experience. But we made no distinction—we were equals. I treasured this collegiality: in their company, I could be myself.

Even with all of these positives, gloom continued to pierce my optimistic nature. I didn't feel like myself. I was usually easygoing and relatively unflappable; now I felt out of control, weepy and miserable. I told myself I finally had the space to grieve my losses without the daily concerns of motherhood. Yet I missed those daily concerns too, and felt aggrieved not to have them. I spent many nights in agitated, sweaty sleeplessness. I thought maybe I was manifesting symptoms of Seasonal Affective Disorder, or SAD, which hits so many residents of the Pacific Northwest during the dark winter months. I told myself to ride it out, that things would get better in the spring. But I was exhausted and emotionally drained.

One morning I ran into Terry, my upstairs office neighbor, at the coffee pot in the office kitchen. When she saw me, she said, "Rabbi, it looks like you could use some of this."

"Oh, I don't think coffee is going to cure me." My eyes filled with tears, and Terry's expression shifted immediately.

"Oh, no. That sounds serious. What's wrong?"

I hadn't planned on confiding to Terry, but I needed help, and forced myself to ignore the distance she placed between us, however unconsciously, by calling me *Rabbi*.

"I wish I knew. Maybe this rainy weather is finally getting to me. I don't feel like getting out of bed in the morning. And then there's the sweating at night. Maybe I'm depressed. Do you think I need a shrink?"

Again I was on the verge of tears. Terry put down her cup of coffee.

"Come sit down. It's going to be all right."

She gave me a tissue and took me in her arms, and we sat that way for a few minutes.

"Hmmm. Lethargy, night sweats, moodiness … sounds awfully familiar," she said. "How old are you?"

"Almost fifty," I sniffled.

She smiled. "I think I know what it is. You don't need a shrink. You need a gynecologist. I think you're going into menopause."

"Menopause! So I'm not going crazy?"

"No. But it does feel that way. I know. I've been there."

"Oh, God. It's such a relief to talk to someone! I can't even tell you … It's been so crazy. I have this nightgown, white cotton eyelet, soft and worn, you know?" I rushed on. "I keep wearing it, and then I have to keep washing it. Almost every day, cause it gets so soaked. But it makes me feel good, that nightgown, even sleeping alone, like I've been doing now for years."

I laughed sheepishly, and she smiled and nodded and squeezed my hand. I hadn't realized how isolated I felt until that moment. I was away from my friends, my doctors, everything familiar. And it wasn't as if I could tell my congregants about the mood swings and the night sweats. Nor Pastor Bill, though he was a wonderful friend. Terry was the first person I told any of it to.

And I chose well: she became a good friend, and she was right in her diagnosis. The doctor confirmed I was in perimenopause and gave me a wheel of pills to take daily. I began my hormone replacement therapy that night, and it took only one day for my energy and optimism to start flooding back. I never suffered any side effects. I was lucky. If only all acute misery could be cured with such a magic bullet.

During that winter, all four of my children came to visit. I was thrilled to show them life on the island and to coddle them with hot breakfasts. I easily slipped back into the role of mothering.

Joy returned to my soul; my muffled cries into my pillow subsided. The longing to have them stay with me forever filled my every *Sh'ma*, the singular bedtime prayer I had learned as a child. *Listen to me O Holy One. You are my Oneness.*

During the next few days, I shared with them the beauty of the place I lived. They loved the ferry ride into Seattle and they watched in awe as Mount Rainier "came out." When a rare two-foot snowfall covered the island my kids were overjoyed, until the meltdown caused heavy flooding and impassable roads.

I wanted to hold onto these moments and memories knowing I would need them to sustain me for the days and months ahead.

But all was not natural beauty in the communities I served. Many of my congregants were independent self-starters who came to the Pacific Northwest to defy the institutions that they had left behind, from Berkeley to Boston. Some didn't want a contemporary, or a woman, in a position of authority. I tried to steer clear of the political turbulence and reinforce the warm community of shared values in Judaism that was growing among those who came to prayer services and attended classes.

Spring was on the horizon, while Don, it became clear, was losing the fight for his life. He had a hospital bed placed in his sunroom, and people came by in waves to say their farewells. He was never left alone. His two children came in from Boston. Carol and her mother, Alice, were always present to greet people, and seemed to find solace by being together. He was heavily drugged, so I wasn't sure that he knew I had come to thank him and say goodbye. Carol and I talked about the arrangements in a separate room.

Don died in the middle of the night on February 13, 1997. His body was taken to Seattle where his *taharah,* his ritual cleansing, would take place. His brother and sister-in-law got on the plane and would be in Bainbridge by Thursday night. The funeral home's assistants were to bring Don's casket back to the island in time for the one o'clock Friday burial.

I was gathering my things to pick up Alice and bring her to Carol's house for the pre-funeral preparations when the phone rang.

"Rabbi, it's Carol. My mother had a heart attack. The ambulance is at her house and someone has to go with her. I can't get there in time. Could you please go?"

I grabbed my purse and the briefcase with my funeral materials for Don, and ran outside to my parked car. This was a matter of life and death. But whose death, Alice's or Don's? Alice was already in the ambulance with an oxygen mask and an intravenous drip. I rushed in front of the police and asked, "Where are you taking her?"

"We're air-lifting her to Seattle. Swedish Hospital."

In the midst of this chaos, I knew I had to be with the living and breathing Alice.

"I am her rabbi. I need to go with her," I said. "Her son-in-law is being buried this afternoon, so her daughter can't be here."

"There's no room on the helicopter, but you can go with the other emergency crew on the ferry. Hurry! It's leaving in five minutes. Meet us on the other side and we'll drive you to the hospital."

As soon I got on the ferry, I called Carol.

With extraordinary calm, she had already thought through the day's events, and she asked me to turn around. "I'm sending two other women to be with Mom," she said. "When they get to the hospital, you come back on the ferry. Someone will pick you up and bring you straight to the funeral."

"But what if she—"

"My mother will be safe at the hospital. She's a fighter—she'll survive. I know she will. And Rabbi, I need you here."

And so I spent an hour at the hospital with Alice, who was in a deep sleep. I sat and thought about how this convergence of devastating events could have come about.

When Carol's friends came to take my place, I caught a cab back to the ferry. Would I catch it in time? I was dizzy with anxiety that I would miss the funeral. When I saw the ferry still sitting in the dock, I felt a rush of relief. The 20-minute ride back to the island gave me a chance to reflect.

This whole situation with Alice and Don had reminded me of another time of loss: the time when Michael's mother was at death's door, and I found out I was pregnant, and a new soul had suddenly inserted itself into the picture. And now Alice lived on, while Don was lost to us all.

How often God sends us these reminders of the ebb and flow of our human lives, I thought. It's all about transcendence: we are rudderless and must give ourselves over to the unexpected again and again. I asked for Don's guidance once more so I could fulfill his last wish.

In the end, it all went smoothly: someone met me at the ferry and drove me to the cemetery, which was crowded to overflowing. A large circle of people from Bremerton and Bainbridge surrounded Don's grave. I sensed that the "children" had already planned for my *not* arriving in time, and when I showed up a few minutes before one, there was a strange murmur of disappointment. The heavens rained down upon us, and groups of two and three huddled under umbrellas.

I had made a promise to Don, and I was here to keep it. My small frame felt as if it were growing in stature as I began chanting Psalm 127. *Esa Einai … I lift up my eyes to the mountains from where my help comes.*

Don's brother sported a long beard and a black hat, and he carried a small *siddur* in his hands, but he never looked at it. He just stared into the crowd, and I wondered what he was thinking, if he knew his brother had gone to such lengths to make him comfortable in his grief.

The specter of Time was still chasing us: the paid Orthodox gravediggers were in a rush, knowing the entire grave had to be covered in traditional fashion before they could leave the cemetery. Shabbat was nearing and they still had to take the ferry into Seattle and find their way home in time to watch their spouses light the Sabbath candles. Don's brother, too, appeared to feel Shabbat bearing down on us as the day waned. He began reciting *Kaddish*, shuckling and bending and gasping between the Aramaic syllables. Suddenly the mourners began to help shoveling, with great alacrity along with the hired gravediggers. The rain had made the sand wet and heavy, and covering the grave had become an arduous task.

People quickly went back to their parked cars. I stood paralyzed in front of the mound, mourning this kind soul who had become my friend and teacher during such a difficult time. Don's grave was only a few feet away from that of Sarah's son. It would be up to us to tell their stories. The cemetery had become quiet, until I heard a screechy cry from above. When I looked up, I saw a sparrow flying past. I, too, wanted to fly away. But I had to stay and pick up the pieces of this shattered community, without shattering myself.

Alice spent the entire week of *shiva* for her son-in-law in the hospital, but she recovered. She would live for another decade. Carol and her children sat the full seven days of *shiva* in their home. The community embraced them and formed a circle of protection around them with abundant food and constant company. Don's death had brought everyone together.

A LESSON FROM KING SOLOMON

I wanted desperately to succeed in my rabbinical role in the Pacific Northwest, to solidify my position on the island so I could stay to complete my two-year obligation.

I was looking forward to conducting the Passover Seders for both the Bainbridge/Bremerton communities. But I was told that most in the community traveled back to their families on the East and West coast, and I could instead take the eight days as my vacation. I bought yet another plane ticket and flew back to be with my family for the holidays.

A day before my trip back West, Michael asked me to meet him for lunch.

"Barbara and I are leaving Greensboro at the end of June," he said. "She wants to live closer to her twin sister in Massachusetts. So I've been looking for jobs these past few weeks, and I've got a few interviews lined up."

"But ... but what about Zachary?"

"Well, that's why I wanted to talk to you. He'll be finished with junior high school, and I've enrolled him in Camp Judea for the summer. After that, it's up to you."

"What? But I have a two-year contract ... and Zachary really wanted to be with you. I didn't think you'd be going anywhere before he finished high school ..."

"Well, we're not waiting any more. Barbara never planned to stay—all her people are in the Northeast. It's not fair to ask her to put it off."

Fair? Was it fair to Zachary? I was backpedaling crazily, trying to catch up to this new wrinkle in my already-complicated life. There were a hundred angry things I wanted to say to Michael, but all I said was, "Have you told Zachary about your plans?"

"We told him a few days ago. To prepare him."

"He hasn't said anything to me. What was his reaction?"

"He's not thrilled. His friends are here. He doesn't want to leave. Anyway, he asked about where you would be."

"But you *knew* where I was going to be! I can't believe you didn't discuss this with me first! This is my *career*, Michael. I went to Bainbridge because I found a job. But it would never work for Zachary there."

"Well, I told him he could choose," said Michael.

"He's only fourteen. How can he choose? We're his parents; *we* have to make the decision."

"I've got to get back to the office," he said. "Let me know what you decide."

I stayed in my seat as I watched Michael exit the restaurant, trying to understand why he felt that it was his prerogative to leave when nothing had been resolved, and why I could never seem to properly stand up for myself in his presence. I covered my eyes and cupped my head in my hands. How would I ever make this choice?

When I arrived back in Seattle, I noticed how clear the skies had become in just a week's time. The sunny crisp air I had fallen in love with had returned; the variegated plants and trees of spring released their fragrance. Hope returned to me, and I was eager to go to my cottage office and see Pastor Bill and my friend Terry. With Don gone, I would have to shape my own destiny. Michael's news was rolling around in the back of my mind, competing with my thoughts about how to create an atmosphere of congeniality and trust among my congregations.

But instead of progress, the news that reached me when I got back to the island moved my goal even further out of reach: in my absence, the Bainbridge community had itself split in two. One faction was in favor of retaining my services, and the other staunchly refused to consider it, wanting to maintain an informal, home-centered service that consisted of lay leaders and communal activities.

Bremerton continued to support my rabbinic authority and asked me to come lead Sabbath services, but the Bainbridge faction returned to their lay leadership. I reached out to Don's wife, Carol, to ask for her advice and support.

"Maybe they will listen to you," I said. "What would Don have wanted?"

"I'm sorry Rabbi. I just can't take sides. These are my friends. Eventually you'll move on, but I'll still be living here."

"You won't even talk to them to reconsider? They're tearing this community apart."

"They just don't want the authority of a rabbi … any rabbi. They've always wanted to do it their way. There's nothing you or I can do to persuade them otherwise."

It was clear that Carol was right. But then why had they brought me here? It was an impossible task.

All I could do now was to focus on those who remained: I tried to keep going with religious school classes and services, to maintain a sense of community. I paid special attention to individuals who still sought me out, bar and bat mitzvah students and people like Ken, the young convert whom I had been teaching since the High Holidays and whose studies were now complete.

One night while I was preparing my sermon for the week, trying to uphold my sense of integrity and ignore the voice in my head that told me it was pointless, Zachary called.

"Mom, I know it's late, but I can't sleep. I have to talk to you."

"Tell me."

"Dad got a job in Pittsfield. It's … I don't even know where it is. He says it's not near Boston or anything. They're moving in June, right after I finish eighth grade. Dad's saying I could go with, but what would I even *do* there?"

"You could make friends anywhere. But do you want to go?"

"No! I want to stay in Greensboro."

I raged at Michael in my head. Out loud, I said, "Oh, Zachary. I'm so sorry that this is happening. But I don't see how it will work now. …"

"I do! I have the best idea! So Dad and Barbara move to Pittsfield. And you, you're staying on the island, right?"

"I … I think so. I've got another year on my contract—"

"I know! So what if I move in with David?"

"David? No, Zachary, that's not—"

"Lots of kids are doing it, you know, so they don't have to leave their school and their friends if their parents move. It'll work out. You'll see."

I thought back to 5-year-old Zachary, with his solution to the problem of my tiny apartment: we would just trade houses with Barbara and Michael, he had said. He was always the philosopher, the problem-solver. But I couldn't let my teenage son do the work of parenting, even if Michael was content to do so.

"I have no doubt you could handle it. You've grown up so much this year. But the thing is, I really miss you. This year's been so hard. I don't want to spend another year without you. And thinking of you alone in Greensboro, without me or Dad, isn't much consolation. "

"But Mom, you know I can't come and live there! I mean, it's awesome and everything, but I would never see my friends. It's away from *everything*."

I started to cry.

"I don't know what to do! I need to think. I'm going to figure this out somehow. It won't be perfect, but we're not going to be apart any more. I love you so much."

"Mom, please, don't cry. I love you too."

It hardly seemed possible. As it turned out, the most important Solomonic role in my life was not the one between Bremerton and Bainbridge, but the one between my rabbinate and my heart.

My heart told me I had to reunite with my son. Working out the details of this reality was not simple, but I could not ask him to join me in exile on this island. I had to leave.

When I confided to my "surrogate family" in Bainbridge, Nancy and Stephen, I was surprised by their response. "Your son needs you. If you break the contract, you break the contract. Everyone will understand. Honesty is best. You might lose some money, but you can always recoup that. What you can't recoup is time with your son."

They emboldened me to talk to the president of the Bainbridge community, with whom I had a very good working relationship. When I told him my story, he was nonchalant, and asked me simply to stay through the final bar mitzvah of the season in the early summer.

I was relieved, grateful for his understanding, but I couldn't help thinking this was too easy. I was right.

At the next board meeting, I got pushback. A Seattle attorney whose son I had just finished coaching for a bar mitzvah stood up and said, "We do *not* accept your resignation. You have a contract and if you want to break it, there will be consequences. You can be sure of that."

"I can't believe you're saying this!" I told the board. "You know me. I didn't make this decision lightly! But I have to consider—"

"You betrayed us, Rabbi," he said. "You won't get away with it."

Here it was again, the inescapable truth: these people were not my friends. True, I had let them down. I was breaking my contract. But it had been virtually impossible for me to do the job they hired me for. And yet I would have stayed. I had been making every effort to salvage what I could from the maelstrom. Now I had something more critical to do than fight this losing battle. I had to get back to my son.

Sure enough, Bob started legal proceedings, and I had to negotiate fiercely just to get him to agree to use a *beit din*, a rabbinical court, to act as a mediator in place of a prolonged court battle. Two weeks later, we all gathered in a fancy Seattle law office.

Three male rabbis formed the *beit din*. They gathered, along with several congregants including my friends Nancy and Stephen, around a formidable conference table and members of the board of directors from Bremerton who came to protect their own interests. I sat at the head, feeling very small. People asked questions and gave their opinions; the rabbis took notes while I was being interrogated.

The attorney's sarcastic tone and innuendos about my "premeditated manipulation" prejudiced the entire proceeding. He was king of the courtroom, giving his final arguments. I was not asked to make a personal statement of my own. I was thoroughly humiliated.

After an hour, the three rabbis retreated to make a final judgment. When they returned, one of them said: "We have reached a decision that will satisfy the communities: You will be permitted to leave after the last bar mitzvah of the season, provided that you return the three thousand dollars you were given for your moving expenses when you arrived."

Permitted? Three thousand dollars? I was alone again, the woman in a group of well-to-do men. There was to be no compassion, and I was not allowed a rebuttal. Bob sat smirking in the corner.

The indignity did not end there. After that, I was *persona non grata* in the Bainbridge community. Word had spread throughout the island that I had broken my contract and that I would be going back East. Next, I received a letter from the Bremerton board informing me that my services would be suspended immediately; practically speaking, this meant that I would not get my last month's paycheck from either party. I was appalled but not surprised that they took advantage when they knew they could. People can be so cruel.

I had one last meeting at the office with Pastor Bill.

"I'm so sorry, Tamara. You deserve better." He embraced me and a steady stream of my tears drenched his blue cotton shirt.

"I've failed," I cried. "I worked so hard. And now I'm being treated like an outlaw. It hurts."

"God has other plans for you."

"What plans? I don't even know what *I'm doing!*"

"Don't you have anywhere to go next?" he asked gently.

"No ... Well, not a job, anyway. I wish I could go back to North Carolina for Zachary's sake, but there's nothing there for me now ... I think I'm going to have to start over somewhere new. But where? And what about Zachary? Oh God. I don't know ..."

"*He's* not abandoning you; He's teaching you," said Pastor Bill. I knew who Bill meant by *He*. Coming from Bill, every word was believable.

"What matters most is that you and your son will be together. You know that. God knows that."

I realized I would miss Bill more than anyone else on the island. He had faith even when I had lost mine. His belief in a benign God gave me comfort. The depth of his belief affected me profoundly, and the thought of it would return to me at the most difficult times.

Still, I knew now that wherever I went, I would always stand a step outside. Rabbis perform rituals, decide matters of Jewish law, act as spiritual counselors and teachers. Like therapists, we are repositories for people's secrets. But this privilege comes with a steep price. They wanted different things from me than from their friends.

They expected me to please everyone all of the time, but I was continually being faced with irreconcilable demands.

It was an endless series of Solomonic deliberations: Bainbridge vs. Bremerton; clergy vs. human; career vs. motherhood; rabbi vs. relationship. There was no resolution. I thought back and saw that I, too, had projected unreasonably high standards onto my rabbis: I wanted them to embody the holiness that would elevate my life and the world around me.

Now I *was* the clergy, and I was walking the border between warring camps, while I clutched the sealed packages that held everyone's secrets. It was true that I was privy to the most sanctified of times: births, deaths, bar/bat mitzvahs, divorces, marriages, mortal illnesses. But outside of the clergy, I could not have a natural friendship.

What was more, my congregants did not expect me to have personal needs and emotions; I was meant to compartmentalize, to act as though I had no other priorities but the happiness of my community. But I was a mother and a woman as well as a rabbi, and I had been operating under the assumption that these roles could all somehow be amalgamated. This was proving to be an impossible handicap, one that opened the door for the doubters to say, "See? Women can't handle these roles. They're too emotional."

It was then that I realized I could no longer be a congregational rabbi. It was not a hill I wanted to die on. I would have to find a new Way.

I was looking for answers to the big question: "Where do I go from here?"

I had only the vaguest idea of what I wanted: a place with more options, where Zachary could thrive, where I could find a new sort of role for myself, though I could not imagine what that would be.

I asked for guidance, walking and meditating on my choices. I walked the 10 minutes from my apartment to the water's edge, and then walked around and around without any destination. I cleared my mind and let the ideas flow, turning the options this way and that. Little by little, a plan began to take shape.

I called Zachary.

"It's Mom. I've made a decision."

"What decision?" he said nervously.

"I know you want to stay where you are, but that isn't going to work for me. I can't take care of us if I can't find a job, and there's nothing for me in Greensboro. I'm sorry."

"Well, I'm definitely not moving to Pittsfield—"

"No, of course not. There's nothing for *you* there. It's the same problem as coming here. So this is what we have to do: we both have to give up something we want, and find a new place to start over together."

"But *why?*" he said, his voice rising.

"It's like Solomon. When it's impossible to decide between two options, you have to find a third one."

He was silent, and I could hear his agitated breathing on the line. But at least he wasn't fighting with me.

"So, I'm thinking Washington, D.C."

There was another long pause. "Well, that's random. Why D.C.?"

"It's really great there. A bigger city with lots to do. The Air and Space Museum," I babbled. "And the Metro goes everywhere. You could get around on your own, without even having to ask me for a ride. We would be closer to my parents and my sister, close enough to drive. And it's still driving distance to Greensboro, too, so you could visit your friends."

"I don't know, Mom. I've got to think about this," he muttered.

Poor Zachary, I thought. He had been in the middle of this tug-of-war for as long as he could remember, switching households, navigating his strange stepfamily, trying to be independent so I could do what I needed to. But he had not lived outside of Greensboro since his birth in 1982. He had his friends, his community, his identity in this small southern town. Now I was asking him to leave that behind, too.

Even then, though, I could tell that he knew I was offering him the best possible option.

The year on the island had been tough for our mother-son relationship, and now we could be together again.

There was no going back for me. I had to make a clean break from my old life. My identity was changing. I would move to Washington, D.C., as a divorced single mother with a 15-year-old son. I would be the stranger again. I would rewrite my story.

As I was packing up my things, I ran into Tom at the checkout counter of the hardware store.

"I'm leaving the island next week. The job just didn't work out," I said.

"I'm leaving, too. Work's been slow. I'm going back to California," he said. "Are you free tonight for dinner?"

"I would love that," I said, overjoyed that he did not hold my past decisions against me. "Let's meet at the Boathouse at seven."

We had a wonderful dinner and talked incessantly about the year that had passed. We laughed at our troubles and our constant challenges. I thought to myself: why hadn't I let Tom into my life that first month on the island? What had I been afraid of? Whenever I think of my year in the Pacific Northwest I feel a pang of regret for that choice.

"I bought this so that you would remember me." He held out an unwrapped box. "Every girl needs an ankle bracelet."

We hugged long and hard beneath the full moon. The next week, I got on a plane and flew eastward, to start again for the hundredth time.

FINDING MY FEET IN THE CENTER

I had no job and no congregation. So I did what people do best in Washington, D.C.: I networked.

I began cold-calling to meet anyone who could help me find me paid work. I substituted for other rabbis; I taught Holocaust studies to high school students at Washington Hebrew Congregation and co-facilitated a healing bereavement group; I led afternoon prayer services at the Hebrew Home in Rockville, Maryland—the first female rabbi to do so. One referral led to the next. Everyone was eager to help. My positive lens on life remained strong, and though money was tight, I trusted that I would find my place (and my prosperity).

From time to time, I received phone calls from people who had a lifecycle event but no synagogue affiliation: baby naming, wedding, divorce, funeral. I would meet with them in a tiny, furnished office I had rented in D.C. for this purpose, and ask just enough questions to get a sense of their lives and losses before I had to officiate at one of the most important days of their lives. Freelancing: it was a strange and wonderful way to get pastoral experience of every sort at once.

People led such complicated lives! For instance: Susan, who was referred to me by a minister, was a 40something PhD medical scientist, a Jewish lesbian who had been involved with a Christian partner for 10 years. She had come from an Orthodox family and felt she had never been given room to discuss her differences; when her parents started to speak to her about marriage, she had run away from home.

Recently, Susan and her partner had become foster parents to a son. With this, Susan, who had never reconciled with her own parents, had begun to realize how much she must have hurt them with her actions. She wanted to give and receive forgiveness from her family before it was too late, and had come to me for guidance. I felt my way forward, using a combination of intuition, tradition, and experience, and together we effected reconciliation.

Somehow, word of my work began to spread through the far-flung D.C.-area Jewish community, and I patched together a living.

At the end of December, I received a call from the executive director of the District of Columbia Jewish Community Center, also known as the Edlavitch DCJCC. It's the hub for the capital-area Jewish community. The director had a remarkable invitation for me: join her team as the Director of Jewish Living and Learning.

"Yes!" I shouted. "I can start right after the New Year."

I loved my work at the DCJCC. My colleagues were in their 20s and early 30s, a constituency largely absent from synagogues in America, but a group that is searching for identity in their work and in their social life. They were energetic and committed to making the Jewish Community Center a vital place. There was a delicious panoply of activities: theatre, film, concerts, literary events, lectures.

Zachary attended Charles E. Smith Jewish Day School, taking a dual curriculum of secular and Judaic studies. His days were full morning to night with school followed by basketball, soccer, or baseball practice, so I had plenty of time to work. Fridays, I got home early and picked him up. Our lives were finally in sync, since both of us had days off during the Jewish holidays.

Being an only child in a one-parent home was tough for him, however. He missed his sisters and the commotion that was generated by a large family. The girls came to visit as often as possible from Boston, and Michael also visited from time to time. But mostly it was just the two of us, comforting and confronting each other on a daily basis.

I often woke him up to attend Shabbat services with me, as my father had when I was a girl. On Sundays, we both had Hebrew school jobs at the local conservative synagogue, B'nai Israel. He got to keep the money he made, and my salary made our life possible. Not comfortable, certainly, but I was frugal, and our situation was not dire.

The music played an Israeli love song while Michael and I walked Naama down the aisle to Jonathan, her groom. Ten years had passed since the divorce. I was not nostalgic, nor was I bitter. We stood together under the *chuppah* as mother and father.

I looked out at the crowd of family and friends. My parents sat in the front row. Several Israeli cousins had come, along with the Bronx cousins. We were gathered in Boston where all three girls had been in school, but we had no ties there. Instead, we carried our ties within us, and we were ready to create new ones.

I turned my eyes back to Naama, my eldest, standing before me with her olive skin, her dark eyes, and her no-nonsense, Israeli attitude, as though our love for the land of Israel was encoded in her skin. She was the mother duckling of our brood: would she still be protective of her siblings now that she was making a new life? It seemed impossible to imagine anything else. The work she had chosen, to be a public health specialist in maternal and child health, told me she would never stop wanting to do good in the world. She was built to help others.

How well she had chosen her mate, I thought, as I turned to look at Jonathan Yager, curly-haired and pale and full of heart. Like Naama, he was pursuing work to reflect his inner self; he would become a cardiologist. He was empathetic, generous, kind. They were both first-born children, strong people who would make one another stronger.

Khana and Shmuel and eight of their nine children, with spouses, had driven up from Philadelphia and New York, but they did not witness the wedding ceremony. They would not be where men and women were sitting together inside the sanctuary. Instead, they waited in the social hall, where they were served dinners wrapped in foil with a sealed kosher stamp. Still, they came. My parents were happy; finally, a *simcha* where we could all participate. The only time Khana's family, all 20 of them, celebrated actively was when they entered the circle of dancers and in a blink of an eye, they rearranged the floor patterns so that the women and the men were dancing in separate circles. It was flawlessly choreographed. After a few songs, the divided circles returned to their intermingled state, and the family left the floor.

Mere weeks after Naama and Jonathan's wedding, Elisheva and her boyfriend, Michael Funk, got engaged. They would move in together, and get married just 15 months later. With the kids living in Boston, me and Zachary in D.C., and the Funks in Atlanta, I lobbied to hold the wedding in Greensboro.

"But nobody lives in Greensboro anymore!" Elisheva said.

"That's true. But we have the synagogue, the rabbi, and a warm place to fly to. Especially in January!"

The idea took hold. Elisheva was nothing if not practical: she always did the thing that made the most sense. She was more concerned about her place in the world than the place where she would hold her wedding; and her groom, Michael, who could sell a shoe to a shoemaker, was carefree and easygoing, and quick-minded enough to see why this plan worked.

Beth David Synagogue was like a second home to us. Our children had had their *b'nei mitzvah* there; it is where I decided to become a rabbi, and where I had been mentored by Rabbi Havivi. It would be a homecoming and a reunion. Rabbi Havivi would officiate, but I would address the couple, too. I was glad Elisheva wanted me to have a part in the ceremony, and I was more ready the second time around.

My sermon to the bride and groom began with a story:

> *"When Rabbi Eleazar of Kosnitz, the son of Rabbi Moshe, the son of the Maggid of Kosnitz, was young, he was a guest in the house of Rabbi Naftali of Ropshitz. They were standing in a room where the curtains had been drawn, and Rabbi Eleazar looked at them with surprise. When his host asked him the cause of his surprise, he said: 'If you want people to look in, why the curtain? If you don't, why the window?'"*

> *All too often it is because of our fears that we envelop our love behind the layers of curtains we surround ourselves with. The treasure we call love is hidden within ourselves. When you want someone to look in and to see deeply into your soul, you must draw aside the curtains.*

It felt right, on that warm January day, to be back in the Deep South. We remembered the wisdom of the Rev. Dr. Martin Luther King, Jr., on the holiday in his honor. It felt right to see my dependable and loyal girl joined to this confident and energetic boy, who wanted nothing more than the right to be the yin to her yang. Beyond that, there was power in being here: I felt healed by the sight of these friends with whom Michael and I had shared so many memories during our married life. Though I had still not found my beloved, Elisheva's wedding helped me forget the shadows of the past and gave me new hope for the future. I was to find that bigger things lay ahead.

I spotted Rabbi Tessler on the checkout line in front of me at the

Giant Food supermarket, and immediately felt shy. I reminded myself that we were colleagues—fellow rabbis—and that, in fact, he was 20 years younger than me. What did I have to be shy about? Was I going to carry the patriarchy around inside myself forever? I knew it was a kneejerk response, my belief that every Orthodox rabbi knew more than me, that I would never catch up. It was, I realized, the way I had thought about my ex-husband as well, as if his *yeshiva* education and medical degree conferred on him some sort of superior respectability that, more often than not, was an illusion.

Rabbi Tessler would surprise me by being more evolved than I was. He turned around and said, "Rabbi Miller! Seeing you here has given me an idea."

"Hello, Rabbi Tessler," I said, noting his unusual use of my rabbinical address. It was strange how often I felt misnamed by people. Those whom I considered friends often insisted on calling me Rabbi, while my male colleagues all seemed to want to call me by my first name. "What sort of idea?"

"I'm going out of town in a few weeks, and I need someone to give the sermon in the morning. You would be perfect."

"*Me?* Give the sermon at Beth Shalom?" I smiled, while my heart skipped around like a six-year-old on a playground. "I'd be honored, but don't you think that would cause a stir?"

"So what?" he shrugged, smiling back at me. "My wife is always telling me that I should let the women speak. And who better than you? I'll have my secretary call you with the exact date."

He didn't wait for an answer. I watched him leave with a bag of groceries in each hand.

When I received the call from his secretary, I realized the weekend in question was the same one chosen by a group of my closest friends from Greensboro to come to town for a reunion. My women friends would be here to witness this historic event in my life. I couldn't decide if that was good or bad, so I left the plan in place.

For the next few weeks, I spent hours studying that week's Torah portion. What would be my theme? I wrote and rewrote my sermon outline. Of course I had given sermons before, but this time was different. I was going to speak in an Orthodox synagogue in front of men and women who hardly knew me. It would be obvious after the first few sentences that I was not of Rabbi Tessler's caliber. Why hadn't I refused? Would some of the men walk out? Would I be shunned for my impertinence? I tried out a dozen different ideas before I hit on a topic that felt right.

The Greensboro reunion turned out to be a boom. My old friends were nothing but supportive, and once they arrived, they coached me.

"Don't be afraid to be yourself. Make it personal," Vivi said.

"Yes, and make sure they know you're *Rabbi* Tamara Miller," Ruth said. "You've earned your title. So use it."

The old, familiar prayers began, sung in the traditional melodies of my childhood, not the newer forms I had learned as I chased after my own brand of spirituality. Still, I had heard these prayers a thousand times as a girl. What was I doing here, a woman rabbi on an Orthodox bimah? I sat with my papers in my lap, butterflies in my stomach, and prayed that I wouldn't make a fool of myself.

"A funny thing happened to me while shopping for my Shabbat dinner at the Giant a few weeks ago," I began. I told the congregation how Rabbi Tessler had cajoled me into giving a *D'var Torah* in his stead. Most people laughed, but a few men in the back walked out as soon as they heard what I was doing there. I looked at the assembly, at the women sitting separately from the men as and saw the old, familiar layout.

I stood strong and spoke fervently about *Parshat Re'eh,* the Torah portion from Deuteronomy 11:26-16:17.

"Parshat Re'eh begins with Moses's speech commanding us: *Look! I am placing before you this day a state of blessing and a state of curse.* When our vision is clear we can see our blessings; when our vision is dim, we cannot differentiate blessing from curse. The long journey to reach the Promised Land allowed us to see what was obscured before: the very act of belief is seeing beyond the set boundaries of our lives." I looked up from my paper and saw rapt faces staring back at me. It was really happening!

When I came off the bimah and into the crowd of well-wishers, I made a beeline for the women's side—my side. My friends embraced me and shouted accolades. "*Yasher Koach*! Good job!"

Good job. Another barrier down.

Being closer to my parents and relatives was another advantage to my new life in Washington. Every few months, my parents would come to Maryland and stay with us in our two-bedroom, two-bath condo, situated on the ground floor, overlooking a small stream.

This is how small the Jewish world is: it turned out my second cousin,

David, and his family lived within walking distance of my condo. When his parents and grandparents came to visit, memories from my Bronx childhood returned. Sometimes my parents showed up on the same weekend, and we would drag the kitchen chairs outside and laugh and talk in Yinglish. It was like constant, enjoyable theater:

JEANETTE (my mother): Ben, go get Jack a chair from inside. *Er steht.* (He's standing.)

BEN (my father, turning to me): Tamara, where can I find another chair?

DAVID (my second cousin): Stay, stay, I'll get the chair!

JACK (my uncle, my mother's brother): *Ich darf nisht.* (I don't need it.)

EDNA (my aunt): Jack, let him get you a chair. You can't stand there all day, can you?

JEANETTE: Oy. Such *tummel* over a chair. Really, Jack, *es passt nit.* (It's unbecoming.)

ZACH: Mom, what are they *saying?* How come you never taught me Yiddish?

TAMARA (sighing): I'll get some more chairs. Zach, you come with me. I'll teach you Yiddish on the way.

It was much ado about nothing. My favorite kind of visit.

For the first time in my life, I had complete rabbinic authority. There was no one telling me what I could or could not do. I had no boundaries unless I created them. I asked myself: *As a Jew, is this what I need? Is this what will nourish me?* That became my guiding principle: nourishment.

I had been fortunate in my own childhood, and had inherited my father's joyful Judaism, his unwavering belief in a compassionate God. I had no need to rebel against my father's world. But as a young woman, I had sat in those pews again, waiting and wishing for something that would move me and awaken my spirit. I never forgot that. I wanted those who had been hurt or had turned away from the Judaism of their childhoods—whose God was outdated and did not work for them, who had decided it was not necessary to have a personal God—to reconsider, to make the journey with me, back into their roots.

As I sat in a staff meeting at the Jewish Community Center, less than two weeks before the High Holy Days, I realized something from the conversations around me: Many of my colleagues had nowhere to go for the Jewish holidays.

"Oh, I don't go to *shul*. I go home to sleep and eat," said one of the young staff members.

"I usually wake up just in time for my mother's Rosh Hashanah brisket and kugel."

"I haven't been to *Kol Nidre* since I had my bar mitzvah," said another, referring to the Yom Kippur evening service. "Though sometimes I still fast."

"I'm staying in D.C., but I'm not sure where I can get a seat," said a third. "I'm not going to join a synagogue just to get into services for two days. Who can afford that?"

I had never once missed Rosh Hashanah or Yom Kippur services, and had not considered the alternatives. How could it be that none of these Jewish folks I worked with had an option they actually wanted to take?

"I don't even need a *shul*," said a young man. "The people around this table are my real Jewish community."

Everyone nodded in agreement. They all looked in my direction. I thought: why couldn't there be an alternative right here at the DCJCC?

I floated the plan to the executive director, who was accepting. "But I have to warn you," she said, "we might get flak from the other synagogues in town. They don't like competition. We have to be careful."

There followed an endless number of meetings and proposals, research, dialogue, questionnaires, and other forms of data gathering—two years' worth. I was told the Jewish Community Center didn't want to risk showing bias by sponsoring a service. I was told there wasn't enough interest to support it. After two years of stonewalling, I realized I was just going to have to exercise my own authority and do it myself.

When I made the decision, I had six weeks to create a High Holiday alternative for my staff and assorted other wandering Jews. I would call it "The Capital Kehillah." *Kehillah* is a word with a lot of layers, but essentially it means a body of people that nurtures community.

I rented a ballroom in the Barcelo Hotel in Dupont Circle (today known as the Palermo), bought a bunch of used prayer books, took out an ad in the Washington *Jewish Week*, and hoped that word of mouth would do the rest. I was thrilled when people simply walked into the hotel and asked where the services were taking place. In the end, there were more than 50 people. They were hungry for something different, intimate, slightly unstructured, but inherently familiar, and totally meaningful.

I hired two musicians, a husband-and-wife team made up of a harpist and a violinist. I knew that musical instruments were not an accepted part of most Jewish services, but I held onto my belief that music could speak to the heart and bypass all barriers.

In no time, The Capital Kehillah became a regular thing. I published a pamphlet and added the words: *To Return Requires That We Take One Step in the Opposite Direction.*

For four years on Friday nights and holidays, with no sacred space to call my own, I felt my way forward, believing that the sacred space was wherever we made it, and certain for the first time that I had arrived somewhere I had always intended to go.

Dating baffled me.

During those first years in Washington, D.C., I realized I just couldn't get a romance to work out long enough to experience one of those stirring Hollywood endings, where you see the couple running toward each other, the sylph-like woman being lifted up in the air, the iconic bear hug while everyone else is clapping and shouting like children on a playground. The music crescendos, and the theater goes dark. Tears of joy on everyone's faces.

Yet I still believed that every date was a possibility for romance: a how-we-met story that would outdo *When Harry Met Sally.* What, after all, was the secret of attraction between two people? And how could I make it happen? Was love, like God, a mystery that was never revealed but was always in the *process* of being revealed?

I tried every avenue: internet dating, blind dates, pickups at parties and fix-ups by friends. Within a short time, I had an entire list of non-starters that scrolled through my mind on lonely nights, like a standup comic's b-roll:

- Millionaire in a Penguin Suit

- Bigger (and Wider) Than Life Itself

- The Guy with Potential Who Learned I was a Rabbi

- The Divorced Grandfather with a Real Estate Problem

- The Ministering Minister

- The Fix-Up Who Needed Repair

- A Jew from Sweden?

- The Guy with Potential Who Learned I was a Rabbi II

- The Therapist with a Prison Record (*Who knew?*)

- The Not-So-Merry Widower

- The Blind Date Who Wouldn't Look at Me

- The Guy with Potential Who Learned I was a Rabbi III

When I was networking for a job, I proudly told everyone of my ordination. But at the endless string of singles events I attended, no one knew I was a rabbi unless I told them myself—which I often chose not to do.

At one of these Shabbat dinners for singles, I found myself surrounded by good-looking men. Mark was on my right, and Gabriel sat across from me: they both worked for the World Bank, I found out during the usual chitchat. I felt a camaraderie with these men that put me back in touch with the fun and freedom of my teenage years. I forgot myself and sang more loudly than usual during the Blessing After Meals.

Afterward, Mark turned to me. "Wow, Tamara, you really know this stuff. You should be a rabbi."

There was a short silence.

"But Mark—she already *is* a rabbi," said Gabriel.

Who had told him? We all laughed. But I knew neither of them would be asking me for a date.

But my most unusual date was one that transcended centuries of boundaries and borders—for the space of a dinner, at least.

"My name is Irfan," said the man, after arriving promptly for the date we had arranged online. He was dark-skinned and dark-eyed, very handsome, with a relaxed and easy demeanor.

"What an unusual name ..." I said. "What nationality is that?"

"Pakistani," he said, smiling gently.

"Really? So you're …"

"Muslim. Yes. But I don't practice anymore. My mother, well, she's still pretty religious. But I married a British woman who had no religion at all. My kids are American. They say they don't have a religious identity."

"And you know I'm Jewish, right?"

He nodded. "I liked your profile on OK Cupid. And the Jewish thing? That's not a problem for me at all. Growing up in Pakistan, I had a good friend, Daniel. He was Jewish. In the neighborhood we all played together, side by side. Muslim, Christian, Jew—there was no difference."

"Are you still friends?"

"No. He moved away. One day, he said that he and his family were going home. *Home? I asked. What do you mean? This IS home.* But he said: *No, we're going to our Jewish home. Israel.* I was angry at him for leaving me."

I smiled at the image of him as a sulky boy. There was something so familiar about him. I was almost alarmed at how engaged I was in his life story.

"So then what happened? Did you stay in Pakistan until you came to America?"

"Oh, no. For high school, my parents put me in a boarding school in east London. They were traveling around the world for work. My father was a diplomat. I was the only Muslim at the school, and there was one Christian boy, but everyone else was Jewish. When it came time for the morning prayers, the Head of School told me that I could join in, or I could sit and reflect with the Christian boy. So I sat in the auditorium and slept. I wish now that I had gone to prayers. I would know Hebrew now."

A dark, handsome man, without any of our tribal baggage, who was clearly a judeophile? It was too tempting. I thought about ending the conversation with some made-up excuse and simply leaving. After all, where could this go?

"Just recently, I called one of the synagogues to ask about taking Hebrew classes," he went on, while I struggled to hide my confusion, "but they said that people study Hebrew in order to chant the prayers and understand the service. They told me that it wasn't for non-Jews. I was disappointed."

I stared at him more openly. He looked Hindu, with his dark features and his soft demeanor. He had that British accent, and a sexy body. I liked every nuanced sentence that came out of his mouth. Could I really entertain a relationship with him? What would everybody say? Especially the kids ...

I roused myself to answer him coherently. "Well, I can understand where they're coming from. The synagogues don't teach the modern Hebrew from Israel. They want their congregants to be able to chant and read the prayer book, which is in biblical Hebrew. That's their main focus. Of course, you could always take Hebrew classes at a college or at Berlitz."

Our knees bumped under the tiny table and I felt a jolt of excitement.

Really, what was so fatal about this attraction? Why would anybody care if I got involved with a Muslim? And why should I care if they *did* care? I had been looking for someone for so long. Why put up barriers and lose a chance like this? He had a spiritual, introspective way about him. He was reflective and vulnerable—a lovely combination. I could really like him, I thought.

But first, the truth had to be told.

"You know, I'm not just Jewish ... I'm a rabbi."

"That's wonderful, Tamara! Only in America can women be accepted in all these different professions. The rest of the world is not so open."

"Yes. It's true," I said, trying not to grin too widely at his response. Finally a man who didn't go pale at the thought! "I've also traveled a good deal, in Europe and Israel and Jordan. I even went to South Africa for a summer to substitute for the rabbi in Cape Town. I was pleasantly surprised at the warm welcome I received there. Of course, they all said I was the first female rabbi they had ever met. But still, I enjoyed these encounters very much."

It was nearly two more hours before we gathered our things to leave.

"Would you like to see me again?" I blurted out. "I would. We have a lot in common, though not everyone will think so."

We hugged like two best friends who had shared much more than iced tea together. We walked out of the restaurant in tandem, still talking a mile a minute.

I really wanted to see him again. I got excited. Fantasies came and went. Movie scenes appeared nightly in my dreams. Then I got scared. How could I justify such a relationship? What if my family reviled me? Two more days went by. Why hadn't he called? Three more days went by. Still he visited my fantasies. Was I just being desperate? Or did I really want to embrace the *other*? It could be labeled as interfaith work, I thought, smiling to myself. But this time it would be personal.

Finally I got this email from him:

I regret that I cannot see you. I'm busy with selling my mother's house and getting her resettled.

I felt relieved.

Maybe he got scared, too. Funny how you can feel so intimate with someone after such a short time, and then look the other way and say goodbye.

But here I am, years later, remembering every word he said. On some cosmic level, I miss him.

I stood on the podium and looked out at the sea of people. Nine hundred of them.

It was the eve of Yom Kippur, the holiest night of the year. I was standing inside the sanctuary of the Sixth & I Historic Synagogue, a 100-year-old sacred space. The synagogue had been converted into an African Methodist Episcopal church and spent half its life that way.

But recently, it had been reclaimed by three Jewish real estate moguls, who undertook a complete renovation. Tonight, this beautifully restored space, with its glowing windows and soaring spaces, was mine—well, mine to share with the Capital Kehillah, which, after four years, was 150 strong, and the 750 other people here to celebrate the first High Holy Day services to be held here in 53 years.

I looked down at my small *Machzor*, the High Holiday prayer book, and reread its inscription: *At last, we meet. Leon. 6/2/94.* Dear Mr. Bernstein. How many kind souls had pushed me down this road?

Farther down the road, the same sacred space would house Sariel's wedding; my third grandson's bris; my 60th birthday celebration; my first grandson's bar mitzvah, my second granddaughter's bat mitzvah; and a funeral I would never forget. But for now, 900 people were looking to me to help make this the holiest night of their year. An electric silence surrounded me as I opened my mouth to speak.

"Every Yom Kippur is holy, but this Yom Kippur has the seeds of an extraordinary new beginning. Together, we are witnessing the return of the Jewish community to this building that has lost its way for a little while—you could say it was wandering in the desert—and now it has found its place again. It may have taken us fifty-three years to return to the majesty that was once ours, but here we are now, and isn't it grand?"

I felt a wave of emotion flooding from the audience into the gorgeous space. I looked up at the refurbished balcony and thought how strange it was that this place of progress and renewal reminded me so much of my childhood synagogue in the Bronx. There she was, the shadow of my 10-year-old self, looking down …

Standing quietly in place, we all listened to the violin and cello begin the strains of *Kol Nidre,* the opening prayer recited before sunset on the eve of the Day of Atonement in synagogues throughout the world.

The ark was opened, and two congregants took out large Torah scrolls and stood on either side of Cantor Rozanski, a World Bank economist who had generously lent his voice for the holidays. I stood off to the side, enveloped in my oversize silk *tallit.* The cantor chanted the Aramaic prayer in its plaintive and touching melody, beginning with the words *"Kol Nidre." All vows.* With great precision and intent, he increased in volume from *pianissimo* to *fortissimo,* repeating three times the solemn words:

"All vows, obligations, or oaths we have vowed, or sworn, or pledged, or bound ourselves to, we repent from this Day of Atonement until the next."

My sermon began with a family story.

My Uncle Joe survived the war, but his Hasidic family did not. He had married my Aunt Ruth in New York City, and created a new family, but his rebellion toward the God of his youth persisted in small ways.

A heavy smoker, he sacrificed his cigarettes, on one day only: Yom Kippur. As soon as the sun set and the last notes of the shofar were heard, he quickly walked out of the synagogue to clutch the hidden cigarette and the lighter that were tucked away inside his jacket pocket. Up in smoke went the cigarette while I caught a glimpse of my Uncle Joe's satisfied face as all the tension went out of him after his annual fast …

I talked about my Orthodox past, and my young self, sitting in the balcony with the other women; how I had looked down at the men below and craved their proximity to the Torah scroll. How they rushed to kiss it! How they escorted it around the aisles of the sanctuary, or turned their bodies toward it with devotion. How joyful the entire proceeding was!

I finished: "Our memories return to us on days such as this one. The past and the present hold hands as today becomes tomorrow's history."

With the help of the Cantor, the entire congregation began to chant in unison: *"Am Yisrael Chai.* The people of Israel live!"

And then something happened that I can't explain. Joy took over. Even decades later, people would come up to me at parties and say, "You probably don't know who I am, but I was there at Sixth & I when…"

165

I reached for the smallest of Torah scrolls, known affectionately as the Baby Torah, and marched around the synagogue as the voices of the crowd reverberated from every corner and drowned out my own. I felt a stab of ecstasy and followed it, sliding out the main door and up the stairs to the balcony, where men and women were no longer separated by gender. I wanted them to touch Torah, to love it as I did.

People followed behind me, as wild clapping urged me on from below. The people in the balcony, their faces lit with surprise and elation, rushed toward me and touched the covered scrolls with prayer books, with open palms, with the fringes of their prayer shawls. The frenzy continued long after my voice could punch out the tune. Eventually I made my way back down the stairs and into the sanctuary. The singing and clapping lasted for 20 minutes.

I was out of breath. I felt as if spirits had taken over the crowded room. It was like no *Kol Nidre* I had ever known. When the ark was opened again and all three Torah scrolls were gently replaced inside the velvet interior, we belted out the final prayer:

"All the paths of Torah are paths of peace. *Chadesh Yameinu ki kedem.* Renew our days as of old."

THE ART OF LETTING GO

As a self-empowered rabbi, I continued to visit the sick in many places around Washington. One of these places was The George Washington University Hospital, a large and innovative teaching hospital in the heart of the city, just blocks from the White House.

I got to know Cassie Billingsley of the hospital's Women's Board. It was her dream to create a chaplaincy program at GW hospital. She became the volunteer coordinator of the Chaplaincy Department and spent two years collecting chaplains of every faith throughout the city. That's how she "collected" me.

Tall, blonde, and very skinny, Cassie overflowed with energy. Her tiny office had once been a closet. She wanted to be available for every pastoral care emergency and had an open-door policy, with one exception. She was a secret smoker, and she would lock her door only to procure for herself another pack from the enormous stash of cigarettes she hid in her office, so her husband would never know. She had married late, and had promised him she would quit smoking, but she was a stubborn and independent woman, and she did what she wanted.

Once she learned about my background, my fate was sealed: she was from Queens, so she felt a sense of kinship with me as a fellow New Yorker. But what was more important, she felt certain that my appearance on the D.C. scene was part of the grand plan. And it was: I would become her only volunteer Jewish chaplain. Every time she called me to the hospital, I came. She was the nicest tyrant I had ever known, and the importance of the work she wanted me to do could not be denied.

But even then, she was not content. She had a big dream, and my occasional visits were not enough to bring that dream to life. Singlehandedly, she set about to raise the funds necessary to employ me as the program's first Director—official, not volunteer.

Cassie was always in a rush, so I wasn't surprised by her tone when she called me one day in June of 2001.

"Rabbi Miller, it's me, Cassie. Can you come by today at four? It's urgent."

"Why? Has someone died? Do you need me to see the patient's family?"

"No. It's much better than that. I've done it! I've got the funding. They've approved your position. There's no time to waste."

"Yes, but, I still have my work at the DCJCC ..."

"Never mind about that! We'll figure it out. This is your calling! Can you come? Four o'clock."

Director of Chaplaincy at GWU? I was too stunned to even be excited yet, but Cassie was right: this was my moment. My work was propelling me forward.

"Come on!" she said when I arrived later that day. "First you need to give blood, then a drug test, and then the psych testing. I've made all of your appointments already."

She was unstoppable. As we dashed from one place to another, her enthusiasm was both alarming and infectious.

"I know it seems like I'm always in your face," she said, with her New York accent, "but I won't interfere with your work."

"I'm not worried about that," I said breathlessly, pumping my short legs to keep up with her long, hurried strides. "I'm worried about how to get it all done! I don't know anything about the administration of the hospital—how things work in this system ..."

"See, that's what I'm talking about! I know *everyone* around here, and I'll have your back. And besides, you know what you're doing when it matters most—with the patients and their families."

"But how do you even know that?" I laughed. "What gives you so much faith that I'm the right person for the job?"

"I've heard such great things about you, Rabbi. And I've seen you in action, too. I've told everyone you're the one to do it! We're going to make a great team."

My first day on the job was her last.

In the midst of my orientation, a man with a look of sadness and confusion in his eyes tapped me on the shoulder. He took me to human resources and sat me down in an office.

I was certain they were going to fire me. It would be the shortest job in my rocky employment history.

"Rabbi Miller," said the human resources manager in a soft voice, "I'm afraid I have some bad news. I've just learned that Cassie Billingsley died at her desk this morning. An apparent heart attack. Her body is in the emergency room. This is a shock for all of us, but I know you two were working closely together on this new program, and we will understand if you want to go home."

"Go home?" I said. "Why would I want to do that? Please, just take me to the emergency room. I would go myself if I knew where it was, but …"

My voice trailed off as I realized what I was going to see there: another mentor who had hired me to bury her.

The man who had come to fetch me was standing quietly by. Now he stepped forward and said, "I'll take you, Rabbi." He introduced himself as Archie, the hospital concierge. He would become a good friend, but that day, he mutely pointed the way toward the room where she lay, and I could see he was frightened to enter. I nodded and thanked him, and went in alone.

I stood and stared at her lying on the gurney: flawless pale face, blond hair, grey suit, white blouse: she looked calm and peaceful, but her body was cold.

I was mesmerized with shock. How could she leave me now? I was totally unprepared. Was there any wisdom to be found here? She had always been in such a hurry: could she possibly have known that she had no time left? I felt a chill at the thought of her sudden disappearance from my life. We had been contemporaries. How did these things get decided?

I wanted to hide in there with her. Her family, the staff, the board would all be waiting for me outside this room. What did I have to offer them?

I spoke aloud to her:

"Cassie, I'm so honored that you chose me to do this work with you. I can't believe you're gone," I cried. "I vow to be worthy of your trust."

I did not take lightly the making of this vow. It was done with a full heart and pure intent. I could not have imagined how it would be tested.

It had been almost a year since my parents had to let go of their home in the Bronx. My father had fallen in the synagogue and broken his hip. It was hard for them to take care of themselves after that, so they moved to Philadelphia, to a place across the street from Khana.

My sister had become more stringent in her Ortho-praxis, and there were adjustments to be made by everyone. Shabbat was sacred, so there would be no cooking, no phone calls and no use of electrical appliances.

Khana cleaned and scrubbed my parent's kitchen to her high standard of *kashrut* and immersed all of the pots and pans in the *mikveh* to purify them. My mother gave in to these supervisions. My father seethed inside, but would not confront her. As always, there was an unnatural truce, filled with pretense.

The large one-bedroom apartment they lived in for the next eight years had a small, square kitchen that could accommodate only their dishes and appliances. There was no breakfast area and no real table, so a shelf was built specifically to hold my mother's two Sabbath candlesticks.

I had witnessed my mother lighting and praying over the Sabbath candles every Friday night for the 22 years that I lived at home. She succeeded in fulfilling this commandment almost 5,000 times during her 95 years; I believe she never once missed this reverent act. When I got married and left the warmth of those Friday evenings, I took the ritual of lighting the Sabbath candles into my home, and it became one of our cherished family traditions.

My father went to synagogue every weekday morning and every Shabbat. But now, living on the fourth floor of an apartment building, he couldn't walk up and down all those steps before and after services. When he told me that Khana had forbid him to use the elevator, I couldn't keep quiet.

"Khana, Dad says you won't let him go to *shul* on Shabbat mornings. Is that true?"

"There's no way that he can walk up and down the four flights of steps with his walker. And he can't take the elevator."

"Khana. He's been going to *shul* all his life. You can't just tell our father, the rabbi, that he's not allowed."

She was silent.

"Maybe we could find someone non-Jewish who could push the button for him," I said, trying to think inside the confines of the sky-high fence she had consented to live behind. Why should she drag my father in there with her?

"But how would that look? What if someone sees Dad in the elevator and thinks that he pressed the button himself? There are other *frum* people in the building who know me. Dad can pray by himself at home."

"Talk to your rabbi, Khana. I'm sure he would give permission. People do this all the time! And have done for centuries. Why should Dad *pray* alone on Shabbat?"

Whose *halachah* is it, anyway? I wanted to say. To me, it is ours—always ours.

But Khana's rabbi agreed with her. It was unfathomable, I thought— and I had no way to overturn my sister's actions or to modify her unyielding beliefs even for the sake of our parents' comfort in their old age. They were always clear in their desire for me not to confront her. I told myself I was honoring their wishes by letting it go.

Letting go is an art we strive to perfect. Separations begin at birth and traverse our lives at every physical and spiritual juncture. But every little fissure in the heart makes room for more love and more longing.

I am still striving to perfect the art of letting go.

I found it difficult to let go of Zachary. All of the practice with my three daughters had not been enough to toughen me.

After high school, he journeyed to Israel for 10 months of study and travel.

"Zachary, please be careful and stay with your group. Don't go out alone at night. Promise me."

"Mom. Anything can happen anywhere," he said, thinking it would calm me. "Life just happens."

The intensified violence of the Intifada further disrupted the already-fragmented lives of Israelis that year. There were bombings at bustling cafes and crowded bus stops; every public space was a potential target. I tried to comfort myself with the knowledge that Zachary was under constant supervision by savvy security teams. I was experiencing a mix of joy and grief with my new inheritance—the position at GWU.

Then, two months after Zachary left, the Twin Towers were attacked in New York City, and not far from GWU, the Pentagon was hit as well.

Zachary called that night from Jerusalem.

"What you said turned out to be true," I said. "Anything can happen anywhere. It was scary, but we are safe."

Of course, I could not know that. Neither of us was really safe. But from 6,000 miles apart, it seemed unkind to let him feel my anxiety—and he was already shaken.

After Israel, Zachary decided to stay close to home and attend the University of Maryland. After he graduated, I thought he would stay in the area.

Instead, the cycle of separations continued: he was accepted to Emory University in Atlanta to pursue a graduate degree. He would be near his sister and her family, I told myself, but still …

I packed him a bagel, an apple, a water bottle, and some peanut butter-and-jelly sandwiches for his 13-hour drive. I watched as my youngest child got behind the wheel of his Honda brimming with his belongings, and as if in slow motion, backed the car away from where I stood.

And then came the most difficult letting go of all.

My father died, of pneumonia, at the age of 95, taking with him the book of himself.

WHOSE *HALACHA* IS IT ANYWAY?

The important thing is not how many separate injunctions are obeyed but how and in what spirit we obey them.
—Baal Shem Tov

I knew not to wait for an inheritance. There were no financial secrets to be revealed. I had grown up in a household where there were no extras; until I was eight, we four had lived in a one-bedroom apartment, my sister sleeping in the living room and I sharing a room with my parents. Their lives and their closets were uncluttered, exposing only one row of neatly arranged blouses, shirts, skirts, and jackets. My mother's extra housecoats hung off to the side.

Our family had doubled up on pots, pans, plates, and silverware only to keep meat and dairy products separate according to the dictum of *kashrut*. During Passover, an eight-day holiday, an array of special dishes and kitchen utensils appeared, but our kosher kitchen was the sign of a deeply held dedication to a religious heritage; it was not about duplication for the sheer pleasure of plenty. Such was the immigrant's life.

After my divorce I relied on myself for my financial well-being. Like my mother, I was a good saver, so much so that my savings account had already outpaced my parents' humble resources that had taken them the life span of two immigrants to secure. A decade before my parents died, they entrusted me to manage their $20,000 savings account. With the help of my financial advisor, we doubled its value in a few years.

In the whole of their lives, with the sort of frugality that would defy most of us today, my parents only asked me to dip into their savings three times: for a new pair of orthopedic shoes for my mother, a dental procedure for my father, and for the cost of repairing my father's *sefarim*, the holy books of his *Mishneh Torah*. The *Mishneh Torah*, subtitled *Sefer Yad ha-Hazaka*, is a code of Jewish religious law authored by Maimonides, one of history's foremost rabbis, known familiarly by scholars as Rambam.

In the summers between rabbinical school classes, while the children were in overnight camp, I had enrolled at the Drisha Institute for Jewish Education in Manhattan for further credits. As during the school year, I stayed with my parents in the Bronx and commuted daily into the city by bus. Whenever I had a question about a certain Jewish law or the meaning of a word in a Hebrew text, I called my father. I thought he was every book that I would ever need. But he always reminded me to turn to the originals.

"You don't need to remember everything," my father would say, "but you need to know where to *find* everything. If you do this, you will be respected everywhere you go."

For him, every book he owned was a treasure chest of esoteric information. Page after page opened a world of discovery.

"Tamara, I found a bookbinder in Washington Heights who has experience repairing *sefarim*," my father said. "Come look at my *Mishneh Torah*. The spines are coming off, and if I don't do anything they will fall apart completely. Since you have your car here, I thought you could help me get these books to him."

The six volumes stacked together were more than a foot high and weighed 20 pounds. I was not surprised that their spines had worn out. My father had turned the pages of these books almost every day of his life, again and again, in his search for clarity.

Washington Heights is a neighborhood in northern Manhattan. In the years after World War II, the neighborhood was referred to as Frankfurt-on-the-Hudson, because of the 20,000 displaced refugees of German and Austrian Jews who had settled there from Frankfurt am Main.

Many of my friends from City College lived there, with their German-immigrant parents. Not surprisingly, Yeshiva University was built in this neighborhood, which continues to house the all-male Yeshiva College, and the all-female Stern College. Both institutions were inspired by Modern Centrist Orthodox Judaism's philosophy of engaging in a dual curriculum of Torah and secular knowledge.

We carefully placed the ragged volumes into two suitcases and laid them in the backseat of my 10-year-old Honda. I was still able to find my way back to this familiar neighborhood of my youth, where, decades before, Michael and I had had our wedding ceremony at the Fort Tryon Jewish Center, a few blocks away from the Harwitt Bindery.

We parked in front of the white brick building on Bennett Avenue, and with our heavy suitcases disguising our precious merchandise, we walked inside. We took the elevator down to the basement to find the owners, Mr. and Mrs. Schnerb, who had been working together for decades repairing documents and books. It was the opposite of a quiet well-organized library. Mr. Schnerb, with *kippah* and modern, clean-shaven face, had been born and raised in Frankfurt and had escaped the Nazis in 1938. Sewing up books and documents had provided for his financial security ever since.

"*Shalom aleichem,*" he said and reached out to shake my father's hand. He nodded to me.

"*Aleichem shalom,*" responded my father.

"*Vos darfts du?*" *What do you need?* asked the mild-mannered bookbinder.

I handed my father each of the six volumes of the *Mishneh Torah*. He, in turn, handed them over to Mr. Schnerb, who intentionally and cautiously placed each one of them in sequential order on top of each another. After taking a few minutes to zero in on the merchandise before him, he calculated the repairs.

"*Ich bin zeyer farnumen mit arbet.*" *I am very busy,* he said. "*Kenen ir vartn zex vokh?*" *Can you wait six weeks?*

I could tell my father was reluctant to leave his companion books for six weeks, but he had no choice. There weren't many craftsmen like Schnerb. Most of them had perished in the Holocaust.

My father took out a $100 bill he had just gotten from the bank and gave it to Mr. Schnerb as a deposit. We would return in six weeks and complete payment of $200 total. This was pricey for my father, but he did not flinch. He wanted to continue his daily studies—and perhaps he was preparing to make the holy books into an offering for future generations.

At the end of the summer, I drove with my father to retrieve his books from the Harwitt Bindery.

"*Bist ir tsufriden?*" *Are you pleased?* Mr. Schnerb asked my father.

"*Zeier gut! Ich bin tsufriden.*" My father's smile broadened to show a grateful customer.

I still remember the celebratory atmosphere that surrounded us. As I watched my father place his refurbished books back inside the same suitcases that brought them there, I realized yet again how these holy textbooks had influenced his life and how much joy he received from them. What was the price tag on that?

At that time, I had just one more year to go to complete my rabbinic studies, but I felt totally unprepared to follow my father. I would never be able to hold the full weight of the wisdom inside these books. My father's traditional upbringing and subsequent ordination contributed to his fierce proficiency in the art of Judaic discourse.

I thought again about gender. If I had been born a boy, I would have gone to Yeshiva at the age of five, and I would have studied the *Mishneh Torah* as a teenager. Instead I was still struggling with Talmudic translations at the age of 47.

Now, as I was sitting shiva for my father, I thought of my father's teaching, his love, and his books. This was my inheritance.

My mother and I sat side by side in the sparsely furnished bedroom where my parents had dreamed together. While Khana stood in back of us, swaying and praying, my mother and I appeared as motionless as the statues on the antique crimson globe lamps on the nightstands behind us. In one hand I held onto a black hard-covered prayer book and in the other hand I squeezed a ball of tissues. My Orthodox sister had draped a full-sized, white, cotton sheet over the huge mirror opposite my parent's bed as a proper sign of mourning.

I waited to say *Kaddish*, the mourner's prayer, for my father, patriarch and rabbi of this immigrant Polish family. I leaned on the double bed that my mother and father had bought 60 years ago for a lifetime of pleasures. On this bed, pneumonia had struck, and silenced my father's Torah.

In the living room, the evening prayers began. "*V'hu rachum*. God the merciful one," murmured my brother-in-law, Shmuel, my four nephews, Yossi, Aaron, Avrummy, and Mordechai, and *yeshiva* students in black suits and white shirts.

My observant sister had arranged my father's *shiva minyan*. They proceeded with the prescriptive texts without my permission and without my participation. To preserve the mandatory separation of men and women, Khana segregated herself, my mother, and me in the bedroom.

I remembered how I had breathed in the silky scent from my father's *tallit* as I had hidden in the men's section of the synagogue, playing with the *Tzitzit* that hung down from its four corners. I remembered how luxurious it felt to sit on my father's lap, absorbing the *Gemara*, the Talmud and all its commentaries, our Jewish textbook of laws and lore that I would study in seminary years later. I had been ordained with my father's blessing and presence.

Hear, Oh Israel, Adonai, Our God, is One.

The chanting of the *Shema* stunned me out of my grief.

The *V'ahavta* prayer followed.

And you shall love Adonai your God with all your heart,
With all your soul, and with all your might …

These prayers strengthened the spine of my childhood theology. I had recited them publicly hundreds of times in congregations across the globe. Yet here in the home of my parents, I was forbidden to utter them in the presence of this community.

I knew the rabbinic rules about public and private prayer. I knew how to obey them. I knew how to alter them. My father had taught them all to me. If my mother had died first, I mused, I would be sitting at my father's side, in the living room.

Wrapped inside our individual shawls, we would have wept while repeating the *Kaddish* by heart.

The prayers in the next room droned on until the silent *Amidah* hushed all human sounds.

I knew that within minutes it would be time for the Mourner's *Kaddish*. Would I defy the dominant men—who weren't even mourners—and recite the Aramaic words out loud for my father?

Tears dripped down my plain black shirt. My heart raced as I remembered my father's words about *halachah:* "The *halachah* was given to show us the path forward," he always said. "If we can't live with the *halachah*, then it's the *halachah* that has to change."

Would I respect and follow my sister's religious edict or follow my own practice? *Whose halachah is it, anyway?* I wanted to shout.

Kaddish arrived as it always does after the final concluding communal standing prayer: *Aleinu.* "To you every knee must bow, every tongue vow loyalty."

I looked up to find an answer from the greater Authority. I looked down to see my mother, curled up like a snail, and then looked sideward, at my sister's hunched back.

I shut my swollen eyes as I pondered my choices. Then I bowed before the God of my father and stayed where I was. I knew he would have expected me to keep the peace.

On the evening of the fourth day of *shiva*, my mother and I found ourselves alone. We sat on the couch, shoulder to shoulder, my arm draped around her slouched body as we breathed in a staccato rhythm.

"You loved him as much as I did," she said.

I found this observation to be accurate, but unsettling. A daughter's love and a mother's love are intentionally different, but at that moment, my mother and I understood each other in ways we had not done before. We became allies in grief, and our affection for each other grew deeper. Our beloved was gone.

I looked up to see our family's handmade bookcase filled with my father's treasured volumes. I wanted to scoop the books up in my arms, hold them to my chest, inhale their ancient aromas into my bones and weep.

Still inside my reverie, I looked back at my mother, but she had fallen asleep. I covered her with her quilt and walked toward the bookcase. I noticed a bookmark sticking out of one of his holy books. I opened the book and recognized the laminated bookmark that I brought back for him from a recent wedding. It was just like him to save this bookmark, and it pleased me to know that it marked the last page he had read before his death.

At the top of the page was the chapter heading: *Taharah.*

Taharah is the ritual cleansing of the dead.

I choked. My father was reading about his own *taharah*. Did he know his life was about to end? After all, at 95 he must have been thinking that any day could be his last.

I took the book in my arms as I swayed and rocked myself, as if I were a *yeshiva* boy *shuckling* back and forth during a particularly poignant prayer. I swallowed the sobbing so as not to wake my mother. My father was gone, but his books would remain on the shelf.

As much as I longed to take the books back home with me, I sensed my mother's need for me to leave everything the way it was before Dad died.

I thought: "If I took a few books here and there, the holes would be visible, and they would remind Mom that Dad is gone."

For my mother's sake, I would wait to claim my inheritance.

YOU ARE THE BOOK

Three things I marvel at
Four I cannot fathom:
The way of an eagle in the sky,
The way of a snake on a rock,
The way of a ship in the heart of the sea,
The way of a man with a woman.
—Proverbs 30:18-19

Sariel broke with tradition. She fell in love with a dark and exotic non-Jew.

Anthony had been born in Los Angeles and had a Mexican background. It was easy to understand why Sariel was captivated by this man—an introverted artist who was also a systems engineer. He was as intense as dark chocolate. How could he resist Sariel, my dreamy, idealistic daughter whose spiritual range included yoga and music and anyone who needed help? Because of her empathic curiosity, she had always been attracted to the "other."

As their relationship deepened, I could see that Anthony was curious about the "other" as well. He was a lapsed Catholic with no connection to his own family's religious background. Indeed, his stepfather was Jewish, so the culture was not entirely foreign to him. The intellectual in him loved the richness of Jewish history and the gravitas of tradition; the artistic, intuitive side of him possessed a natural spirituality. He was open to anything that moved him.

There was a part of me that resisted his "otherness," but most of me saw and accepted this as the future of my tribe: more and more, we would have to find ways of joining our disparate lives together. Sariel and Anthony had a deep and passionate connection; it would not be denied.

One day, Sariel called and asked if she and Anthony could meet with me.

"We want to get married, and Anthony has decided he would like to convert. Can you help us?"

"Of course I can help you," I said, though I had grave hesitations about the extent of my role here. "I can find you someone to take you through the process."

And so began a nine-month course of study for Anthony and Sariel. They were quite diligent about their attendance, and the class afforded the three of us opportunities to talk about faith, belief, practice, anti-Semitism and the Jewish survival story.

When it came time to decide who would officiate at the wedding, it seemed I was the only one who did not see the answer clearly.

"Mom, just do it yourself," said Naama. "After all, it's going to be at Sixth & I."

"Exactly. You know everything about that place and you don't have to ask permission. Just do it your way," Elisheva said. "I wish you could have done *my* ceremony."

"Yes! We know your style: a little quirky but lovely. I want you to marry us. Please, Mom!" said Sariel.

"All right," I said. Maybe it was time for me to step up. It was true that there was no place I felt more comfortable than at Sixth & I.

I assumed that the rabbi who taught the course would become the sponsoring rabbi for Anthony's conversion. But Anthony did not feel a connection to him. About three months before the wedding, I began to get uneasy.

"Anthony, do you have a date for your conversion yet?"

He shook his head and looked abashed. "You're the only one I trust," he said. "Why can't you do it?"

"It's not the right thing for me to do," I said. "It would be like a doctor treating his own family. I can't convene a *Beit Din* for you. But I think I know someone you'll like a lot. Don't worry. We'll get this straightened out."

Harold White was the first rabbi in Washington, D.C., who willingly performed intermarriages. He was known nationally for his efforts to

180

cultivate interfaith understanding and interfaith marriage. He was the first Jewish chaplain at Georgetown University, a Jesuit institution, and served there for over 40 years. When I first came to town, Rabbi White had made a point of inviting me into his office and spent over an hour getting to know me. He was a rabbi's rabbi, and I felt safe in asking him anything.

"Why do you do interfaith weddings, Rabbi White?"

"I want everyone to have a rabbi they can go to. I want to make it possible for them to have a dialogue about their spiritual journeys."

He suffered greatly for his stance, though now I see just how prescient he was. Interfaith work is the challenge of the century for the Jewish people. I was one of hundreds of rabbis struggling with how to incorporate interfaith families into their communities; and now it was a deeply personal encounter.

"The goal of inter-religious dialogue," he said, "is not just to look for similarities, but to see the differences and be able to embrace them. People can ask their best questions only as they become their best selves."

I tried to send Anthony to him, but somehow the timing didn't work out. Rabbi White said he'd be happy to meet with my future son-in-law, but Anthony told me their schedules did not mesh. Looking back, I can see there was more to it than that.

A few weeks before the wedding, Sariel and Anthony came to visit. I sat on the couch and they pulled two chairs around to face me.

"I'm just not ready to convert," Anthony said.

I was speechless. This was one of those moments in my life when the wind shifted out of nowhere, and I saw myself steering my boat alone on a restless sea.

"Mom, you'll still do the wedding, right?" said Sariel into the thick silence.

"I have to think about it," I stalled. "I know you're telling me this out of your own truth, Anthony. But I'm disappointed. I thought you were committed to this path. Can you tell me what went wrong?"

He shook his head. "I'm just not ready."

When I was a rabbinical student, the policy of the Academy for Jewish Religion was to forbid interfaith weddings. But it was understood that after ordination, we had our own authority to decide whether such an act would be consonant with our principles. I continued to revisit this topic on a case-by-case basis, but one thing that had been ingrained during my studies was that Jews do not court converts. They must come of their own free will and demonstrate the seriousness of their intentions to take on the burdens and the joys of being a Jew.

Converting men and women to Judaism is one of the most meaningful and rewarding parts of my rabbinic practice. I get to elucidate my Jewish heritage and pass it down to others who would not have received it in any other form. The entire process of studying intimately with another person and redefining faith and religion is meaningful for both of us. I had wanted to become a rabbi to talk about things that mattered: my work with converts mattered; our continued relationship mattered.

Would Anthony ever find his way to Judaism? How could I perform their wedding, not knowing the answer to that question?

My mother, whose health had been failing ever since my father died, urged me to embrace Anthony. "You'll see," she said. "He'll add something special to your family."

I knew Sariel and Anthony would have a Jewish home—and a spiritual one—and it was true that Anthony had a colorful background and unique perspective. But I couldn't help noticing that my mother said *your* family, not *our* family; she knew my sister, Khana, would never accept Anthony, so some sort of breach was inevitable. Still, my mother felt a strong connection to him. Perhaps she was telling me in her own way that the heart is what matters most.

My father had met Anthony several times before his death and had seen the writing on the wall. "Conversion is never easy, Tamara," he had said, "but it's going be okay as long as Anthony converts before they stand under the *chuppah.*" If he were still alive, what would he tell me to do?

I couldn't help feeling that I had failed Anthony and the memory of my father. But maybe it was only *I* who needed Anthony to be Jewish. Maybe it wasn't what *he* needed.

What did my daughter need?

"Of course I'd like it if he became a Jew, but it doesn't change anything for me, Mom," Sariel said.

"I'm just having trouble wrapping my mind around this. I feel like there was an understanding between us that he would convert before the wedding."

"But you marry other interfaith couples! Why can't you marry us? Anthony will find his way in his own time. You know how painstaking he is. I can't force him to convert."

"No. And I wouldn't want you to," I said, ashamed of the fact that this was not entirely true. Why was my daughter unable or unwilling to convey to her beloved the importance of this choice? I couldn't understand why this was negotiable.

With the wedding only weeks away, I had to decide. If I said, no, would my family understand? Could I give them an ultimatum, and would that even be fair? And if I did officiate, would it set an untenable precedent for my rabbinate? I knew in my heart of hearts that if my father were still alive, I would have accepted whatever advice he gave me.

I went back to Rabbi White.

"What am I going to do? I can't seem to make a decision. The voices of my Orthodox past are interjecting with the realities of the present."

"I can see how confusing this must be for you, given your background. I know you don't make these decisions lightly, and even more so when your own children are involved. But you have a true opportunity here, Tamara. You can be their connection to Judaism. Keep them close, celebrate their love for one another, so your family stays in one piece, so you can know their children, so they can turn to you without reservations."

In the midst of this storm of indecision, a 28-year-old named Isaac was referred to me for counseling. It was clear that he was in deep spiritual pain. With some prodding, I learned that Isaac had grown up under the shadow of his father's alcoholism, with a mother too timid to protect him from the consequences.

"It must have been a miserable way to grow up," I said, surprising myself with this emotional language. It was a hard story for me to hear just then.

He shrugged. "It was all I knew. It started before I was even born."

"And yet … there is still a lot of bitterness in you."

"Well … something happened around my bar mitzvah. I got obsessed with the idea that he had to be sober for that one day. For my sake. Was that so much to ask?"

"Of course not. Though I'm sure you know now that alcoholics struggle with their self-control, and that it's worse at times of family stress. But you couldn't know that when you were thirteen."

"Exactly. It was all I could think about, that my dad would prove how much he loved me by showing up sober for my big day. I was so worked up that I even confided to my rabbi during one of my lessons. It wasn't something we ever said out loud, but I just blurted it out. And the Rabbi told me to pray hard, every day, and if I was sincere in my prayers, God would make it happen."

"Oh, dear."

I winced at my own inappropriate response, though Isaac didn't seem to notice. He was somewhere else in his mind. He had taken a tissue from the ubiquitous box on my coffee table and was twisting it into shreds that fell on the carpet. I watched his agitated movements and thought that I wasn't in a very good place to be counseling this wounded boy.

"So, you can guess the rest, right? I prayed and prayed, but still my father turned up drunk," he said, sounding as raw as if it had happened yesterday. "He embarrassed me in front of all my friends. I was mortified and ... well ... devastated, if you want to know. I mean, I was used to my dad letting me down, but God? What was the point of that whole charade? My bar mitzvah ... the rabbi ... it was all useless. I haven't done a single Jewish thing since then."

"I can understand how that would have seemed like the easiest choice at the time. And it must have been very hard for you to come see me today. So what can I do to help?"

Isaac took a deep breath. "I haven't seen my dad much in the last 10 years. I got away as soon as I could. But then last week he called and asked me to come down and see him. It turns out he's sick. Cirrhosis of the liver. He doesn't have long. So ... what should I do? I still haven't forgiven him."

What could I say to Isaac? How could I help him find the comfort he was seeking? I made an inadequate response and told him I wanted time to think about his situation so I could give him the best possible counsel. I asked him to come back later in the week. He looked surprised but he agreed.

I was deeply disturbed by this encounter. It caused me a disproportionate amount of anxiety—even more than my conflict over Sariel and Anthony's wedding. I couldn't see that my anxiety *was* about their wedding—and my father's legacy. I felt I was not qualified to give advice or to make these life-altering decisions.

I wanted to call my father, my rabbi, and ask him to look inside the book of himself and tell me what to do. In desperation I scanned my library shelves, looking for words of wisdom to help Isaac, to help myself. But nothing seemed right.

I cried out to the spirit of my late father.

What do I do, Daddy? How will I help this boy find peace in his soul?

You don't need me, came my father's warm, gentle voice in my head. *You are the book that will touch his soul.*

Was that true? I wanted to be the book my father saw in me. After all, he had bequeathed me his rabbinical soul. Still, I could not imagine filling his shoes. What wisdom did he think I had acquired? Would his faith in me be enough to guide me? As I debated about my role in my daughter's wedding, Isaac returned again and again. He told me his truth in every way he could. I listened and watched. We conversed about the details of his childhood, and I acknowledged his grief. Still he returned. I began to doubt my father.

What could I say to right this wrong?

In the end, I simply said, "Isaac, there is no denying that you were hurt. But do you want to carry that pain around for the rest of your life? What would happen if you let it go?"

"I don't know. How can I?"

The look on Isaac's face told me he had never considered that possibility before. What would his life be like if he no longer had to nurse this wound? He had come to me hoping for a witness, but I was offering him permission to begin a new chapter of his story that had nothing to do with this old pain.

"You just let it go. No one else has that power. Only you."

In his tears of relief, I saw anger give way to hope. In coming to me, he had taken the first steps back to his heritage; and in the weeks to come, he took the first tentative steps toward his father.

Isaac's reaction to my simple words had a startling effect on me as well: in empowering him, I suddenly felt I could trust myself to make a choice about my own dilemma. I did not know what would become of Anthony's spiritual journey, and in some ways he was my toughest teacher. But I knew I could welcome him into my family and still remain true to the voice of my father within me. I could just *let it go*.

So Michael and I walked our third daughter down the aisle in the resplendent sanctuary I knew so well. I walked up the four steps to the bimah as the mother of the bride, but I stood under the *chuppah* as the rabbi officiant for my daughter and her husband-to-be. I faced the full house of friends and family and smiled at my mother, sitting bravely without my father in the front row.

I chanted the first blessing. "*Baruch Atah Adonai*, Holy One of Blessing, bless this *kallah* and this *chatan*, this bride and this groom."

The sound of shattered glass was heard again, and then the traditional *Siman Tov und Mazal Tov* as Sariel and Anthony ran down the aisle, holding hands and dodging soft candies we tossed to send them on their way to a sweet life together.

MY FATHER'S BOOKS

On the weekend of my father's *Yahrtzeit*, the one-year anniversary of his death, I stood next to my mother in their kitchen, and the two of us lit the candles together. My childhood memories melted into the wax.

My mother leaned on me as she waved her hands in front of the flame to usher in the light of the Divine. With her eyes closed, she continued the tradition of her foremothers, mumbling the customary Hebrew blessing, while her heart cried out with grief.

Afterward, she turned to me. "I can't go on without him. What for? Even my siblings are gone. Don't you think it's my turn?"

I was afraid, and I told her I would come again the next weekend.

She said, "No. I'll be fine."

"Mom, I want to come. Why don't you want me here?"

"I just don't want you to drive back and forth by yourself in this weather. I'm fine. Stay at home. I'll call you if I need you."

My mother died the following Sabbath in the early morning hours before dawn. I was not with her when she lit her candles for the last time, but I believe my father's spirit stayed to bless and temper her Sabbath sorrow. He resided in the tears that fell onto my mother's apron and sanctified the windowless space. I can picture my parents leaning on one another and waving their hands toward the light. Perhaps the glow of the flame was my father's soul longing to be at home again with her. Perhaps it was my mother's soul, longing to be at home in his. Maybe both.

Because our mother died before dawn on Shabbat morning, Khana chose not to notify me of her passing until after nightfall. During the day I had gone to the synagogue for a bat mitzvah. I had come home, taken a nap, read and prepared for the evening's party at a nearby restaurant. I was dressed up and looking for my car keys when the phone rang. It was Khana.

"Mom died this morning. The funeral is tomorrow at eleven o'clock."

I couldn't quite understand the message or its meaning, so I shouted into the phone.

"What do you mean, Mom died this morning? It's eight o'clock at night. Where is she? What happened? Why didn't you call earlier?"

"It was Shabbat. I couldn't call you," she said. "It's not like you could do anything … she was already gone."

How had I accepted my sister's dogma for all these years? Of what more would such dogma rob me? Could I accept these injustices, again?

I went into the bedroom and took off my fancy dress and my high-heel shoes; I called my family, and we arranged for our car trip to New Jersey the following morning. I got into bed and cried until the morning sun reached my heavy eyes.

It was time to bury my mother, on this cold February day, next to my father at our family's plot. My grief overcame my anger and eventually my anger became combined with my grief. I did not see my mother's body before she was buried. I imagine her saying, as ever, "Forgive your sister. She is the only sister you have."

We left at six in the morning to make the four-hour road trip to the Beth-El Cemetery in Paramus, New Jersey. I rode with Naama, Sariel, Zachary, and Anthony. I had no official role in the burial. I uttered not a word. I did not even say *Kaddish*.

Instead, my sister's ultra-orthodox rabbi mumbled the prescribed prayers with the men standing with him on one side and the women standing huddled together on the other. My parents had warned me: I was not to interfere. Again, I was silent for their sake. I told myself that it would be the last time I caved in.

Following the funeral, we all drove 20 minutes to my nephew's house in Passaic, New Jersey for the *seudat havra'ah,* the traditional condolence meal. After we ate and drank together in the basement of my nephew's home, the conversation turned to my father's books. I was facing Shmuel.

"I'm going to take them," I said mildly. I knew my father had left no written will.

"Those books belong to me," Shmuel said.

"What do you mean? How can that be? My father has had those books for decades."

"Well, they're mine. I got them as a wedding present. I knew your father was a big fan of the Rambam, so I told him that he could borrow them until I wanted them back."

"Oh, really?" I said, my temper rising. I had no idea if it was true, and it didn't matter any more. "Did you know we refurbished your books at a bindery in Washington Heights a few years ago? He used them so much that the bindings wore out, and he paid two hundred dollars to fix them. Where were you then?"

"What's the difference? I'm taking them."

I felt that someone had punched me in the stomach. I wanted to throw up, and my paper coffee cup began to shake in my hands. I put the cup on a nearby table so it would not spill all over me. I took a deep breath. I refused to cry. I wanted to slap him across the face, but he was inches taller than me. How dare he claim my father's holy books?

Etti, Shmuel's second daughter from his first marriage, saw my flushed face and plunged into rescue mode. She was all too aware of her father's temper.

"Tatteh," Etti said. "Why don't you let Tamar have Papa's books? They were with Papa for a very long time, and they are all that she has left. Why don't I call the Jewish bookstore in Queens when I get home? I will find out how much the set cost. She can buy them back from you, and you can have the same set, only it will be brand new."

Everyone was listening to Etti's hurried speech. Shmuel was silent. Perhaps he did not want to be caught in his own malicious tactics. He turned his back on me and walked away. This was how it had been these last eight years, with Shmuel living across the street from my parents' high-rise apartment building. There was a constant tug-of-war between what is right, and what is righteous. These are not always the same.

"What is the purpose of religion, if it doesn't lead to ethical behavior?" people will often ask me.

Legal observance doesn't make you ethical; it can only teach you about ethics. There are religious people who are unethical and non-religious people who say that being good and doing the right thing *is* their religion.

Shmuel defied all logic. He was an angry man who never knew where to put his anger. Everyone around him had at one time or another experienced his wrath.

We drove home in separate cars to start the week of *shiva*. My sister and I sat *shiva* separately in our own homes with our own individual friends and family. This time the grieving process was different. There was no parent to comfort and there was no parent comforting me.

I was an orphan.

"Now they are together," said the many visitors who came through my home during that week. They meant it to be comforting, but I had my doubts. There was no scientific evidence of an afterlife. However, I must admit that just entertaining the possibility that my parents were enveloped in each other's arms had its own emotional appeal. During times of loss and crisis, why not entertain the mysterious?

A month later, my cousin Shaindle came from Atlanta to help us empty my parents' apartment. She had not been able to make her aunt's funeral at such short notice. But here she was, at the wheel of my car; I was happy to have her company on the three-hour drive to Philadelphia.

"You know," I said, "there aren't many things that I want or need. Khana can keep the furniture or give it away. She already has my mother's Passover china. I just want my father's *sefarim:* the *Mishneh Torah* and a *Tanach* or two. I think I once bought him his own copy of Rashi's commentary on the Five Books of Moses."

"So, you worked things out with Shmuel?" she asked me.

"Oh, yes!"

Shaindle prodded me. "I thought you told me that he wanted to keep your father's books for himself. Said something about them being his to begin with."

"Yes, but remember, Etti came to my rescue?" I said. "I sent him a check for two hundred dollars. Case closed."

My cousin was skeptical. "Did he cash the check?"

I write very few checks and I hardly ever reconcile my register. So I had to say, "I don't really know."

"Aha," she said. Her tone made me uneasy.

It was late afternoon when we arrived at my parents' apartment. Half of the furniture had already been removed. Several of Khana's sons were carrying out bags of clothing and kitchenware in shopping carts they had borrowed from the nearby grocery store. I looked at the mess in front of me. My mother, who valued organization and cleanliness, would have been very upset at this chaotic sight. I didn't like it either. My grief caught me unprepared.

Khana sat on a kitchen chair in the middle of the living room. She looked tired and sad. When she saw Shaindle she got up and they hugged.

"Shaindle," she said. "I'm so glad you came. Thank you for bringing Tamar." All three of us cried.

Shmuel's voice boomed in my ears. "Boys. Don't just stand there. Fill up the bags and take them to the trash. Now! Yaakov, I need help with this lamp. Be careful with it. I want it for my desk."

He was relentless in giving directions to his sons, who would not, or could not, obey him. The louder he shouted, the less engaged they became. Yaakov and Mordechai, Aaron and Yossi moved around the apartment in a directionless frenzy. I imagined they had feelings of loss as well. They were very attached to my parents, to whom they showed affection in their own ways.

In all the chaos, I didn't notice that Shmuel had moved from one side of the room to the other, where the bookshelves stood away from the wall. With the skill of a robber, he had honed in on my father's *Mishneh Torah*, and before I knew it, he was gesturing to his sons and they had started dumping the books into the shopping carts. I heard a sharp ringing sound as the tomes hit the unprotected metal. *Thud. Clang. Thud. Clang.*

"Shmuel," I screamed. "What are you doing? Those books belong to me."

"What are you screaming about?" he said. "I told you before, those books were mine from the start. I'm just taking what belongs to me. Do you have a problem with that?"

He put his hand inside his jacket pocket and pulled out an envelope. My check! He held it up and tore it into tiny pieces, wearing a malicious grimace.

I had a flashback to the shredding of my own *get*, my Jewish divorce decree. There is something so demeaning about such scenes: they take away every ounce of agency we might have accumulated in our lives as women. In that case, Michael had not even been present. Two witnesses—men, of course—and the rabbi authorized the severing of our marriage. Michael was allowed to choose a proxy to deliver the decree to me, but I had to stand there and take it. Now I felt that powerlessness again in the face of my brother-in-law's bullying.

"Case closed. Let's go, boys."

I froze in place like Lot's wife. Fear held me hostage. Shaindle put her arm around me. Khana sat dumb. She did what she always did. She gave in to her bully of a husband.

Finally she said, "I'm sorry, Tamar. There's no reasoning with Shmuel."

Shmuel and his sons had left us, three women in mourning, to clean up their mess. But there was no whitewashing the injustice.

This would be my last memory of the last place my parents had lived, the place where my mother had lit her candles and my father had pored over the pages of his beloved books.

I sat on a folding chair, put my hands over my eyes, and wept convulsively. How had I let my brother-in-law trick me out of my birthright? His deception was Biblical.

If my parents could witness this scene, I thought, they might have whispered in my ear once again: "Let it go. You need to protect Khana from Shmuel. If you interfere, she will suffer the consequences of your actions."

I don't know what hurt more, losing my father—which was inevitable —or losing his books, the result of pure malice. But I let it all go. I left holding a ceramic coffee mug etched with my father's Hebrew name, and the oval Sabbath plate I had brought my mother from the Old City.

What is our responsibility in fighting injustice? When do we save ourselves? When do we set aside fear and fight? What did it mean that my parents wanted me to keep silent with Khana? Did they not see history repeating itself in our tiny world?

I had claimed my rabbinical inheritance from my father—I was beginning to believe that it had been inside of me all along, and I told myself I didn't need a holy text to show me the way forward.

But "being the book" is not just about having answers for others—it is about finding your own voice.

INSCRIBED UPON THE HEART

I stand alone under the *chuppah* holding a Torah. The heavy scroll nestles like a baby on my chest.

It is the eve of the holiday of Shavuot, the anniversary of the giving of the Torah on Mount Sinai and the day of my own birth. I am surrounded by my chanting community—people I have spent weeks with over the course of years, learning to invoke the sacred through this Jewish renewal practice. They have gathered to honor the mystical tradition of *Leil Tikkun*, the all-night Torah learning that is meant to be a reenactment of the preparations for a wedding; the holiday itself an homage to the glorious marriage between God and Israel. The Torah is the written *ketubah*, the marriage contract, signed and sealed every year on this day.

I stand alone under the *chuppah* and hear the 40 voices surrounding me with one incantation:

"Nattati et Torati b'kirbam, v'al libam echtavenah. I will give my Torah into their inmost being and inscribe it upon their hearts." (Jeremiah 31:33).

I want to be worthy of this sacred task, to give myself over to the guidance of Rabbi Shefa Gold, the "priestess" of our group, who has taught us how to chant, and tonight has enjoined us to renew our covenant with God.

Rabbi Gold tells us: "Each one of you will choose four people to hold the poles of the *chuppah* for you. They will bear witness to your promise for the future."

The chanting is seamless as we inscribe each person's promise into our hearts before handing off the Torah to the next person. Midnight comes and goes, we climb higher into our collective state of faith in one another.

But my heart is greedy: I am holding back, keeping my strongest intentions for myself. Right now there is something else I want even more than communing with my God: I want to find my Beloved. Tonight, I want to summon him to me. When my turn comes, I do not hesitate, but pick a phrase from Song of Songs to be my chant:

Sham etayn et dodai lach. There, I will give you my love.

Shefa has taught us: "Build your intention to love the One, and love will emerge everywhere in your life."

I want this to be real. *If love will emerge everywhere, then let it emerge for me now.* I hug the Torah more tightly to my heart and say the words aloud: "My promise and hope is to open my heart so I can find my *basherte,* my soulmate."

I hear myself saying the words, hear my community chanting the Song of Songs for me, and ecstasy surges from my head to my fingertips. I know with certainty that everyone here wants my happiness. This is not too much to ask. The desire for my beloved is also part of the Divine.

And I would receive all I asked—but not in the way I had imagined.

My work as a chaplain and a freelance rabbi meant that I was continually called upon to participate in the lifecycle events of people I did not know. This was never simple, though joy was always far easier than grief. I had given end-of-life advice to many dozens—if not hundreds—of people by then, but I never grew immune to the gravitas of confronting death in such an intimate way.

I had learned over time that there was a crucial difference between a psychiatrist (like my former husband) and a chaplain: where the doctor is meant to maintain an emotional distance from the patient, the chaplain is charged with entering into each person's pain and dwelling there. Only then can we hope to walk them through their suffering and bring them to a place of peace. In the period around the deaths of my parents, this challenge took on a whole new level of intensity.

Sorrow was written on me with fresh ink. Even so, I could not close the door to my community: birth and death never rest.

This is how it came to happen that I received an email from a High Holiday congregant named Bruce while I was sitting *shiva* for my mother:

I know you are in the midst of your own grief, but when you're ready, my wife and I would like to talk to your about her end-of-life arrangements. She has liver cancer. We were at your Yom Kippur services for the past few years, and she liked the way you spoke and led services.

I had sent out an email to the Capital Kehillah to let my community know that I was once again an *avelah*—a mourner. I had no idea who Bruce was, but I was immediately impressed by his empathy in the midst of his own impending grief. So when I completed my seven-day confinement, I contacted him immediately.

A few days later, he picked me up from work at GW hospital and drove me 20 minutes to his home in Alexandria, Virginia. I didn't know what to expect when I arrived at the apartment, and I braced myself as I always did when I was about to meet someone at the end of life. The memory of Fanette was a phantom that accompanied to every such visit: would my first glimpse of this person be my last? I was relieved when I walked into the bedroom and saw Elizabeth poised in her bed, propped up by several pillows. In her mid-60s, she was radiant and beautiful, with blonde hair and a serene brow. Only her sallow complexion betrayed her illness. She smiled graciously and held out her hand, which I gently cupped in mine.

"Rabbi Miller, it's good of you to take time out of your busy schedule to come and visit with me. Please have a seat. Bruce, could you get Rabbi Miller a drink?"

"A cup of tea would be perfect," I said, thinking of Fanette and her rugelach. I could see she wanted to talk to me alone, and I needed to compose myself.

"As I'm sure Bruce told you, I'm dying of liver cancer. It started in my breast twelve years ago and traveled from there. So I have known for a long time that I would not get to grow old. But I have tried to have a full life."

She stopped briefly to inhale. "I wanted to live as long as possible for our son, Matthew, who was born to us late and is still in college."

We were contemporaries, Elizabeth and I, and we shared this, too, the joy and worry of a late-in-life son. I was on the verge of tears.

"And for Bruce," she went on. "Twenty-one years. Did you know Bruce and I had both been married before? We found each other late. It was a miracle that Matthew was even possible. I'm so blessed to have both of them! I don't know how people do it without a loving and supportive family."

We talked about her final wishes for her memorial.

"Judaism is very important to Bruce, and we've shared many of the traditions. My only regret is that I never converted. But I want you to do my funeral and give Bruce what he needs Jewishly."

"Of course. I will be there for your family." I choked on my words.

Then she said something to me that I would revisit a hundred times in the years to come:

"Please. Take care of Bruce for me. I worry about him even more than our son. Matthew has many friends at school. But Bruce will be alone. He will need someone to lean on."

I saw Elizabeth several more times until her death eight weeks later. Every time, Bruce would pick me up from GW hospital and bring me back, so we had a lot of time to talk.

He recounted what it had been like for him to live with someone whose days had been numbered for over half of their time together. They had tried to be mindful of every moment. Elizabeth had been in a support group for people with cancer, and that was both a blessing and a curse, he said, because she had watched the group shrink over time and had felt the palpable presence of time.

"We looked like a normal couple," he said, "but there was this undertone of grief that never went away. We were always wondering how long we had."

"And you?" I asked. "What do you do for support?"

"I don't know … I have my two sisters. They live far away, but we talk a lot. And I have a couple of good friends here. John and Terry. But of course it's impossible for them to really understand. It's been lonely. And I feel like I can never do enough."

"You're a wonderful husband."

At the funeral, I sat hugging my hard-covered Rabbi's manual and listened to Bruce eulogizing Elizabeth while tears flowed down my face; I patted my mascara with a cotton handkerchief from my jacket pocket.

"We searched for years to find the perfect diamond to express my love for her," Bruce said, standing with his arm around his son. "I wanted so much to make her happy and for her to have this token of my love. But she always hesitated. 'It's not quite right,' she would say. Now, as I think about it, I realize that *she* was the diamond. How could any physical treasure match her?"

I had presided over many funerals at the Sixth & I Historic Synagogue but never before was I so weepy. Was it the recent loss of my mother just two months prior, or was it witnessing this man's sorrow over losing his beloved?

"Elizabeth and I had a good life together, but, as it happened, not a very long one. We will miss her." Bruce faltered and ran out of words. He held his son and a sacred silence swept through the sanctuary.

"I want one just like him," I heard my mind whispering. "Such devotion. Such love. Such sweet sorrow."

What does it mean to fall in love with a congregant at his wife's funeral? In hindsight, I suppose I should have seen that such a beginning would lead to further complications.

But at the time I was grieving, and all I could feel was the birth of hope.

I couldn't get Bruce out of my mind. In the weeks after the funeral I started to call him several times, but I always hung up. I knew I was not being rational.

Finally, I got hold of myself. After all, this was a purely professional call, right?

We decided to meet for Sunday brunch near my place. We hugged. We ate. We talked about Elizabeth over tomato-and-mozzarella flatbread, red wine, and a platter piled high with *babaganoush* and pita cut into triangles.

"You really helped me during the most difficult time in my life. Knowing that Elizabeth got such comfort from you eased me as well. I am forever grateful."

That was so like him, to thank me. To think of someone other than himself.

"It was a privilege. Elizabeth was very special. We had an instant connection."

"Yes, she liked you very much. And the memorial service was just the way she would have wanted it."

His loneliness enveloped him like a cloud. Matthew had returned to school and Bruce's dog, Romeo, accompanied him on long walks down by the river near his home. His two sisters called regularly. His friends rotated visits, but it wasn't enough.

"I hear her voice in the morning advising me on what to wear. At night, I look at her pillow and I can't understand where she is now. It's only at work that her presence recedes into the background, but otherwise it hurts so much that sometimes I want to go under the covers and just sleep forever."

"I'm sorry. I know, this is the hardest time. But it will get better."

"Will I ever laugh again?"

"Yes, you will. I promise."

I wanted to say more, to assure him that he would enjoy life again, but I was afraid my secret wish would show through: I wanted to be his new love. And I knew too much about the stages of grief to interrupt his process. If I pushed him too early, he would be dismissive, if not angry. Bruce still needed to cry in his own bed and go through the ugly reality of his new existence. How could I protect him from the inevitable waves of pain? On the other hand, he had been preparing for this loss for a very long time, and I felt certain that he would adjust. He was a very grounded person.

Another month passed. We went out to dinner. He chose a nice fish restaurant in Dupont Circle; his demeanor was already a little less depressed. He talked about work and about Matthew's new girlfriend. Work was his antidote. He loved his job as CEO of a trade association in Washington, D.C., and because he had been there for over 10 years, he was given a great deal of slack, which, of course, he refused to take advantage of. I was struck by his integrity.

He continued with his hectic work schedule and called me often. We saw each other again after three weeks, then after two. Then he was off to another state or country for business-related travel. I missed his voice when he was gone.

Everyone loved Bruce, including the waitresses.

"I remember when I was a young waiter at a country club in Detroit. Hard work. Tips were all I got. Somehow it was enough to pay for my college books."

He was a big tipper. Courteous and complimentary.

And so it went. Inch by inch. Date by date. We held each other for a long time before parting, and even progressed to kissing goodnight, but beyond that—we both knew to take it slow. He trusted me. He confided in me. And he still talked about Elizabeth. He talked about how they had met and their quarrels, and the cancer that was always present, even during years of remissions. Sometimes, when his grief flooded him, he withdrew for a week at a time. He was never rude or dismissive. He just asked me to wait until he was ready to connect again. I never grew tired of waiting. And he always returned.

We marked Elizabeth's *yahrtzeit* by inviting some friends over to his house. I facilitated a mini-*shiva* in remembrance of her life. Bruce passed around photos and offered up stories.

"How do you think Bruce is doing?" I asked his best friend, John.

"He has his ups and downs. Sometimes he lets me come over and he sits on the couch and we cry together. I call him every day. I'm worried about him, but I don't tell him. I try to put a positive spin on everything. He's my best friend."

I nodded and smiled, but I realized that Bruce had not shared with his best friend the fact that we had been seeing each other. What should I make of that?

The act of loving him felt good. Like a summer rain, his attention provided a welcome relief from my longing. I felt more at home with him than I had felt with anyone else since the early years of my marriage. I went through my day wondering what he was doing. Should I call him at work? I wondered if it would disturb him or he would appreciate the distraction, and whether I should identify myself as "Rabbi Miller"—always easier to get his secretary to put me through to him—or as "Tamara," which was more truthful when it came to how I felt. How I hoped *he* felt. I wandered through Macy's searching for a perfect gift to give him. Was I right in thinking he was slowly coming to return my feelings? Could it be that this man, wounded and grieving, was really my beloved?

This is how he looked: Not very tall, maybe five-foot-four, which suited my five-foot frame perfectly. Slim and athletic. His gold-rimmed glasses accentuated his salt-and-pepper hair, still full enough to hold a *kippah* without a clip. His dimples gave him a never-ending smile. I thought he was all-out cute.

Compulsively I went over my wish list, an actual piece of paper I kept in a box in my closet. He was generous. Check. He had a Jewish education. Check. He had a spiritual side. Check. We could dance cheek-to-cheek. Check. He had a sense of humor. Check. He was trustworthy and dependable. Check. He made me laugh. Check. He had a deep soul. Check. Check. Check.

Looking back, I must have known that I had to take the chance with him then—maybe it was all the recent loss, or the passing of my 60th birthday—but I could not have imagined what would come next. I only knew I had to seize the day. I held onto him and he held me back. Time passed.

HATE ON HOLY GROUND

The shooting of Stephen Johns at the Holocaust Museum happened on June 10, 2009.

I had been seeing Bruce for a year. The days that followed the shooting left me beset by tears and nightmares about the Holocaust. I woke screaming in the middle of the night. It was a relief to have someone to lean on, to not have to be alone after witnessing such pain and hate.

I would call Bruce at night and whisper hoarsely into the phone. "I can't stop thinking about it. What's wrong with people? It's getting all mixed up in my head with the past."

"Tell me," he would say, and I would talk about Paul Bermanzohn and the Greensboro Massacre, those heart-wrenching conversations with Paul's Holocaust-survivor parents, and inevitably, I would come around to those dark blue numbers tattooed on the arms of our neighbors, the specter of death that had always taken up a place at our Bronx kitchen table.

One night, about a week after the incident, once again facing a night on which I was too agitated to sleep, I gave up trying. I sat down at my computer. I wrote all that I had been thinking.

In the morning, I sent the piece to Rabbi Herzfeld, who suggested I send it to the editor of the "On Faith" blog at the *Washington Post*. With a click, the company published my essay. (I did not write the headline.) It was June 25, 2009.

Holocaust Comes to the ER

By Rabbi Tamara Miller, Director of Spiritual Care, George Washington University Hospital

There are no good protocols for the unexpected and the unfamiliar. Early Wednesday afternoon on June 10, my on-call chaplain stood inside my office doorway. The trauma pager beeped. The phone rang. Something big was going on in the emergency room. Something terrible had happened at the U.S. Holocaust Memorial Museum …

The word "Holocaust" reminds me that I am a Jew in hiding from another anti-Semitic act, another planned suicide bombing, another round of hate rhetoric. So when they said there had been a shooting at the Holocaust Museum, my genetic history caused an internal earthquake. I felt violated and incensed that on this holy ground of remembrance and sanctity, someone dared to defame and disregard the very truth of that living museum and memorial.

But I had no time to analyze or condemn the attack. In a moment, I was in the emergency room holding hands in prayer with the wife of Stephen Johns … Three chaplains kept vigil with the Johns family and friends.

Inside the operating room, doctors of every faith and cultural background gathered their medical skills to save their wounded patient whose big heart had stopped beating. Outside the operating room, there was waiting and wailing, praying and punctuated sobbing. When the news of Stephen's death was pronounced, we all went into our own magical thinking and reimagined a different outcome. Then reality reared its fearful face.

On Rosh Hashanah it is written and on Yom Kippur it is sealed. Who shall live and who shall die? Who in the fullness of years and who before? It had already been written. It had already been sealed.

Stephen Tyrone Johns died in the Divine arms of the medical personnel, his young life truncated by a shotgun powered by evil. The mourning has just begun.

Unrelieved by my truth telling, I continued to feel the effects of the tragedy: my back went into spasm and my walking became compromised. I limped robotically through my days. When my back pain increased, I went to see an orthopedist, who prescribed a week's disability for rest and relaxation: "You are coming out of a traumatic experience, and you need peace and quiet. You are carrying your stress in your lower back."

While on disability leave, I attended the funeral for Stephen Tyrone Johns with a fellow chaplain, at Ebenezer AME Church in Fort Washington, Maryland. We bore witness together with 2,000 other attendees. I looked around the huge sanctuary and recognized Holocaust survivors, one other rabbi, and ministers from every faith background, along with the Johns family and the extended hospital community.

"Stephen Tyrone Johns was the six-million-and-first person to die in the name of prejudice and racial discrimination. We have much work to do to combat this sinister thinking in the world … In memory of all those who have died at the hands of murderers, we add Stephen's name. We are one in purpose," shouted Pastor McCoy into the hallowed silence.

His words shook me to the core; they sounded like the portent of further sorrow.

Rabbi Herzfeld and I had exchanged a glance across the sanctuary.

By the end of that week, still in shock and pain, I was suspended from work. I never got my job back. Fifty-one days after that fateful shooting at the Holocaust Museum, a security guard escorted me out of the hospital, my workplace of 10 years. I was banned from returning.

It was a Friday afternoon. I walked around my apartment in a daze. Then I picked up the phone and called Bruce.

"Did they say why they fired you?"

"No, not in so many words. They just gave me a letter and a check."

"Did you open the letter?"

"No."

"Well, open it now. Read it to me."

Rabbi Miller has been fired for misconduct. Her termination is immediate. July 27, 2009.

"Tamara. You need a lawyer. Don't do anything yet—let me see who I can find. I think you have a case of unjust termination on your hands."

"Can you come?" I pleaded. When he came in the door, I collapsed and cried with gratitude. It was my turn for consolation.

I never received an official explanation for my dismissal. I was told by a fellow co-worker that by publishing the name of a patient in that blog piece, I had violated a healthcare regulation intended to protect confidentiality. It was true that my article was personal, but the media had disclosed specifics of the event minutes after the shooting occurred. There was no way the hospital could argue that I had been first to reveal the victim's name.

My attorney suggested I was let go because of my outreach efforts to the African-American community. I had been helping recruit more black chaplains in an effort to offer more diverse spiritual care to the hospital's patients, who were of many races and religions. He said my recent campaign for equal pay as a female chaplain may not have helped my situation.

I had a choice. I could walk away quietly and disappear from public view, or I could stand firm and speak out.

Within a few days, I received letters, phone calls, and emails—offers of support from friends and strangers alike. They were incensed by the hospital's stance.

Someone offered to start an online petition. An attorney called and offered his expertise on a *pro bono* basis. My fellow staff chaplains subsequently resigned. Uncomfortable with confrontation, and still in a state of sadness, I contemplated total withdrawal. But I could not do it. The truth needed to be told, even if it was at a financial and emotional cost to me.

We went public on the major networks; Pastor McCoy and I gave an interview on the *Kojo Nnamdi Show*, syndicated on National Public Radio; the story appeared on the front page of *The Washington Post*. With the help of some dedicated people, we staged a lunchtime protest in front of the hospital building that drew a crowd of college students, professors, doctors, and passersby. What moved me most was the presence of my fellow co-workers, many of them black, who came down from the hospital floors to add their voices to our chants of solidarity: "No more injustices!"

Several of my black former co-workers conveyed a message to me personally over these days: "We're sorry this happened to you, Rabbi, but it happens to us all the time. Nothing you can do about it."

That meant a lot to me—yet it spoke to me about the pervasiveness of injustice, as well.

In spite of—or perhaps because of—my now-public situation, Rabbi Herzfeld had called to ask me to facilitate a meeting with Pastor John McCoy and Officer Johns's widow, Zakiah. "I want to personally offer my sympathies to the family," the rabbi said. "I have condolence cards from my congregation. And we have collected money for his widow."

Rabbi Herzfeld had long been recognized in the D.C. Jewish community for his public stance against injustice, and I was honored he had asked me to stand with him now. Still, my anxiety was as high as the humidity on that summer day the rabbi and I arrived outside the Word of God Baptist Church in Southeast Washington, D.C.. I was eager to go inside.

"Just a minute," the rabbi said. "We have to wait for someone."

"Who else is coming?" I asked.

"Rabbi Avi Weiss is flying in from New York. He is in a cab right now and should be here momentarily."

"Rabbi Weiss?" I repeated, taken aback. Rabbi Avi Weiss is very well known within the rabbinic world as the Modern Orthodox head of the Hebrew Institute of Riverdale in New York. Under his leadership, the first Orthodox female rabbi, Sara Hurwitz, was ordained, and the Yeshivat Maharat was established for the purpose of bringing other women into the Orthodox Jewish clergy. He is a maverick and an outspoken activist against injustice wherever it appears. If the timing had been different, I have sometimes thought, I might have been one of his students.

How did I get here? I wondered, as I watched Rabbi Weiss approach. But still, I felt I was exactly where I belonged. And Rabbi Herzfeld would soon confirm this in a most unexpected way.

Rabbi Herzfeld quickly introduced us, and, we walked briskly into the Christian house of worship.

We were welcomed by the Minister of Comfort, a statuesque woman who guided us into a generous space for our *shiva*-like gathering. *Good idea, I* thought to myself; *all congregations could use a Minister of Comfort.* Several people sat around a bare wooden table: Stephen Johns's widow Zakiah; her grieving father; a friend of the family; and the church's Minister of Education.

Pastor McCoy was standing by and embraced me as I came in. Together, we had witnessed the sudden loss of a young life and the outcry of a beloved. Several weeks had passed since that day at GW hospital.

Rabbi Herzfeld spoke to Zakiah first.

"I extend my deepest condolences on the death of your husband. Please accept these belated but heartfelt offerings from my community sympathy cards made by children and adults alike, and some money we collected to help with expenses."

Zakiah wept as she accepted the gifts, and her father put his arm around her.

Rabbi Weiss spoke next.

"Mrs. Johns, I was in my study when I heard about the shooting, and I immediately called Rabbi Herzfeld, who used to work with me in New York. He told me the terrible story about the loss of your husband's life during the hate crime that was committed. I also bring you a monetary offering from my community.

"But the real reason I came," he continued fervently, "is to say: we stand with you in solidarity. Your husband, who made it his daily work to guard this critical part of our history, went on to save many lives when he gave up his own. We have so much in common. We need to fight these injustices together."

Zakiah nodded and thanked him, but I could see she was still stunned with grief. Pastor McCoy said, "Stephen is not the first black man to be buried under these circumstances, and he won't be the last. Your presence here, rabbi—" his glance took in all three of us— "brings some solace to our community, struggling under a weight with which you are all too familiar."

Rabbi Weiss agreed, and then changed the mood by making another offering. "A great scholar once said: *There are gates in Heaven that cannot be opened except by melody and song.*" He began to sing a song by the late Shlomo Carlebach, known as "The Singing Rabbi." It was familiar to me. He began softly and wordlessly, then sang the melody as he translated the words, so all could join him in the chorus:

> *"For the sake of my sisters and friends, for the sake of my brothers and friends, please let me pray, please let me say ... peace to you. This is the House, the House of the Lord, I seek only good for you."*

Even Zakiah joined in and seemed to find some comfort in the lilting melody. Our voices blended together as we thought of the 39-year-old man whose voice would not be heard again. Before we got up from the table, Rabbi Herzfeld surprised me by asking Reverend McCoy to help me.

"A week ago, Rabbi Miller was fired from the Spiritual Care Department because, they say, she violated patient confidentiality by writing about the shooting and attending Stephen's funeral. We may need your testimony to overturn their decision."

Pastor McCoy's calm changed to dismay and disbelief. He looked at me with affection, and assured me he would write a letter to the hospital praising my work with the Johns family. I saw myself through his eyes: another injustice.

His testimonial did not change the outcome for me, but our connection lasted far beyond that day. We reconvened a few months later when Rabbi Herzfeld invited the Pastor and his congregation to dinner at the synagogue, where a gospel choir, Glory to God, was coming to sing from New York. On that night, then–Secretary of Defense William Cohen and his wife, Janet Langhart Cohen, spoke from the pulpit. They told the story of Janet's play *Anne & Emmett,* a play that imagines an encounter between Anne Frank and Emmett Till, both teenagers from very different times and places, both robbed of their lives because of bigotry and hate. The play was to have premiered at the Holocaust Museum on the same day the shooting occurred.

The Glory to God gospel choir sang a Hebrew song they had learned from Neshama Carlebach, daughter of Shlomo. At one point, we all joined the choir on the dais, raising our voices together.

I thought: *A bond is growing between our African-American and Jewish communities that no act of hate can break apart.*

Two months after I was fired from the hospital, I started writing my weekly blog, *Spiritualetters,* to gather a virtual community around me. wanted to be a builder, not a breaker.

My initial blog posts were audible questions to myself.

How do we acquire faith?

Is it a learned behavior from a parent or grandparent? Is it a discovery found in books and lectures? Or do we meet faith at the crossroads of a difficult dilemma? Do we abandon faith when we ourselves feel abandoned? "I believe" is more than a statement of faith. It is my daily mantra that plays on several wavelengths in my mind and on my heart. I practice believing. I acquire faith.

Can everyone dance?

It is easy to dance and sing, smile and laugh, when we are content.

What takes practice, is dancing and singing, smiling and laughing when we are despondent. Rabbi Nachman of Bratzlov encourages the dance practice as a form of therapeutic resistance to sadness and suffering. Yes, everyone can dance, if only in thought.

Writing became my new spiritual practice. I would sit in front of my computer and stare into my heart. Sometimes the idea came quickly with a few taps on the computer, and the story would write itself. But sometimes the writing continued deep into the night.

When I finally sent the letters them to my subscribers, vibrations of love reverberated throughout my small universe, and I was reconnected to friends and family and all the people I worked with and ministered to during those rewarding years at GW hospital.

During this time, Bruce was a constant source of support for me; ever since the Museum shooting, something had shifted in the dynamic between us. I can't recall when the tipping point came, but one day Bruce came to my apartment and something was different. He was noticeably nervous. He wandered around the living room looking at every piece of art and touching every book on my shelf.

"Bruce. Relax. Would you like a glass of wine?"

"Oh. Yes, that'd be great," he breathed.

It had been a year- and-a-half since we met; 15 months since Elizabeth's death. I knew that it had been several years since Bruce had been intimate with anyone. I can't say Elizabeth was actually in the room with us, but I could hear the echo of her voice: "Please. Take care of Bruce for me." I had no way of knowing if this was what she had meant, and yet I was certain she would have approved. Whatever ambivalence I felt, I knew I was the right person to be in his life. Now it was time for me to stop being his rabbi once and for all, for us to be a woman and a man together.

For more than a year after that, I gave my time and energy to two opposing forces in my life: growing my relationship with Bruce, and fighting against injustice. Bruce was still sometimes very emotional when we were together, and sometimes even cried, but then, so did I. We both had our challenges, and we were overcoming them with an increasing sense of partnership.

The fight for justice was a different story. Among other battles, my personal one showed no progress. As Rosh Hashanah of 2010 approached, an unproductive, two-hour mediation in the courthouse brought reality into sharp focus: I was never going to win. There would be no severance pay for me. I would not be returning to the patients who had trusted me with their pain and suffering. I was David and the hospital was Goliath, but I had no hidden slingshot that would change the course of my suit against the bureaucratic machine.

I called my attorney. "It's time for me to move on. Do whatever you can to settle. In the new year, I need to spend my energy on goodness, not on hate."

I had lost the illusion that racial integration has a firm foothold in this country. After my political work following the Greensboro Massacre, I had lost trust in a system that allowed members of the Ku Klux Klan to go free after murdering five young people in cold blood on the morning streets of Greensboro, North Carolina.

I had lost my naiveté about ethical behavior in the workplace. I had lost a meaningful occupation. I felt in some ways that I had lost my identity—the status I had in the community because of my job—not to mention financial security. I felt betrayed by people I had trusted. I learned that loyalty is not a two-way street.

But I also had many gains in the year since my termination.

I gained a friendship with an African-American pastor who offered me spiritual succor in a difficult time.

I gained a new self-identity, one of empowerment instead of victimization in the face of discrimination.

I gained a new perspective about my calling to do inter-religious work.

I gained an appreciation for the strength of my support network; I felt at times that I was being held up only by my nurturing friends, who encouraged me in my efforts to right a wrong.

I have no regrets about speaking out the way I did, or about letting it go when it became obvious that continuing to fight would hurt me more than them. I know that my true nature is not one of antagonism, but overrode my discomfort for just causes: to champion diversity, to talk about pay-based gender discrimination, to fight bigotry and hate. In the words of Martin Luther King, Jr.: "Our lives begin to end the day we become silent about things that matter."

LOVE LETTERS, LAST LETTERS

It was six o'clock in the evening when my landline phone lit up with Bruce's name.

"Bruce! I'm surprised to hear from you. You're supposed to be at a convention in Florida."

"I wasn't feeling well, so I came home early."

"A cold? Flu?"

"I don't know. I'm just ... lethargic. John says I look a little yellow. But not to worry, I have an appointment tomorrow with my internist. I promise I'll call you after."

"Maybe it's nothing," I said. "You really have been burning the candle at both ends. Maybe you just need to slow down."

"It's true, I've been stressed at work. We'll see. I'm going to lie down now. I'm really tired."

"Yes, rest as much as you can. Let's talk tomorrow."

A week later, I walked into the lobby of GW hospital and got a visitor badge from the security guard. It had been nearly two years since I had stepped inside these familiar corridors. I easily found the surgical waiting room where John, Bruce's friend, sat with his hands covering his face.

"John?" I said. "What's going on?"

"It's not good. I know it. We just buried Elizabeth. I can't lose Bruce now."

It had been almost three years since Elizabeth's death, but I supposed that fear had warped John's sense of time. I was inwardly terrified, too but tried to keep calm for his sake.

"Have you seen Bruce? What did his doctor say?"

"I haven't seen or spoken with anyone. I just know it's bad."

I sat down next to him but he never looked up. He was crying into his cupped hands. It was hard to see a man crying like that.

"John. It's just a biopsy. We may not know anything for a few days. Please. Let's try to be positive. Even if it *is* cancer," I allowed myself to say the awful word, "there are all kinds of treatments. New ones. Better ones. Here, take my hand."

John took my hand, and slowly, his sobs turned into deep sighs.

"Rabbi Miller, what are you doing here?" I heard a voice say.

I was startled. I was here as Bruce's girlfriend, but there was Dan, one of my favorite operating nurses from the old days, calling me back to my other role. I stood up to greet him, and he gave me a hug. "We've missed you."

"Thanks for saying that. I've missed being here, too. Actually, I'm here to see my friend who was scheduled for a biopsy. Can you check if he's back?" I gave him Bruce's full name.

"Oh! I'm his nurse. He just got back. He's a little groggy. But you can come and see him. I'll show you which bed he's in. And don't worry. I'll take extra good care of him."

Without speaking, John and I followed Dan. When we saw Bruce lying pale as the sheets on the hospital bed, with intravenous tubes injected into his arms, we stopped at the edge of the open curtains.

"Hey, you two," Bruce said. "I didn't feel a thing. But you look awful, John. Didn't you sleep last night?"

"Let me remove some of these tubes," said Dan, "so I can discharge him and bring him downstairs. Why don't you meet us in the hallway by the elevators?"

"I'll go bring the car around," John said.

"I'll stay here with Bruce," I said.

"I'm going to leave you now," said Dan. "Take care of yourself, Bruce. Rabbi, always good to see you."

Bruce chatted away about the hospital, the anesthesia, the nurses. He joked about the good care, and I knew he was teasing me.

"Let's get out of here," he said. "I don't like hospitals. Been in too many of them and so have you, right? John will take me home and put me to bed. Why don't you call me later? I don't think we'll hear anything until the end of the week."

He squeezed my hand.

"It'll be okay," I said more to myself then to him. "I think *you'll* have to take care of John. He's very fragile."

"I know. He's so sensitive. But that's why I love him so much."

We kissed each other gently.

I opened the door to John's car and Bruce got up from the wheelchair and plopped himself into the front seat. He immediately closed his eyes, resting his tousled grey hair on the headrest. I watched the car slowly edge toward 23rd Street.

It was not okay. It was stage four pancreatic cancer.

Bruce told me on the phone. I did not see him in the days right after the diagnosis; his days were a flurry of further medical tests and lawyer visits. He made last-ditch inquiries. He wrote a will.

I was working as a chaplain and spiritual counselor at the Center for Integrative Medicine. I don't know how, but I continued to go to work and minister to my patients, many of whom had cancer, too. When it got to be too much for me, I sought the advice and friendship of my colleagues there, who knew all too well what could be ahead, for Bruce and for me.

Bruce wanted more time. He decided to have a Whipple surgery, a high-risk, complex procedure—but if it worked, it could give him up to five more years. My supervisor, John Pan, the Center's founder and director, said, "If it were me, I wouldn't do it. It's a brutal surgery, intrusive and very painful. He'll suffer a lot, and there's very little chance it will work. He should let it go, die with his dignity intact."

I didn't know what to think. I wanted more time, too. But I couldn't bear the thought of him suffering.

When I finally saw him again, he picked me up from work and took me to the café behind the Kennedy Center for the Arts, one of the Washington, D.C., cultural hubs. We had an hour of intense conversation about everything. His son. The surgery. How he felt.

"I'm a realist," he said. "Chances are, I won't survive the surgery."

My first instinct was to deny what he was saying. I wanted to protect myself from the sadness of it. But I let the warm night swallow my words, and moved closer to him. I took his hand and remained silent, waiting.

I called Bruce several times that week, but it always went straight through to his voicemail. I wanted to visit him at the hospital, but he had asked me not to. He didn't want me to suffer, either. I didn't know what to do. To make matters worse, I had months ago planned a trip to Israel for a family bat mitzvah and an important rabbinic conference, before I had any idea what was in store for Bruce. Now the date was approaching fast.

He didn't seem to want me by his side, but how could I leave?

For weeks following surgery, he was in constant, debilitating pain. He was full of medications that made him sleep for hours on end. When called to check on his progress, one of his sisters would answer the phone.

"He's not himself, Rabbi. He's either sleeping or moaning. It's difficult to watch. All I can do is tell him you called, but don't expect a return call. He's just so weak."

"Sure, I understand. If you need anything, anything at all, please call."

Rabbi? Again, there was a divide—I was being regarded less as a woman, or as a partner, or even as a friend.

Days would go by without any news, but I kept calling. A week later, I was about to hang up when he picked up the phone on the fourth ring.

"Bruce? I've been so worried about you, but I haven't been able to get through at all. What's going on?"

"To tell you the truth, Tamara, I can't seem to catch my breath between the sharp pain and the meds. I'm basically in a sort of hell. The doctors want me back in the hospital."

"Oh, no. This is awful, just awful. I'm so sorry this is happening to you. Why won't you let me come and see you, be with you, comfort you?"

"I just don't want you to see me like this. A skeleton. There's nothing you or anyone else can do. I've got to get to the other side of this post surgery healing, get to the quality time the doctors promised me. I'm counting on it."

I felt shut out. I wanted to hold his hand, to whisper a prayer, to sit next to him while he slept and watch over him. I knew from all my chaplaincy work how hard it was to be in pain, to lose a once-active life. I wanted to enter into his pain and to relieve him of it.

But Bruce wanted to shield me from his world of physical indignities. Could I honor his request without guilt, hurt, judgment? Would that be the most empathetic thing I could do? To face Bruce in his suffering would inflict another level of devastation on both of us; it was hard enough to experience it from afar, through my imagination. I thought again about Fanette and all that she had taught me. Would Bruce bring me a different sort of wisdom?

My prayers kept me company: "God, please stop his suffering. *El na r'fah na lah.* Please, God, I beg you. Heal him." I believed in the power of my prayers to keep me from despair. I needed to pray even though the outcome would not change.

Several weeks went by, with a phone call here and there, until one day I received a meticulous hand-handwritten letter. I held the heavy linen-stock envelope in my hands for a long time before reading. A tremor of fear went through me.

I couldn't bring myself to keep that letter, but in my memory, it goes something like this:

> *Dear Tamara,*
>
> *How can I thank you? How can I leave you?*
>
> *But the more I suffer, the closer I am to Elizabeth. The cancer has brought her memory into the limelight of my diminishing life. The present is calling on my past, and giving me permission to move forward.*
>
> *Please forgive me for anything hurtful I have said or done to you. I now must concentrate on my health and my son. I hope you understand ...*
>
> *Love, Bruce*

I cried into the night and the next day. It was Shabbat so I had no place to go and no appointments to keep. I read and reread this strange "Dear Jane" letter. What would I have done if I were in his place? My grieving began that day. There was no denying his death would come. How would I survive losing him? I often wonder what would have happened if I had just shown up at his apartment. Would that have caused us both more distress? But I never found out.

After that letter, I understood that Bruce had never really let go of Elizabeth; no matter what he told himself or me, he had not viewed me as a life partner, nor had he asked his family to view me that way. In the end, he had relegated me to my spiritual role: receptacle for his secrets, comforter of his grieving soul.

I did not see Bruce again. In my mind, he just faded away. No funeral. No eulogies. Whether I felt noble or not, I decided to honor his request to leave him with his dignity intact. It was his way of saying goodbye. For myself, I took the gift Bruce offered me, of remembering him as he truly was: a generous, animated, light-hearted, selfless human being.

MY *SAVTA*, MY RABBI

There are many different kinds of prayer: some are words of petition, others are words of gratitude. Sometimes our prayers fail us, and we need the words to come from a different mouth.

I took my absence from Bruce's death as a personal failure. Why was it so hard to know when to let go, and when to fight? But when in despair, I called Reb Zalman.

Rabbi Zalman Schachter-Shalomi, known to all as Reb Zalman, was one of the founders of the Jewish Renewal Movement and acted as my spiritual advisor; he believed that Torah should be received as a continuous infusion that we as spiritual leaders dispersed throughout the world. He believed in the power of ritual to transform human experience. He would say: "Let's download some Torah together," or "I'm deploying you to bring Torah to the people."

Once again, he comforted me in his intensely personal way. "Your friend's suffering will not pass into the next life. He has quietly completed his holy tasks, and his life has been a blessing. Accept the wisdom he has bequeathed you, and use it to make your life a blessing, too."

What would that mean, *to make my life a blessing?* It has taken me most of my life to answer the question.

What happened with Bruce was not the first—and certainly not the last—time I would be tormented over what role I was playing: the rabbi or the friend? The mother? The grandmother?

But it was certainly the most difficult time I would face this conflict. My life is a blessing precisely because I continue to integrate all these roles to allow the ebb and flow of the mother and the rabbi and the beloved and the grandmother. It's true that this process is often laced with sorrow, but sometimes it is pure joy.

The birth of my first grandson, Adin Isaac, made me a *savta*, a grandmother. Thirteen years later, as Adin's bar mitzvah approached, I knew I would officiate.

I wracked my brains to find a format unconventional enough to suit the occasion, and I finally recalled how, years before my ordination, I had seen Rabbi Steven Sager, the congregational rabbi of Beth Shalom in Durham North Carolina who had become my beloved mentor, do something completely unexpected: he engaged bar mitzvah students in a public dialogue on the bimah. This seemed a perfect approach for my effusive teenage grandson.

Adin gladly accepted this out-of-the-box proposition, and we began posing the questions and writing down the answers together. The morning of the bar mitzvah, I remembered that first Rosh Hashanah when I looked into the crowd of 900 people and wondered how I got here. I imagined my grandson might feel the same way now.

Later that same year, my granddaughter, Noa Rebecca, celebrated her bat mitzvah with a tribute to curiosity—and I stepped once again into my dual roles. She read from *B'reisheet*, the first chapter of the first book of Genesis. Noa was poised and confident, full of joy as always.

Her sincerity, so touching in a 12-year-old, was manifest in the set of her shoulders. She wore the prayer shawl that my oldest daughter, Naama, had worn at her own bat mitzvah, 30 years before. It had been handmade by a family friend, Rachel—but because Rachel was Orthodox, her own daughter would never wear a prayer shawl.

It was a reminder of the contradictions that shaped our past and continue in our lives. On the collar of the *tallit* was a Hebrew inscription from Proverbs: "Wisdom begins with awe."

After reading from the Torah, Noa delivered a teaching she had prepared, which ended with these words: "I understand Eve's curiosity and her hunger for that apple full of knowledge. I learned that the Torah, such an ancient text, really does have relevance for me in this modern age."

At the end of her thank-yous, she took a breath and said, "I would especially like to thank my *savta*, my Rabbi."

My *savta*, my Rabbi.

When I was ordained, 20 years ago, grandchildren were not even a twinkle in my eye.

But now, many of my classmates are grandparents. We are elders, but not in the rabbinate. At least the women are not. In the future, there will be many granddaughters who will be calling their *savtas* their rabbis. But the *savta*/rabbis of the present time are still few. I am one of them.

At Noa's bat mitzvah, we stood at the intersection between history and family. These roles are slowly being interwoven into a one-of-a-kind tapestry: I can see the unbroken chain of my granddaughters' knowledge stretching far into the future.

That future is all the sweeter for our constant awareness as a people of how close we came to losing our future entirely—a theme that ran through my life like a bright red thread, but one that I would never allow my eyes to focus on.

We live our lives always close to loss. As always, I felt this acutely whenever I talked to or visited my sister, Khana, who had known so many losses.

After our parents died, I no longer needed to make the monthly trek to Philadelphia. But my sister and I continued our relationship through phone calls, occasional visits, and my attendance at the numerous wedding and circumcision ceremonies.

When my nephew, Yaakov, was struggling with physical weaknesses attributed to his psychiatric medications, I drove with my sister to his group home in the outskirts of Philadelphia. The reality of his bus accident in Israel had continual repercussions; this was the most recent.

For Khana's 70th birthday, I drove to Lakewood, New Jersey with my daughter Naama, her husband, Jonathan, and their four children to mingle in a room overflowing with her descendants. Her nine children, her six sons- and daughters-in-law, her nearly thirty grandchildren, and a dozen great-grandchildren sang her praises.

Khana sat like Queen Esther, holding court at the head of the table but holding, instead of a scepter, a wooden cane. She looked radiant. So much love surrounded her.

I added my words to the celebration:

"It may not appear possible that we are sisters. We took different paths, yet we come from the same roots. We are both entrenched in our

Jewish faith and our communities. We believe in the power of the Divine spirit and we believe in family.

"Our parents taught us to care for one another and leave the door open for the stranger, the orphan, the widow. Both of us are committed to doing good in the world. We are both entrenched in the values of our traditions. May the Holy One hold you close, Khana, and bring down the blessings from On High. You deserve them, each and every one of them."
I hugged her collapsed body as my tears fell. Today, I was a sister first.

As I became more and more comfortable with the reality of integrating my disparate roles, it grew increasingly obvious that there was one more amalgamation I had to confront: my Holocaust heritage, both familial and tribal.

This was surprisingly challenging for me. Despite all I had experienced of violence, injustice, suffering, and death, I still viewed the world through a positive lens. I preferred to walk away from conflict. Examining the Holocaust would bring all the conflicted thoughts, the violence, the greatest suffering imaginable directly into my mind and spirit, in a way I couldn't evade.

How could I make meaning out of the suffering of my forbears?

WHEN JEWS GO ON VACATION,
WE ARE NEVER JUST ON VACATION

How was I to face the dark inheritance of the Holocaust and allow it into my daily spiritual life? Once again, I was wrestling. And a man named Jakob would help guide me.

I met Jakob in 2012 at a Hebrew *ulpan* class in Jerusalem's Conservative Yeshiva. *Ulpan* is an immersive Hebrew course people take for any number of reasons: academic, functional, or spiritual, and I had a little bit of each need. Our class came from the Netherlands, England, Hungary, Germany, and Ramallah. A few Americans were sprinkled through, just enough that we mingled our Hebrew with our English phrases. The teacher was constantly bringing us back to *Ivrit b'Ivrit: Hebrew in Hebrew.*

Jakob was always the first to arrive in class, and despite his obvious shyness, he positioned himself directly to the left of the vivacious redheaded Israeli teacher. By the time I got there, the only seat available was on the opposite end of the table from this serious, reticent man. Consequently, we didn't interact much. My curiosity was piqued when on Tuesdays and Thursdays he left the class a half-hour earlier than the rest of us; the teacher paused to explain the next day's assignment to him and then he was gone. So I asked.

"Jakob lives at a monastery, and he's in charge of lunch on Tuesday and Thursdays," explained one of our classmates.

In my mind, I attempted to put these facts together: he wears a yarmulke while studying Hebrew. His intense demeanor and gracious smile convince me that he is a holy man. Did I mention his horned-rimmed glasses and his immaculate homework pad? He is one of the best students in the class. And by the way, he is a Bavarian Benedictine monk.

By week two, we had made huge leaps in our comfort with the spoken language, and we started socializing with each other outside of class. When we had Shabbat dinners together or attended a concert, we attempted to speak Hebrew, but more often than not, our mother tongues returned to our lips. Jakob could speak German, Afrikaans, English, and French. We were all envious of his linguistic range. Still, he joined us in English with reluctance. He was a purist: if he was to learn Hebrew, he said, he needed to speak it often and exclusively. Only after we teased him and made him laugh did he give in to the majority.

The teacher asked each of us to find someone to work with on a project; along with our partners, we were to present a 10-minute debate to the class in fluent Hebrew on a prescribed topic. Jakob surprised me by walking up to me and asking in Hebrew, *Can we work together?* Secretly, I was delighted, but I answered in Hebrew, simply: *Yes, of course.*

Our assignment was to discuss the pros and cons of learning languages in foreign countries. We got together several times to work on it, and quickly discovered that we shared a vast acreage of common ground. I was an American rabbi in search of a proficient Hebrew accent and a spiritually meaningful life. He was a German monk in search of the biblical source language to translate for his Brothers back home—and a spiritually meaningful life. We had both struggled, and through that hardship, had come to devote ourselves to a clerical path.

For Jakob, the fact of my gender—not disturbing to him but certainly an oddity in his world—opened the door to new perspectives. He had a way of creating intimacy, making me feel seen and understood just by lowering his voice. During those sessions, I fell in love with my monastic friend. After a lifetime of being offered love, seeking love, falling out of love, and experiencing several relationships, this was a new kind of experience—simple and natural. Jakob and I were soulmates.

What does it mean to fall in love with another human being? Not all love is romantic, but all love is part of the great romance. Jakob and I met on the dance floor in a sacred dance with the Divine. Our connection was not about gender; I simply took a more intuitive and emotional approach to the spiritual life than he had known up to that point. He felt free, with me, to speak his truth. It was in this soulful space that we met.

After six weeks of daily classes, the time came to say goodbye. Jakob and I stood face to face in the *beit midrash*, where we had prayed and studied together. We looked into each other's eyes and I said in Hebrew, *"It's difficult for me to separate myself from you."*

Without hesitating, he said, *"Then why don't you come to Germany?"*

I laughed and thought to myself, "This is crazy wonderful. A German monk is inviting me to visit?" It had never occurred to me to visit Germany for pleasure, but coming from Jakob, it sounded like an opportunity not to be missed. All I said was, *"Maybe I will."* We hugged with great feeling.

It took us two years to see each other again, and it was during this time that I discovered the real reason I had come into Jakob's life.

It soon became clear to me in the course of our ongoing email correspondence that he was struggling with his spiritual choices. I was surprised to learn of this development because I had felt such a strong commitment from him during our time in Jerusalem. What was going on? He told me his time there had led him to question the validity of his religious path; it was in the Holy City that he felt most at home. Since returning to his rural monastery in Germany, he had been teaching the Psalms to his Benedictine brothers in the original, and had begun saying his morning prayers to himself in Hebrew as well.

He looked to me as a spiritual counselor—a safe repository for his shifting perceptions.

He did not need my advice, only my understanding. A transformation was already under way. He received a call that his old apartment in Berlin was about to be vacated; even these small signs were pointing him in one direction. After conferring with his Abbot, he left the monastery where he had lived and worked for ten years, said goodbye to the Brotherhood he had once idealized, and moved back to Berlin.

In time, further revelations from Jakob traveled to me through cyberspace: his mother had been born and raised as a Jew, but before World War II she had married a non-Jewish German and moved to South Africa where Jakob was born and lived through his early childhood. He had been raised as a Catholic, and he was a teenager before the facts of his heritage were revealed to him.

Now he was finally coming to face it: he was a biological Jew. He told me that he had realized he did not have to leave the spiritual path altogether —only that he was meant to be on a different one. But he understood that in his case, biology alone would not be enough to satisfy the Israel Rabbinate. He began to fly back to Jerusalem every few months, to study in earnest for his conversion.

I had to see him. But I couldn't quite imagine traveling to Europe alone. I was afraid I would see the specter of the Shoah around every corner.

Around that time, I got a call from my friend Sharon. "I was thinking of renting an apartment in Paris this summer," she said. "Want to come?"

"What a funny coincidence! I've been trying to make plans to visit a friend in Berlin. And I was thinking about visiting Prague while I'm there. Maybe we could see it all."

I knew where I was going, and the inheritance that waited in Germany and France. Yet I was still set on avoiding facing the Holocaust. Sharon and I told each other that this would be a vacation. We would not be going to visit Camps or any other reminders of the bleak parts of history.

Yet in a Prague hotel, something changed. A couple began to talk to us about their experience visiting Theresienstadt, or Terezin, as it is called in Czech. It was as if they were compelled to speak of it, but they didn't appear harmed by their experience—more awed. Sharon and I had the same thought—we had to visit.

Terezin was both a ghetto and an internment camp, where 60,000 Jews were sequestered in a space meant for 7,000. What made it extraordinary was the number of artistic, intellectual, and cultural figures who were sent there as a way station to the death camps of the East: the great theatrical director Gustav Schorsch, the symphonic wunderkind Gideon Klein, the conductor Raphael Schachter. It was said that there were enough great musicians there to create two entire symphony orchestras at any given time. Performances were mounted on a regular basis, both because the occupants were driven to continue their artistic endeavors even in the face of imminent extermination, and because the Germans allowed it. Theresienstadt, they declared, was their showpiece to demonstrate their supposed magnanimity to the rest of the world; they called the ghetto their "gift to the Jews."

There had been eight synagogues in the ghetto, but today, just one remains, revealed after the Velvet Revolution, in 1989, eradicated the rule of Communism and made it possible for Theresienstadt to be investigated more fully.

The sign posted outside the room for the tourists' benefit read, "8 people only can enter at one time." Not even enough for a *minyan*, I

221

thought. When I think "synagogue," I think pews and pulpits, social hall and chandeliers, a babble of voices. How many human beings had crowded into this tiny chamber and said their Mourner's *Kaddish* in hushed tones?

We stepped into the dim space one person at a time; even with my short stature, I could feel the curved ceiling bearing down on me, and some in our group had to stoop simply to enter. It was a bit like a wigwam, with plaster walls. What surprised me the most were the colorful paintings on every available surface. Martina told us that a Terezin inmate named Artur Beringer—a cantor, religious educator, and artist—had happened upon this vacant, vaulted room and transformed it into a *shul* with his paintbrush. The walls themselves were their book.

Remarkably, it is all still visible. He had painted a six-pointed Star of David among many other stars on the ceiling. He had painted two Shabbat candlesticks on the wall in cerulean blue that could be blessed in lieu of real candles. He had painted a Hebrew inscription that people could face as they prayed. I recognized the words: *Dah lifney mi'atah omed.*

Know before whom you stand.

What did the Jews of Theresienstadt pray for? I wondered. Did they know that they would be transported to Auschwitz and perish there? Did they believe that God could find them in this hidden synagogue?

Back in Prague, we wandered the cobblestone streets, looking down often to check our steps. I stopped when I saw four brass squares glittering among the grey and white ones.

"Here lived Robert Katz, born 1901 — deported 1942 to Terezin — murdered at Auschwitz April 1944"

Nothing more. I couldn't possibly conjure up a person based on this inscription. There was no information about his life before his deportation and his horrific death. Yet the irony was that this stumbling block would symbolically return him to the neighborhood where he once lived, worked, loved. Here was history beneath my feet.

In German, such blocks are called *Stolpersteine,* or "stumbling blocks" because before the Shoah, people who stumbled over a protruding stone in a street might say: "There must be a Jew buried here." Hatred of the Jew was so pervasive that they were blamed even for the simplest misstep. More than 27,000 of these stumbling blocks have been laid in locations all over Europe. There are 300 *Stolpersteine* in Prague. The four brass squares in front of me were placed lovingly in a row like flowers in a garden.

Now the idea of these stumbling stones is to make people stop, remember, and reflect. They cannot simply continue smoothly on without thinking about the Jews who once lived in their midst. The importance of these stones for me was not remembrance—how could I ever forget?—but presence. I began to allow for the idea that I could stand in this place of loss and replace it with my living self.

At the Berlin Hauptbahnhof, or Central Train Station, in the throng of people swishing past us, Jakob and I found each other, and hugged again for a long time, as only good friends do.

Sharon and I had arrived on a Friday, and our first order of business was to shop and cook for our Shabbat dinner together. Sharon went to bed early, but Jakob and I stayed up talking late into the night. He was still looking to me for the part of the religious experience he had not, as a purist, allowed himself: up that point, he had been spending his time with Orthodox rabbis, learning traditional texts in a *yeshiva* setting. But he was lacking a Jewish family that could take him beyond duty to belonging. In the warm environment of our temporary Shabbat home, we effortlessly slipped back into our soulful space, finishing each other's sentences and laughing about it.

"Your letters have astounded me. I'm dizzy from all these changes. I can't imagine how you're feeling," I said.

"It has not been easy," he said, leaning in and whispering in his unique way. "Everything is a struggle, a contradiction. My Christian friends feel betrayed, but my Jewish friends are skeptical. In Jerusalem I feel part of something special, but I also love Berlin." He paused. "In a few days you, too, will fall in love with Berlin."

I smiled. "Well, I'm not skeptical about your path to Judaism. I think you're very brave, and right where you're supposed to be. But me falling in love with Berlin? That's a different story."

On Shabbat, we went to three different synagogues—a cross-section of Berlin Jewish life in 25 hours. Jakob had lived in this city for 20 years and he never had to think about where he put his feet. With him as my guide, I didn't either. He related the rich history of each building, and I provided as much religious context as I could.

As I prayed, I thought about the very first woman rabbi, Regina Jonas, who was ordained in Berlin in 1935. She wrote her thesis there, on the subject, "May a Woman Hold Rabbinic Office?" It is the first known attempt to find a legal basis for women's ordination in Jewish law. She was sent to Theresienstadt in 1942 and performed rabbinical functions there until 1944, when she was sent to Auschwitz, where she perished that same year, with no successor.

I introduced Jakob to Rabbi Tzvi Blanchard, my colleague from the States who was teaching at Humboldt University and could serve him as an invaluable guide to the Berlin Jewish community he was preparing to join. He now knew the prayers in Hebrew as well as Russian and German and English, and was beginning to see the world from a Jewish perspective. I could see how Judaism suited him.

"Where would you like to go tomorrow?" he asked.

"Wannsee," I said, surprising myself.

He nodded, never one to shy away from the complicated history of his city.

Wannsee, a resort villa nestled in a Berlin suburb, was where Hitler and 15 of his high-ranking officials came to work out the details of the Final Solution. On January 20, 1942, in a 90-minute conference around a long dining room table overlooking the lake, the extermination of the European Jews was set in motion.

How could this be? The beauty of the setting seemed to fly in the face of this truth. Only in the past 25 years had it been turned into a museum; we walked around looking at photographs of the Shoah's skeletal bodies. We did not speak, but I knew we were of one mind about our experience.

For the next six days I saw Berlin through Jakob's eyes. We went through the Brandenburg Gate, visited the new Holocaust Museum, stood before the tomb-like memorial in the heart of the city. We saw spectacular collections of modern art, went to the symphony, ate falafel at an Israeli café. Little by little, I began to see Jakob's Berlin in all its complexity, a troubled but beautiful city reborn out of the ashes of World War II.

I let go of my fear and felt a sense of healing, for which I thanked him. We agreed that such healing was about more than buildings or museums or views—it was about the power of friendship, as an antidote to sorrow, and the joy of finding a fellow pilgrim who is also trying to make sense of the world.

In the early morning of the last day, Jakob led us to the train, pulling our suitcases behind him. As we waited for the train to arrive, he sang us the goodbye song made famous by Marlene Dietrich in the 1960s.

> *Ich hab noch einen Koffer in Berlin,*
> *deswegen muss ich nächstens wieder hin;*
> *die Seligkeiten vergangener Zeiten,*

sind alle noch in meinem kleinen Koffer drin ...

... I still have a suitcase in Berlin,
So I must go there again soon;
Happy memories of times gone by
Are all still there in my little suitcase ...

When he finished singing, he shrugged. We couldn't seem to find the right words to let go.

"Again, it is difficult for me to leave you," I said. I knew I would be leaving so much more behind this time—a whole suitcase full of memories. The train to the airport arrived, and the doors opened before we could really hug each other. I rushed on board and the doors closed again far too quickly.

When Sharon and I landed at the Charles de Gaulle airport, we decided to experience the full urban City of Love, so we opted for the metro instead of a taxi. After a hot and exhausting trip—which included an incomprehensible mid-stream change of trains—we exited the metro station, trying to keep track of our suitcases and other belongings amidst the hubbub. At the turnstile, we fumbled for our exit passes. A man pushed past me, yanking at my shoulder bag as he ran. My wallet, camera, Kindle, were all lost in an instant.

This was a minor precursor to a greater loss. We arrived at our rental apartment in Le Marais, the historical Jewish quarter of Paris. I checked my email, and I was shocked to find that Reb Zalman had died. My friend Sharon sympathized as I shared how I had treasured my beloved mentor's wisdom.

We walked to the police station, and I filed a report in a sad fog; afterward, we ambled along the Seine. We gazed at hundreds of "love locks," padlocks that had been affixed to the sides of the bridge by lovers who wanted to leave their mark. I was still shaken, but Sharon's calm presence comforted me.

Over the next few days, I pushed through my discomfort to visit the Louvre, the Pompidou Center, the Shoah Memorial, seeing others' loves and losses from over the centuries. We feasted on falafel and homemade knishes in Le Marais. France's Jewish community is the largest in Europe.

After five days and dozens of miles on the streets of Paris, we welcomed Shabbat for rest and reflection. It was a warm and rainy day in

July when we made our way to the 9th arrondissement to attend mornin services at the oldest and most impressive Jewish house of worship i France, the Grand Synagogue, or Synagogue de la Victoire.

This edifice, built in 1847, sits on a narrow pebbled street an overtakes the entire block. On that dreary morning only about 50 men an women were seated in the tomblike catacomb, though almost two thousan souls can pray together in this sanctuary. It is an architectural jewel, bui with Rothschild money; it protects the Jewish community from furth destruction, like the Lions of Judah that stand sentry over the Te Commandments carved above the Holy Ark.

Before we could pray, we had to deal with the stark realities of Jewis life in Europe. The security guards asked us to hand over our passports, an I felt fortunate that I had kept mine in a separate place from my othe valuables, and that we had thought to put them in our backpacks, whic were now emptied most meticulously. Afterward we were escorted insid women to the left, men to the right.

Generations of French Jews had prayed here, shielded from th political climate of the day. What were the Jews thinking when they bui this "cathedral" to their God all those years ago?

Future prosperity. Economic security. Demographic growth. Cultur continuity. Eternal light.

I was startled by the luminosity of this womb-like structure. Dozen of menorahs with nine bulbs each circled the space. Chandeliers hung fror every corner. Light fixtures on the walls illuminated our way to the women section downstairs. Facing sideways toward the bimah, I could see the me performing their fastidious morning choreography, singing and chanting th traditional Hebrew prayers, which reverberated off the walls and ceilings. I was beautiful. I was reminded of my old Bronx synagogue where the blen of those male voices brought the prayers of the past into this melodiou present.

The following day, still fresh from our day of rest, we sat in ou favorite falafel place in Le Marais, at a table we were sharing with an Israe mother and daughter. When we mentioned our visit to the Jewish Museun of Art and History, the mother said, "Oh, you couldn't convince me to g into that place. Look what happened in Brussels—four people dead." Th shooting in May at the Jewish Museum of Belgium was still fresh in all ou minds.

Just then, the owner of the restaurant came over to our table an urged us to leave immediately. Speaking in hushed Hebrew, as if it were secret language, he said the French police had warned shopkeepers of a large pro-Palestinian demonstration against Operation Protective Shield in the Gaza Strip. The protest was coming our way, and it was getting violent. Without a second thought, we rushed out all together and dispersed into the crowd, the peace of our Shabbat forgotten in the swell of our fear.

That night we read on the Internet of the fallout from the protest: it was like a tiny Kristallnacht. Synagogues and shops were targeted by the anti-Zionist crowd, which moved on to disrupt the 200 Jews attending a memorial service for three boys who had been kidnapped on the West Bank. Those events had triggered the summer conflict of 2014.

Now, clashes erupted between the protesters and the young Jewish men who guarded the *shul*. Bats, tables and chairs, homemade bombs, and other weapons were hurled at the group, and at least three Jews were taken to the hospital. More French police and Jewish groups quelled the stampede, and finally, calm resumed. It wasn't until several hours later that the people inside the besieged synagogue were able to return to their homes.

The next day we visited the Pere Lachaise Cemetery and stood over the graves of Oscar Wilde, Gertrude Stein, and other cultural giants. Visiting the dead restored us to a mood of contemplation, and as we were walking back, we passed the gates of a large synagogue: the Don Isaac Abravanel. Reading the sign affixed to the gate, we realized this was the very site of yesterday's violence. I thought: when Jews go on vacation, we are never just on vacation. We are always learning, remembering, reliving our history. Despite our sorrow, each of these events is an opportunity, a reminder that we are all connected through time.

Six months later, the memory of that visit came back to me while I was watching a televised memorial service for the four Jewish victims of a terrorist attack inside a kosher supermarket in eastern Paris. Four more lives lost. It was the weekend of January 9, 2015. Prime Minister Netanyahu and President Hollande were seated side by side inside the Grand Synagogue, which was filled to capacity and pregnant with security. I wondered how all these dignitaries and their escorts had made it through the narrow passageway to enter this worship hall, now made famous again in the harsh lights of the television cameras. Those lights could not capture the full impact, the sheer radiance of the interior the way I remembered it. There were cheers from the audience after Prime Minister Netanyahu's speech. The cavernous space echoed with the sound of 1,800 people reciting Mourner's *Kaddish*.

I sat in my living room and watched the spectacle, but the memories of that peaceful Shabbat morning flowed through me. I prayed again to hear those sweet harmonies. I prayed for sacred healing to rise like the majestic stairway to the blue-velvet-covered ark.

I prayed that the Lions of Judah would continue to protect their cubs from enemies, but I feared that the hate-filled past would repeat itself.

THANKSGIVING

I believe that everything in life is a vehicle for transformation. That's not to say we always get into the vehicle and drive—but it's sitting there idling all the same. My summer travels became a process of revelations that entered into my soul and reside there still. I reached an altered state of consciousness and it wouldn't let go of me. But how would I make this trip matter beyond its scope in time and place?

For decades, I had resisted looking directly at the Holocaust, even though the stories of survivors were my childhood fairytales. But now my parents were gone. I had lived the fallout of Officer Johns's murder. I had finally spent some time in Europe, seeing the realities of Jewish life there.

On the heels of my unconventional friendship with Jakob, I could see the future more clearly than the past. I was grateful that we met each other at the nexus of our own personal histories in Jerusalem, the center of the universe. But most important, I knew I must find a way to amalgamate the understanding I had gained into my rabbinical and interfaith work. I understood this work as my personal heritage.

When people asked me about my trip to Europe, instead of gleefully announcing my "great time," all I could say was, "I had quite a history lesson. Something's changed for me."

My mind was a jigsaw puzzle of images both beautiful and disturbing.

After I returned, I underwent training so I could volunteer at the U.S Holocaust Memorial Museum. I practiced for another few months before I found my niche. The museum was offering a six-week educational class for docents for the special exhibit *Some Were Neighbors: Collaboration and Complicity in the Holocaust.*

This exhibit explores how countless ordinary people, from all walks of life within the Reich and across Europe, were instrumental in the fulfillment of Nazi racial policies. To lead visitors, to try to understand, I undertook to learn more history. More facts. More synthesis.

I couldn't help noticing that the motto of the museum had changed from "Never Again" to "What You Do Matters." I took it as an ongoing charge.

On Thanksgiving Day in 2015, the U.S. Holocaust Memorial Museum was unusually quiet. The security guards flanked the doors, and two employees sat at the information desk. Small groups of people wandered the lobby and spoke in hushed tones to their companions. The austere brick structure took on a holy face.

I had come to give a tour of the *Some Were Neighbors* exhibit. As usual I stood in front of the information desk holding up the placard notifying people of the tour.

A young boy came over to me and asked, "Could you tell me where the picture of Special Officer Johns is located?"

Four young people then encircled me. I asked them about where they called home, and where they were traveling. All were born in America, but they told me more about their backgrounds, too: The two boys were Ethiopian; one girl was African-American; and the other girl, who wore a hijab, was Muslim.

"We're here to do extra credit for our high school class assignment," one of them said. "This is one of the questions we have to complete."

"What a coincidence!" I said, trying not to startle them with the intensity of my emotions.

"You came to the right person. I know quite a bit about Stephen Johns. I was the chaplain on call when Officer Johns was shot by a white supremacist. Mr. Johns was taken by ambulance to the George Washington University Hospital. The memorial is at the front of the building. Let me take you there."

We stood in front of the picture of Stephen Johns, ever handsome, ever young, offset by a draped black background. I told the students what had happened the day he died:

"Stephen was on guard at the front entrance. He saw an elderly man with a long coat approach the museum, and walked toward him to open the door. The man took out his shotgun and shot Mr. Johns at close range. In a matter of seconds, the other security guards shot the perpetrator, probably saving many more lives. Both men were taken to George Washington University Hospital and both underwent surgery. The shooter survived, but Mr. Johns didn't make it. My only glimpse of him was when I went with his family to view his body before they took him down to the morgue."

The students were silent. Then one of the girls said, "He was only 39." I nodded. "Not everyone gets to die of old age."

They followed me back to the information desk where Arthur, a longtime employee of the museum, was perched. "Arthur, these students are doing some research. Were you here during the shooting?" I asked.

"Yes, I most certainly was," he said. "I was up on the fifth floor when I heard something I had never heard before. At first I thought it was the air-conditioner breaking down, but later I realized that the noise came from the shotgun that shattered the glass doors and killed my friend Stephen. We were told to stay put until security came to walk us down the stairs to the ground level. We walked out the back door onto the grounds of the National Mall."

The four students, standing shoulder to shoulder, listened intently while continuing to write in their notebooks. They were quiet and respectful. Their faces were sad—and although this was appropriate, it also concerned me. I didn't want to leave them alone with their thoughts. I asked them, "Do you have any Jewish friends?"

Three of them shook their heads no, but the girl wearing the hijab said, "Actually, I moved here from New York, and my best friend there was Jewish. We had such a good time together." She smiled wistfully, and I smiled back at her.

I said, "It's important for all of you to get to know Others when you can." I wondered if they could hear the capital letter. "Do you have time to see the exhibit downstairs?" I asked.

They looked at each other and then at their iPhones. "My dad is coming to pick us up in a half hour," one of them said.

"Perfect. What if I give you a quick tour of the exhibit, *Some Were Neighbors?*" I said. "It shows how the Holocaust spread to countries across Europe, because so many ordinary people collaborated with the Nazis."

They nodded solemnly and followed me down to the exhibit. We talked about how ordinary people took hateful actions against their neighbors, while others risked their lives to save both neighbors and strangers. There was a quote etched into the wall before us by Raul Hilberg, a refugee from Nazism and a Holocaust scholar.

I read it aloud:

> *At crucial junctures, every individual makes decisions and ... every decision individual.*

I hoped they understood what I was trying to tell them.

When the tour ended, they asked if they could take a picture with me for their class project. They handed over an iPhone to a young couple, then thanked me and rushed out to get their ride back to Virginia, to share Thanksgiving dinners with their families.

I later learned that the picture-taking couple was from Munich, Germany, as were so many of the visitors to the Holocaust Memorial Museum. I imagined what a wonderful dialogue they could have had with the students.

If only there were more time.

ACKNOWLEDGMENTS

Writing a book is not the solitary activity I thought it was when I sat in front of my computer all those many nights and weekends. First, it was just me and my thoughts. Then my past came alive, with descriptions and stories of people and places.

I want to thank my family and friends; you have provided me with the stories that came out of our shared living experiences. I hope this book will bring back memories of nourishment and nostalgia. Maybe a tear will fall, or a smile will form, when you read my Torah.

My writing became cleaner because of my teacher Michelle Brafman and the writing workshops she led at the Edlavitch Jewish Community Center in the District I was fortunate to receive a Jenny McKean Moore scholarship, which allowed me to join a writer's class at George Washington University, led by novelist Tim Johnston. My wonderful classmates gave me honest and constructive feedback.

My assistant, Salem Pearce, entering her final year in rabbinical school was also my writing mentor. She helped give form to my early *Spiritualetter* blog and was my technical guru.

Paula Amman, writer and editor in the Washington, DC, area, reviewed my ideas and gave me encouragement and further input.

But it wasn't until I found and hired editor/writer Rachel Feingold that I began the memoir in earnest. She was instrumental in seeing beyond the blog into a larger story. And so I began expanding each story, forming chapters, and connecting the dots of my life. We spent many hours together digging into my past, to answer questions readers might have. She was my accountability coach for a year.

I also want to acknowledge my colleagues from CLAL's *Rabbis Without Borders* who listened as I read my stories aloud at their annual retreat. Their laughter was mixed with silent recognition that I had hit an emotional bullseye.

Then came the decision to publish. Enter Esther Goldenberg of Three Gems publishing and her editor Sara Wildberger. Together, the pushed me to the next level of editing and revisions. Their perspective was invaluable in the development of the memoir.

I am grateful to all these angels who came into my life at just the right time for just the right reason. I am a finer writer and a more effective storyteller because they shared their creative gifts with me.

I give thanks to the God that Moses encountered at the burning bush, the "I Am That I Am" who sends us all on a mission to find our holy destiny.

ABOUT THE AUTHOR

After decades of congregational work in synagogues across the country, Rabbi Tamara Miller served as the Director of Spiritual Care at George Washington University Hospital in Washington, D.C.. In 2000, she founded *The Capital Kehillah*, the first outreach community for Jewish spirituality piloted by a female rabbi and housed at the Sixth & I Historic Synagogue. She is a fellow and an alumna of the New York City based think tank, CLAL'S *Rabbis Without Borders*. Rabbi Miller was ordained by the Academy for Jewish Religion whose pluralistic approach to Judaism crosses all denominational lines. Rabbi Miller is the proud mother of four children and ten grandchildren.

For more information or to connect, visit www.RabbiTamara.com.